Eye Movement Desensitization and Reprocessing (EMDR) in Child and Adolescent Psychotherapy

Eye Movement Desensitization and Reprocessing (EMDR) in Child and Adolescent Psychotherapy

Ricky Greenwald, Psy.D.

JASON ARONSON INC.
Northvale, New Jersey
London

This book was set in 11 pt. New Baskerville and printed and bound by Book-mart Press, Inc. of North Bergen, NJ.

Library of Congress Cataloging-in-Publication Data

Greenwald, Ricky.
    Eye Movement Desensitization and Reprocessing (EMDR) in child and adolescent psychotherapy / Ricky Greenwald.
       p. cm.
    Includes bibliographical references and index.
    ISBN 0-7657-0217-7
    1. Eye movement desensitization and reprocessing for children.
    2. Psychic trauma in children—Treatment. 3. Child psychotherapy.
    4. Adolescent psychotherapy. I. Title.
    RJ505.E9G74 1999
    618.92'8914—dc21   99–12196

Printed in the United States of America on acid-free paper. For information and catalog write to Jason Aronson Inc., 230 Livingston Street, Northvale, NJ 07647-1726, or visit our website: www.aronson.com

Contents

PART II: THE TECHNICAL REPERTOIRE

PART III: SPECIAL APPLICATIONS

Preface

Eye movement desensitization and reprocessing (EMDR) is a recently developed individual psychotherapy method that entails a unique integration of exposure and client-centered principles. To oversimplify, it features having the client concentrate intensely on the most distressing part of the upsetting memory while moving the eyes from side to side (by following the therapist's moving hand or other object) at the rate of about one round trip per second, for a variable duration of about 20 to 60 seconds. Following a set of eye movements, the client is asked to report whatever "came up," possibly including changes in the imagery, thought, emotion, or physical sensation (all are common). This report becomes the focus of the next set of eye movements. For example, if the client reports, "Now I'm feeling more angry," the therapist may say, "Concentrate on that," for the next set. This procedure is repeated until the client can identify no further distressing elements of the memory and can embrace a more positive or adaptive perspective regarding the memory. For full effect, related memories may also require similar treatment, as more than one traumatic memory may be driving the presenting symptoms.

Here is a synopsis of the history and current status of EMDR for children and adolescents. EMDR's brief history has been marked by considerable excitement as well as controversy. Shapiro's (1989a,b) initial reports, which included step-by-step instructions, presented "EMD" as a rapid treatment for traumatic memories, sometimes even curing posttraumatic stress disorder (PTSD) in a single session. When Shapiro observed that practitioners of her new technique were not using the method the same way, she came to appreciate the complexity of the method, including the "reprocessing" element, which was added to the name (Shapiro 1991b). She expanded her workshop to include more detailed instruction as well as small-group supervised practicums, and suggested this supervised training as a minimum requirement for responsible practice (Shapiro 1991a).

Outcomes in published reports of EMD and EMDR initially varied considerably, probably due to variations in the quality of the intervention. This led to a division between appropriately trained clinicians, who knew from experience that EMDR worked, and appropriately skeptical clinicians and academicians, who had not been convinced by the empirical data. This gap was magnified because EMDR-trained clinicians had greater access to positive reports before they were published, as well as a better understanding of the flaws that figured prominently in those studies that showed EMDR in a less favorable light (Greenwald 1996).

A number of more recent studies featuring a higher fidelity to the revised EMDR protocol have been quite positive, consistent with Shapiro's initial findings. In fact, EMDR's efficacy is supported by more controlled studies than any other psychotherapy treatment for trauma (Shapiro 1996a). EMDR has become widely recognized as efficacious in the treatment of trauma (Chambless et al. 1998, Feske 1998, Greenwald 1996, Shapiro 1996a, van Etten and Taylor 1998) and is considered by many to be the treatment of choice for traumatic memories and related applications. Controversy does continue, with some die-hard

EMDR opponents straying ever further from the data to make their points (Greenwald in press).

The need for formal, supervised training in EMDR has been strongly endorsed by those therapists who have undergone such training (Lipke 1994). The emergence of treatment fidelity as a key factor determining outcome (Greenwald 1996, Lee et al. 1996, Shapiro 1996b) has highlighted the importance of training. Indeed, some now question whether the currently dominant model of training is sufficient for mastery of the method (Greenwald 1996, 1997a). The responsible clinician who plans to use EMDR is urged to pursue the most comprehensive training opportunity available.

Although after EMDR a memory may become less vivid, during treatment the EMDR process seems to facilitate enhanced recall of memory details. Caryl McBride (personal communication) studied EMDR's utility in enhancing recall of abuse memory details for children who had been identified as victims of abuse. Following the standard interview given by the state agency, EMDR was used to elicit numerous additional details, many of which were then independently corroborated. This well-designed study showed very strong results with the first twenty children, but then funding ran out. As far as I know, it has not been continued or reported. McBride's findings are consistent with the results of Lipke's (1994) survey of 442 EMDR-trained clinicians, in which 86 percent described EMDR as more likely than other methods to lead to the emergence of repressed material.

The underlying mechanism of EMDR is not known. Shapiro has suggested that the procedure somehow induces accelerated information processing, whereby dysfunctionally stored traumatic material can be accessed, rapidly integrated, and thereby depotentiated. Along these lines, some have speculated that the purported accelerated information processing effect may be related to REM dreaming (e.g., Greenwald 1995, Stickgold 1998). Taking a different tack, and not addressing the possible effect of the eye movements, others have pointed out that the EMDR procedure is quite comprehensive in incorporating virtually every element believed to be effective in trauma therapy (Hyer and Brandsma 1997, Sweet 1995). The question of how EMDR works is far from resolved, and in particular the role of the eye movements remains a mystery.

Although most studies have focused on trauma and/or PTSD, EMDR has been applied to numerous conditions, including dissociative disorders, grief, somatic problems, anxiety, depression, and addictions (Shapiro 1995). Generally the approach is to locate and reprocess the distressing memories at the root of the disturbance. However, some applications also rely on the apparent enhancement effect of EMDR on other techniques, including hypnosis, visualization, affirmation, and learning. This range of application is consistent with Shapiro's (1995) proposition that EMDR facilitates accelerated information processing. While awaiting further reports on EMDR's possible range of applications, its stature as a trauma treatment can no longer be denied.

EMDR FOR CHILDREN AND ADOLESCENTS

EMDR's use with traumatized children and adolescents also appears to be quite effective, although the documentation specifically relating to this population is more limited. Hundreds of cases have been informally reported with generally positive results (Greenwald 1993c). Published case reports on EMDR for children have been uniformly positive and consistent with findings on analogous treatment of adults, except that child treatment may be even more rapid (Cocco and Sharpe 1993, Cohen and Lahad 1997, Greenwald 1993b, 1994a, 1998b,d, Grosso 1996, Mendoza-Weitman 1992, Pellicer 1993, Rodriguez 1997, Shapiro 1991a). For example, Greenwald (1994a) reported that all five children treated with one to two EMDR sessions several months after a hurricane recovered to their pretrauma symptom levels, with gains maintained at 1-month follow-up.

Controlled studies are also beginning to be reported. Since most of these have not yet been published, I will briefly review them here.

Chemtob and Nakashima (1996) reported very positive results in using EMDR with children traumatized by Hurricane Iniki in Kauai who had failed to respond to a generally effective previous treatment program. The design featured a delay control group, independent assessment with several standardized measures, and five therapists with varying levels of EMDR training and experience (level 1 minimum, plus specialized child EMDR training). The treatment protocol was clearly specified, and a number of efforts were made to ensure fidelity. Participants averaged a 58 percent reduction on the primary trauma measure following three sessions, with results holding several months later. Significant reductions were also found on anxiety and depression measures as well as visits to the school nurse.

Puffer and colleagues (1998) reported on a study of twenty children and adolescents, ages 8 to 17, who were nonrandomly assigned (according to convenience of scheduling) to EMDR treatment or delayed-treatment groups. Treatment was a single session; the focus was a single trauma or loss. The first author conducted all treatment and assessment, using several measures pretreatment, posttreatment, and at 1- to 2-month follow-up. There was no change during the 1-month no-treatment delay, and significant improvement between the first and last scores on all measures. On the best measure of trauma symptoms (Impact of Events Scale), of the seventeen participants starting in the clinical range, eleven moved to normal levels, and three others dropped twelve or more points, while the other three stayed the same. Problematic design features include lack of independent assessment (although no subjective scoring was involved) and use of a therapist with only partial EMDR training. Also, three participants had ongoing sources of distress, making recovery unlikely. Still, the results were quite positive, although somewhat more variable than in other studies.

Sandra Wilson and colleagues (personal communication) have completed data collection in a study of a three-session trauma-focused EMDR treatment with seventy children, ages 8 to 11, diagnosed with PTSD (n = 27) or PTSD symptoms (n = 43). This study features a randomized design with a delayed-treatment group, multiple well-trained therapists, and blind, independent assessment using multiple standardized measures. Although statistical analysis has not been completed, preliminary review of the data is extremely favorable for EMDR. Wilson noted that the occasional EMDR failures were consistently diagnostic of ongoing sources of distress.

Rubin and Bischofshausen (1997) reported on the first twenty-seven participants in a larger randomized study in a child guidance center, with EMDR being added to the eclectic treatment for the experimental group. The participants had a variety of diagnoses, and all had a trauma history. Therapists were social work interns with the full EMDR training who received monthly supervision by an experienced EMDR-trained child therapist. Independent fidelity ratings ranged from adequate to good. A possibly problematic feature was the use of relatively insensitive measures, especially given the diversity of the sample. The preliminary results on various measures were either neutral or favored EMDR, with some differences reaching significance. Final results have not been reported.

Weinberg and Caspers (1997) reported on a pilot study in which EMDR was applied in an innovative way to children with learning disorders. They randomly divided six boys (grades 3 to 4) from the same resource room into two groups. Participants in both groups received a 10-minute individual treatment session twice a week for eight weeks, focusing on recent difficult or upsetting situations that occurred in school. The experimental group was given EMDR during these sessions, whereas for the control group the situations were just discussed. All three of the children in the EMDR group, as well as one in the control group, made rather dramatic gains on various measures of reading and writing skills; the two others in the control group showed little change. Their follow-up study (Weinberg and Caspers 1998) reported similar findings, except that in the second study not all of those receiving EMDR responded as positively as in the first one. These studies included serious limitations such as the small *n* and the use of children with untreated major trauma, who therefore might not reasonably be expected to respond fully to the treatment intervention, which was focused on more minor school-related experiences.

Several researchers have targeted traumatic memories with EMDR in the hopes of reducing criminal or acting-out behaviors. Soberman and colleagues (1998) provided three sessions of EMDR focused on a primary identified traumatic memory, as an adjunct to standard care, to about half of 29 acting-out boys ages 10 through 16 who were in residential or day treatment. This study featured random assignment, multiple trauma-focused, and behavioral measures from multiple sources, independent assessment for most measures, and a fully trained and experienced EMDR therapist. Design problems included use of a single EMDR therapist, who also administered the self-report forms, and no independent verification of treatment fidelity. The trauma measure referencing the treated memory showed much greater change than the global trauma measures, probably indicating that additional trauma remained untreated. The EMDR group did far better than controls and nearly halved their primary identified problem behaviors at 3-month follow-up.

Datta and Wallace (1996) reported on the EMDR treatment of ten incarcerated adolescent male sex offenders who themselves had also been sexually abused. Following an average of three EMDR sessions focused on their own trauma history, in addition to standard care, participants showed significantly increased empathy for victims of abuse, such empathy presumably being incompatible with further abusive behavior. At one-year follow-up, the empathy gains were maintained, as well as the reduced distress (SUDS) and increased self-esteem (VoC) related to the targeted traumatic memories. Similar gains in empathy were not shown by control groups. Design problems include lack of independent assessment as well as the fact that the empathy measure's validity has not been fully established. Additional data on individual participants indicate that many showed objective behavioral gains, including spontaneous attempts at victim restitution, increased scores on IQ tests, improved school performance, and exemplary behavior in the community.

Scheck and colleagues (1998) reported on the EMDR treatment of a high-risk acting-out community sample including both adolescent (ages 16 to 19, n = 18) and young adult females (ages 20 to 25, n = 42). All reported a trauma history, and over three-fourths met criteria for PTSD. Participants were randomly assigned to the EMDR group or the Active Listening (AL) control group, each of which received two treatment sessions focused on the traumatic memory. Independent, blind assessment of five standardized measures at pre- and posttreatment indicated that both treatments were helpful, but EMDR much more so. In fact, following treatment, those in the EMDR group fell within the normative (nonclinical) range for all measures, whereas only one outcome score fell in that range for the AL group. Three-month follow-up of a subsample showed maintenance of gains. This study found no differences in the responses of the young adults compared to the adolescents (Judith Schaeffer, personal communication), in that EMDR was equally effective.

What we are finding, in summary, is (1) that EMDR seems to be about as effective with children and adolescents as with adults, but may be even quicker; (2) that the EMDR treatment of traumatic memories can affect a wide range of behaviors; and (3) that a somewhat different technical repertoire is required to use EMDR with children. Although further study is needed, available data are consistent with the assumption of downward age extension of efficacy. Because EMDR is apparently safe as well as effective (Greenwald 1993c, Lipke 1994), and because it does not interfere with the use of other approaches, clinicians may responsibly choose to use this method with children and adolescents without awaiting further research (Greenwald 1998b). Supervised training and practice is required for client safety and for consistent effectiveness. Since a somewhat different repertoire of EMDR interventions is required with children and adolescents, this should also be mastered for optimal results. It should be noted that the research supporting EMDR's effectiveness reflects use of the standard EMDR protocol, with the child/adolescent studies also staying fairly close to the standard. The numerous technical variations available for use with children and adolescents should be used when necessary, while keeping as much to the standard protocol as possible.

Acknowledgments

Thanks to my grandparents for setting such good examples, and to the rabbi at the graveside, who said, "Love is taking responsibility."

Thanks to Marlene Miller and Lisa Sieverts for helping me learn to feel responsible for all children—even the ones I don't know.

Thanks to the many clinicians who have shared insights, cases, and questions over the years. This work to some degree represents the accumulated clinical experience of a community of psychotherapists. At the risk of inadvertently omitting mention of many deserving of recognition, I would like to acknowledge some of the members of this community.

Thanks to Francine Shapiro and Robbie Dunton for their pioneering contributions to the development of child applications of EMDR. The basic child protocol that Francine has presented in the Level I trainings and the innovations that Robbie has so freely shared within the EMDR community serve as the foundation for this book's EMDR-related technical innovations. Francine's invitation to simplify and to be creative with children has been accepted by many practitioners, with good results. Robbie's numerous insights, as well as her "chest of drawers" and "container" metaphors, have served as a beginning repertoire for many. Thanks also to both Francine and Robbie for their encouragement and support over the years.

Thanks to those who contributed material to this book (some inadvertently): Michael Abruzzese, Joy Armstrong, Sue Bishop, Ari Blatt, Judith Boel, Pamela Carlton, Georgia Carpenter, early Child and Adolescent Specialty Group members (Jane Hadley, Jack Hennessey, Virginia Lewis, Linda Martin, Liz Mendoza, Elizabeth Myers, Alice Ruzicka, and others), Nick Cocco, Purna Datta, Philip Dutton, Frederico C. Grosso, Michael Harris, Faye B. Heller, Jeanne Hoffman, Greg Keck, Joan Lovett, Theresa Marshall, Terry Martin, Joanne May, Rick McMahon, Carol Naumann, Linda Neider, Sandra Paulsen, Jerry Powell, Stephen Reiter, Caroline Sakai, Anne Samson, Zvia Silberman, Diane Spindler-Ranta, Jean Sutton, Yoshinori Takasaki, Bob Tinker, Shannon Tolson, Marilyn Vargas-Lobato, Silke Vogelman-Sine, Jane Wakefield, and Jesse Work.

Thanks to those who offered editorial suggestions on some portion of this book: Michael Abruzzese, James L. Bibb, Judy Boore, Robbie Dunton, Ruth Grainger, Jill Robbins, Jeanne Hoffman, LaVay Lau, Dianne Lynn, Dennis McLaughlin, Carol Nowak, Sandra Paulsen, Phil Robbins, Don Rosenberg, Francine Shapiro, Roger Solomon, and Silke Vogelman-Sine.

The preface was adapted from an article originally published in *Clinical Child Psychology and Psychiatry* 1359–1045 (199804) 3(2): 279–287; 002869 by SAGE Publications (London, Thousand Oaks, and New Delhi), portions of which are reprinted here with permission.

Introduction

One of the greatest honors of my life came several years ago in a phone call from my mother, who is a psychotherapist. "Rick, do you think you could do some EMDR sessions for a few of my clients?" My mother, in addition to being very experienced and competent, is one of my therapy heroes. I always learned more from talking over cases with her than I did from most of my classes in graduate school. This request was also a bit of a shock in another way. I had been telling her about eye movement desensitization and reprocessing (EMDR) for some time, and getting back variations of "That's nice, dear." And now she wanted my help in getting a few of her clients to the other side of trauma-related treatment impasses.

My mother observed one EMDR session I conducted. Afterward, of course, I asked her, "What did you think?" She said, "Well, it was very interesting, seeing [the client] change so quickly like that. Weird, really. But, you know, you were doing a lot of the same things I do." I replied, "It's just therapy, Mom."

I like EMDR because it seems to help people with certain types of problems feel better quickly. But EMDR isn't *instead* of therapy, it *is* therapy. It's one tool used by a therapist. Sometimes I compare EMDR to penicillin. Like penicillin, EMDR seems to do what it does better than whatever was available before. And like penicillin, EMDR may play a key role in some treatments. Of course, therapists who are trained in EMDR still need to be good therapists, to be knowledgeable in their areas of specialization, and to use EMDR competently as well as selectively, according to clinical judgment, in the context of an overall treatment plan. One doesn't do only EMDR.

I think of trauma, broadly defined as incompletely processed upsetting experiences, as one of the primary sources of children's mental health and behavioral problems. In this book I extend trauma theory to explain the notion that problems come from experience, and I show how I might conduct an entire course of treatment using the trauma orientation to organize various family and individual interventions. EMDR is used for much more than just addressing trauma. In therapy the case formulation drives the overall treatment plan, and EMDR is used when it fits in.

This book focuses on using EMDR with children and adolescents. EMDR is a fairly new method and most of the variations used with children and adolescents are even newer. Much of the technical material in this book has never been published before.

The book is written for those interested in learning about or doing therapy with children and adolescents. The trauma orientation to conducting therapy, combined with various applications of EMDR, makes for some innovative and effective approaches to common treatment issues. To use EMDR in treatment requires formal, supervised training, which a book cannot offer. But for those readers who have completed training in EMDR, this book is also a technical guide to using EMDR with children and adolescents.

The approach to treatment that I present reflects the way in which I have incorporated child trauma–related concepts into my clinical practice. The 1990s has seen a burgeoning interest and knowledge base in the child trauma field, a movement I have been a part of. Early in my career, I began understanding many problems as being related to unprocessed loss, which could be addressed in individual as well as family contexts. Later, I incorporated my growing awareness of trauma as an extension of this approach, consistent with the experiential source of symptomatology as well as with principles of treatment.

I first learned to use EMDR in 1992. I then had two opportunities to volunteer as a mental health worker following major hurricanes. I had to draw on my full repertoire of clinical skills with children and families, as well as my specialized training in critical incident response and in EMDR. The work took place in ad hoc settings such as food stamp lines, school playgrounds, and other people's offices. The experience of treating so many people with acute posttraumatic reactions, often with considerable efficiency and success, was invaluable. The acute trauma setting provides access to clients during the window of time in which, with help, even a major trauma may not have to result in posttraumatic stress disorder (PTSD). I felt I was helping individuals and families solve problems before they really took hold, problems that might otherwise have led to years of suffering. I had never had so much impact so quickly, nor had so much fun working. I even thought about becoming a disaster psychologist.

Unfortunately, most disaster psychologists have to volunteer for a long time, and for long stretches at short notice, before they can make a living at it. Instead, I pursued my interest in child trauma, while continuing to work as a generalist with children and families. Somewhere along the way, my original unprocessed-loss orientation developed into an unprocessed-trauma orientation, which sees loss as one type of trauma-like experience. Over time, I found myself applying principles of trauma treatment to my cases on a routine basis. However, it wasn't until I began providing clinical supervision to beginning therapists that I realized that I had developed such a systematic approach to child and family treatment.

One source of technical data for this book is an informal EMDR Institute in-house publication (Greenwald 1993c), written for those already trained in both EMDR and child therapy, that provides guidance in adapting the adult-oriented EMDR method to younger clients. When I interviewed child EMDR practitioners for that booklet in 1992, two things struck me. First, I could find only about thirty people in the United States who were using EMDR with children (I may have missed a few). Second, there was wide variation among practitioners in terms of techniques used as well as success rates. Many simply didn't know what to do, while others had developed an array of creative approaches. There was no accepted repertoire or standard of care available for using EMDR with children, and this was reflected in the hit-or-miss nature of the reported outcomes. (Actually, only a few people reported failure, but many others were simply unwilling to try.) That booklet included techniques and protocols based on practitioner interviews, minutes of the Child and Adolescent Special Interest Group meetings, conference presentations, published articles, and a number of my own innovations and case studies.

The event of this book's publication reflects a number of changes in the field. Now that EMDR has such strong empirical support, the professional community is showing much more interest. Practitioners want to know what EMDR is, how it is used, and whether they should learn how to do it. Also, now that so many thousands of clinicians have been trained in EMDR, and because training is now available from so many sources, this book's publication makes the technical information more widely available. Finally, there have been numerous further developments in applying EMDR to children and adolescents, which are included here. New source materials include conference presentations, published articles, numerous conversations with colleagues, Internet discussions, and my own consulting and clinical experience. I have done my best to include everything available regarding EMDR's use with children and adolescents.

Part I addresses EMDR in child and adolescent therapy. Chapter 1 features several vignettes, including case histories and selected session transcripts, to provide a basic idea of what goes on in a trauma-focused EMDR session with children and adolescents. A number of cases or segments of sessions are presented throughout the book. As per standard practice, names have been altered, along with other identifying information, to protect the privacy of those involved. Some vignettes represent actual cases whereas others represent composites.

Chapters 2 and 3 present a generic trauma-informed approach to child treatment to show how EMDR can be creatively used even for problems that are not typically viewed as trauma based. The trauma orientation does not replace other ways of understanding child problems (e.g., systems, behavioral, psychodynamic, or physiological perspectives); rather, it organizes them in a particular way. I present integrative treatment approaches, including EMDR, guided by the trauma orientation. I describe interventions for a specific presenting problem—disruptive behavior disorders. Children with these disorders are commonly referred for treatment, and they are one of my special interests. However, the overall approach, along with many of the interventions, can easily be adapted to work with other types of presenting problems. Chapter 2 features a comprehensive treatment approach for disruptive latency-aged boys, including family and individual therapy components as well as possible medical and educational interfaces. Chapter 3 features an integrative individual therapy protocol for adolescents with conduct disorder.

Part II addresses the technical repertoire for using EMDR with children and adolescents. It reviews the standard (adult) EMDR protocol, and gives detailed rationales and instructions for child- and adolescent-specific variations.

Part III addresses special applications of the trauma orientation and EMDR, along with context-specific considerations, for a variety of ages, presenting problems, and treatment contexts.

The chapters address infants and toddlers, very young children, family therapy, and bed-wetting. Chapter 12 covers special considerations for additional specialized populations and other treatment contexts.

The appendices provide resources for tracking down a variety of information on child trauma and EMDR, including child trauma measures, parent education handouts, scholarly articles, and training opportunities (Appendix A). A review of child trauma provides the foundation for the book's clinical orientation (Appendix B).

The text itself is nearly free of citations, for two reasons. First, the approach I describe is based on integrating the trauma orientation with generally accepted clinical principles. Second, regarding the EMDR-specific technical innovations, I don't actually know where a lot of the material comes from. The grapevine among EMDR practitioners is such that it is often very hard to track down exactly where a particular technique originated. In many cases, I'm not even sure anymore if I made something up myself, heard about it somewhere, or, just as likely, heard about it and then modified it. Where a specific source is known, it is credited.

This book serves several functions. First, it provides an introduction to a trauma-based integrative approach to child and adolescent psychotherapy, incorporating the selective use of EMDR. It also provides a practical reference for clinicians seeking both theoretical and technical guidance on how to use EMDR with children and adolescents, and it serves as a documented standard of care for training and research purposes. I hope the book provides some encouragement, as well as raw material, for those who wish to further develop this approach. There is plenty of room for progress, and I look forward to including the reader's findings and innovations in a future edition.

PART I

EMDR IN CHILD AND ADOLESCENT THERAPY

1

Child and
Adolescent Trauma

Eye movement desensitization and reprocessing (EMDR) is best known as a treatment for traumatic memories, and the vignettes in this chapter portray this classic use. But it is unusual to use EMDR as a stand-alone treatment for discrete traumatic memories, although it is occasionally called for, as in disaster relief settings. More commonly, trauma work with EMDR is done in the context of a broader treatment approach. A more detailed description of the EMDR method is given in Part II.

The EMDR protocol entails a sequence of steps to prepare the client for the potentially difficult processing of upsetting memory details, to facilitate this processing, and to support recomposure and consolidation of gains. Additional techniques are used to problem solve in difficult sessions.

Variations of the standard (adult) EMDR protocol may be used when necessary with children, depending on age and other demands of the case. The protocol is often simplified, and some components may be modified.

The following vignettes include a combination of case history and selected verbatim in-session dialogue, as well as commentary. The cases presented here and elsewhere in the book represent my personal style as a therapist.

CASE VIGNETTES

Russell

In response to Hurricane Iniki, which struck the Hawaiian island of Kauai on September 11, 1992, disaster relief centers were set up around the island to assist the residents in their recovery. As a mental health volunteer, I used EMDR to treat ten children in the second week after the storm. A disaster relief center is a chaotic setting for conducting therapy. Crowds of people mill around a school yard or community center and wait in various lines to obtain food stamps, clothing vouchers, emergency loans, emergency housing, and hot meals. I obtained my occasional EMDR clients by hanging around and chatting with people, some of whom were parents concerned about their children's post-hurricane reactions. Treatment was limited to a single fairly brief session (15 to 30 minutes) in a semi-quiet nook or corner.

I had met Russell's mother when I treated her daughter for nightmares the day before. The mother now reported that the girl had had a good night's sleep with no bad dreams. However, she was concerned about Russell, the 5-year-old younger brother, who also had had bad dreams since the hurricane, and had begun to wet his bed again after a year of being dry.

Russell was the most difficult and unusual of the ten children I treated. The case illustrates the importance of talking first with a parent to get pertinent information about the child. The therapist must take considerable responsibility and initiative when treating young, inarticulate, traumatized children. I sought to develop rapport with Russell by accepting his assertion that he hadn't been scared, and by seeing bed-wetting as a normal response to trauma, before suggesting that he might have this problem. After the traumatic memories were processed, I *installed* a success memory as well as a role model, to fortify recovery of continence.

Installation

The installation entails having the client concentrate on a positive image and/or thought during eye movements. Difficulty in installing a positive may be an indicator that some upsetting aspect of the targeted memory remains unprocessed. The installation is used to strengthen and consolidate the gains made during the treatment.

Therapist: Your mother says that you've been having some bad dreams since the hurricane. Do you want to do something with me to try and make them go away?

Child: I don't have bad dreams.

Therapist: Oh? How come your mother said you did?

Child: Well, I didn't have one last night, but I did the night before, and another time.

Therapist: Oh. Well, would you like to do something with me to try to stop them from coming back?

Child: No.

Therapist: Okay. Do you want to try to make the bad memories from the hurricane not feel so bad?

Child: No.

Therapist: No?

Child: I don't have any bad memories.

Therapist: Okay. Where were you in the hurricane?

Child: I was in my house.

Therapist: Was it scary?

Child: No. I wasn't scared.

Therapist: You know, a lot of kids I've been talking to were afraid they were going to die during the hurricane, and you know what happened to them?

Child: No.

Therapist: Well, a lot of them are having bad dreams now, or wetting their bed. Your mother said that you've been wetting your bed, too. Is that true?

Child: Yeah.

Therapist: Do you want to try something to see if it will help you to stop wetting your bed?

Child: Yeah.

Therapist: Okay, here we go, for a dry bed. Tell me the worst thing that happened during the hurricane.

Child: When the car sank in the water.

Subjective Units of Distress Scale (SUDS)

The SUDS is a subjective rating of how bad the targeted memory feels right now. The SUDS rating is used to track progress during treatment. For adults and older children, a 0 to 10 scale is used. For younger children, the hand-spread method is simple and sufficient.

Therapist: When you think about the car sinking, how bad does it feel, really bad, like this (hands outstretched), pretty bad, like this (hands halfway out), or just a little bad, like this (hands closer together)?

Child: Like this (waves hands out); the whole room.

Alternative Methods of Inducing Eye Movements

Many younger children have a difficult time following the therapist's fingers moving across the visual field. The hand-slap method allows the child to slap each of the therapist's hands alternately. This procedure induces the eye movements—the child has to look where he is slapping—and is easier for young children to accomplish.

Therapist: Okay, think about when the car sank, and (therapist holding own hands out, palms up) hit my hand here. And now this one. Good, go back and forth, just use that one hand. Good. Okay, now take a big, deep breath, like this. And when you breathe out, breathe out all the junk. Good, you're a good breather. Now do that again, big breath, and breathe out the junk. Now think of when the car sank, and show me how bad it feels now.

Child: (hands about halfway out).

Therapist: Okay, we're going to do it again. Think about when the car sank, and hit my hands like you did before. Good. Now take a deep breath, breathe out the junk. Again. And show me how bad it feels now.

Child: (touches hands together).

Therapist: Good. Now, tell me another bad part about the hurricane.

Child: When the roof falled down.

Therapist: Think about when the roof falled down, and show me how bad that feels.

Child: (hands outstretched).

Therapist: Okay. Now think of that and hit my hands. That's enough. Now take a deep breath. Again. Good. Now show me how bad it feels.

Child: (hands a little apart).

Therapist: Okay, think about it again, and hit my hands. Now take a deep breath, and another. And show me how it feels now.

Child: (holds hands together).

Therapist: Okay, what's the next bad part from the hurricane?

Child: Nothing.

Therapist: No other bad parts?

Child: No.

Therapist: All right. Now think about how good it feels to wake up in a dry bed. Feels good, huh?

Child: Yeah.

Therapist: Okay, think about how good that feels. And hit my hands. Good. Now breathe. Again. Good. When did you stop wetting your bed, before?

Child: When I was 4.

Therapist: But now that you're older, you don't do it so much anymore, huh? Now that you're a bigger kid.

Child: Yeah, I'm 5 now.

Therapist: Tell me who you know that seems really big and strong, someone you know? Or maybe someone on TV?

Child: Hulk Hogan [a wrestler on TV].

Therapist: Would he wet his bed, or is he too big for that?

Child: He's too big.

Therapist: Okay, I want you to think about Hulk Hogan, and think about sneaking up behind him, you're so close that you can feel him breathing. And really slow, sneak up right inside him, so you can feel what it feels like to be him. And hit my hands. Now breathe. Good. Now think again about how good it feels to wake up in a dry bed. Hit my hands. Breathe. Good.

Child: Where's my mother?

Therapist: Let's go look for her, and tell her how well you did.

Discussion

In this case, I had to take considerable initiative in selecting the targets as well as the first installation (how good it feels). Russell was not articulate, would not admit to being scared, and was only motivated about one thing: not wetting the bed. Once I agreed to this goal, Russell did all he was asked. It was important for me to have my own ideas about what precipitated Russell's recent bed-wetting, and about the relationship between continence and maturity.

This treatment context afforded little in the way of opportunities for pretreatment assessment or posttreatment follow-up, factors seriously constraining treatment efforts. Still, I thought that providing EMDR treatment was both ethical and useful despite such constraints. This decision was largely based on the assumption that children's recent traumatic experiences, leading to sudden behavioral changes, can be appropriately and successfully treated in an individual psychotherapy modality. Also, as families were under stress, and children's posttraumatic symptoms constitute additional stressors, successful treatment might contribute to overall relief in the family.

Considering the limited information base on a given child, and limited opportunity for follow-up, the single-session treatment should be designed for maximum possible effect, beyond simply processing the trauma memory. I took every opportunity to reinforce Russell's sense of strength, mastery, and maturity. I used EMDR to install the good feeling of waking up dry, and, evoking Hulk Hogan, to help Russell feel big and strong. I also emphasized his strengths in other ways, for example by pointing out his age and maturity, and praising the quality of his participation. More subtly, I reinforced this message through the process itself, by having Russell actively hit my hands to effect eye movements, by not challenging his denial of fear, and by fostering client control of the session by not starting EMDR until he had identified the motivation for doing so. This "shotgun" approach to fortification of client strengths may compensate for the therapist's inability, given the transient nature of the treatment setting, to target these interventions more precisely.

Paul

On August 24, 1992, Hurricane Andrew devastated much of South Dade County in Florida. Almost four months later, many area children were still suffering the psychological consequences, generally related to prolonged fear during the event as well as subsequent loss experiences. At that time I was part of a volunteer crew of therapists specifically offering EMDR to assist in emotional recovery from the hurricane. Clients came from a variety of sources, including school referrals, posters at supermarkets, a story on the local TV station, and word of mouth. Again the single session was standard, although people did occasionally come back for another. I used EMDR with five children in this setting (Greenwald 1994a).

Paul was an eager, intelligent, 11-year-old boy who had changed markedly following the hurricane, becoming apathetic, easily frustrated, pessimistic, and irritable. Although Paul expressed no motivation for treatment, and checked his watch frequently, he was cooperative. The treatment focus was the scariest hurricane memory, of huddling in a closet with the house falling apart around him. Paul found himself reexperiencing many memory aspects, one after another, almost like watching a movie in slow motion, over and over again. In addition to fear, he expressed helplessness, saying, "I can't do anything." However, he eventually expressed full confidence in the statements, "We're gonna make it better than before," and "I'm gonna get through this." His SUDS level went from 8 to 0 very gradually as he reexperienced different memory segments. The reexperiencing of a segment was often preceded by a physical sensation. For example, when asked what he noticed in his body, he said, "My ears are hurting," and then in the next set of eye movements he reexperienced the noise and the air pressure from the storm. He commented, "I get better and better at handling this the more times I go through it." Finally, he was able to imagine weathering another hurricane, but with less fear and more comfort and companionship.

Individual Differences in Processing Traumatic Memories

Some clients doing EMDR tend to maintain a focus on the initially selected aspect of the memory, perhaps moving through various types of emotional responses over the course of the session, or perhaps simply experiencing a decrease in target-related distress. Other clients tend to run through the entire sequence of events in the memory, often a number of times, even if some particularly distressing aspects of the memory may require more attention. Those clients working on memories of events that occurred within the past few months may be more likely to "run the movie," but this may also occur with older memories.

Another variation in individual response to EMDR involves the focus on the memory itself; some clients maintain an exclusive focus on the targeted memory, whereas others jump around from one memory to another. When more than one memory is driving the symptoms, all source memories should be processed with EMDR for maximum effect. However, the method seems to work best by focusing on one memory at a time, at least for the most important of the memories targeted within a given theme. One of the challenges in conducting EMDR well is to know when to follow the client's lead, even into another memory, and when to bring him back to the initial focus.

Discussion

At one-week follow-up, Paul's mother reported a great drop in symptoms, "just about back to normal." At four-week follow-up, Paul's mother reported that a sadly anticipated family change had taken place: Paul's father had taken a job out of state, and was with his family only rarely. Despite this, the symptoms were down to nearly prehurricane baseline, a small additional improvement. This type of response is fairly typical, in that treated children seem to be able to handle new challenges that might previously have been experienced as overwhelming. Paul's mother reported that he had caught up on his schoolwork and was doing well again, and that he had a "better attitude" in general. For example, he was more forgiving of himself, and didn't feel so bad after making a mistake. And, corny but true, he was looking forward to Christmas again.

Shirley

When I was working in a large community mental health center, a female colleague who knew I was trained in EMDR asked for a consult regarding Shirley, a 15-year-old girl who had been raped the year before, and was still having pervasive fears, nightmares, and intrusive imagery. The therapy relationship was well established after several months, but Shirley's remaining symptoms seemed resistant to treatment. We discussed the possibility of a consultation, and after obtaining sufficient information I agreed. Although I did not require a lot of detail on the event itself, I did learn that the girl was not a high risk for dangerous behavior, that her pretrauma functioning was fairly good, and that she had friends as well as parents to look out for her. I also knew that I could count on this therapist to provide any follow-up support that might be needed.

Shirley's parents were both concerned and protective, and asked to meet with me during one of their sessions with the primary therapist before agreeing to let me see Shirley. I responded to questions about my background and about EMDR, and I also gave them reading material. I explained a theory of trauma processing and how EMDR seemed to get stuff "unstuck" and help the person get through it quickly. We agreed that if Shirley decided to try EMDR, it would only be for one or two sessions, with the primary therapist present and continuing therapy afterward.

> ## Explaining Trauma and EMDR to Parents and Teens
>
> Here is what I typically tell parents and teens about trauma and how EMDR can help. I might give additional information on EMDR, but the focus is on trauma theory. I like this explanation because it is consistent with current scientific knowledge, and because clients invariably nod their heads in recognition as

I describe the various elements of the posttraumatic reaction. It can help to include examples consistent with their own experience. This is what I say:

> When you have a really bad experience, there are two things that you can do with it, two ways you can go. One way is to keep the memory right in front of you, keep on thinking about it, talking about it, having feelings about it. This can be hard but it's like each time you do that, you take a little bite, chew it up, and digest it. Then it's part of your nutrition, it helps you to grow. And the part that feels bad keeps getting smaller. When they say you get stronger from going through hard times, this is how it happens.
>
> Unfortunately, sometimes people go the other way. The memory is just so bad, feels so bad, that you just want to push it out of the way, put up a wall against it, just to feel okay, to get through the day. That works, at least for a little while; it does provide relief. The problem is, the memory doesn't go away, it's always there, as fresh as the day it happened, still waiting to come in, to get chewed up and digested so it can become part of the past. And then every time something reminds you of that memory, it says, "Hey, me too, can I come in now?"
>
> Here's an example. Most of us, if someone bumps us by accident as he's walking by, well, maybe we get a little irritated for a second but it's no big deal, just "Excuse me" or "What's wrong with him?" and that's the end of it. But someone who's got a lot of anger pushed behind that wall, bump into him like that, he's got the normal small reaction that we do, plus all that stuff behind the wall says, "Me, too," and now he's so mad that he's ready to fight. And that's the problem, that stuff behind the wall, it can jump you at any time, make you overreact, make it hard to handle things that should be easy. And sometimes it just kind of leaks through, makes you feel sad or scared or discouraged or whatever. It's always waiting at the door. And you can get busy, think about other things, get drunk, whatever, but it's always there, waiting to come in.

So sometimes when people get sick of having these problems, they go to a therapist for help. And with the therapist's help, you reach back behind that wall, take out a little piece, chew it up, digest it, and get that much stronger. This works. The thing is, it can take a long time, months or longer, and even then you might not get through the whole thing. With EMDR, it's a lot like other therapy, you reach back behind the wall, take out a piece, chew it up, the whole thing. It's just that with EMDR, you go through the pieces a lot faster, maybe get through a whole bad memory in just a couple of sessions, sometimes more, sometimes less. Also, EMDR seems to be more thorough, so you're not as likely to have stuff left over behind the wall. The thing is, going through the different parts of the memory so fast, it's very concentrated, and it can get pretty intense sometimes. For some people it's just too much and they have to stop, take a break. But a lot of people would rather just get through it and get it over with.

Two weeks later, I met Shirley. She was very quiet and shy-acting, but seemed determined to try this new thing to see if it would help. Although her primary therapist as well as her parents had discussed EMDR with her, I also did so myself, mostly to give her the chance to get used to me. I made it a point to say that some people found the process emotionally painful. I also assured her that she would not have to tell me anything she didn't want to tell me, and that she could stop whenever she wanted to. She asked few questions, mainly nodded, and finally indicated that she wanted to try it. I told her that I would be available for her session in the following week, and that when we next met it would be okay if she had more questions for me, or even changed her mind.

We met the next week, she had no further questions, and she still wanted to go through with it. It's tricky being a male therapist working with a teenaged girl who has been raped. Many girls this age don't like to talk to a man about anything to do with sex, and when feelings such as fear, shame, or guilt are tied in, it's even worse. Having her own therapist there helped a lot, but I still made an effort to help her feel comfortable and in control. I showed her that she could make the procedure stop. I helped her to access a strong part of herself, and I allowed her choices regarding degree of disclosure in the session. Of course, the more safe and in control the client feels, the more likely she will be willing and able to persevere through difficult parts of the process.

Preparing the Client

A central component of trauma treatment is to help the client feel that she is in control, and therefore safe in the session. It is from this base of safety that traumatic material can be faced and worked through. Several aspects of client preparation contribute to this sense of safety and control:

Predictability: Tell the client what to expect in the EMDR session, including possibly high levels of distress. If she is prepared for intense distress, then if it happens it's not a surprise.

Volition: To feel safe, the client needs to know that she is not stuck in this reexperiencing process, that she can change her mind at any time. The *stop means stop* intervention, demonstrated below, is a graphic and effective way to convey this sense of control.

Coping capacity: The client must have a means of coping with the potentially distressing material. This may be accomplished by discussing problem-solving options should she become upset, by training her in relaxation or self-soothing procedures, or by helping her gain access to existing inner resources such as a sense of strength.

Therapist: I told you last time that some parts of this might get pretty bad for you. Remember, if you decide to stop at some point, that doesn't mean that you're weak or can't do it. It just means you need a break. Then we'll stop and figure out together what to do next. The first thing I want to do is practice stopping. If you were a cop, how would you stop traffic with your hand?

Child: (puts arm out with hand facing forward).

Therapist: That's it. Now I'll move my hand back and forth, and you give me that stop signal (moves hand back and forth). Go ahead, make me stop (client gives the signal; therapist stops). Good. Let's try that one more time (motions repeated). Good. So if you ever decide to take a break, you know what to do.

Child: (nods).

Therapist: Before we get to work on the memory, I want you to just imagine for a minute that the whole thing was a bad dream. If you had to go back into that bad dream, what would you need to be safe, to be okay?

Child: Would need to be stronger, to be able to protect myself.

Therapist: What's the strongest animal you can think of?

Child: A tiger.

Therapist: I want you to picture a tiger, a really strong one: what size it is, the colors, how it stands or moves. Concentrate on that, and now move your eyes like we practiced (therapist moves hand from side to side, child follows with her eyes). Good. What was that like?

Child: Kind of weird.

Therapist: Okay. Concentrate on the tiger again, now move your eyes (eye movements). How did that go?

Child: Good, I guess.

Therapist: Do you feel more safe, less safe, or about the same?

Child: More safe.

Therapist: Okay. This time when you concentrate on the tiger, also say to yourself, "I'm safe" (eye movements). Now, more safe, less safe, or the same?

Child: More safe again. The tiger won't let anyone hurt me.

Therapist: Good. Now, as we get into the memory, remember, whatever happened last year, now it's your memory, you can do what you want with it. If you want to bring the tiger in, it's up to you.

Child: Okay.

Setting up the Targeted Memory

The standard adult protocol for setting up the targeted memory can be used with most adolescents. It involves eliciting an intense, multimodal focus on the most disturbing segment of the memory. The client is asked to identify the most disturbing image, as well as associated cognition (or negative belief), emotion, and physical sensation. (The adult client is asked to rate the felt validity of a more positive belief, but I skipped that part here.) The client is also asked to rate the current level of distress, using the SUDS, associated with the memory.

Therapist: Okay. Now I want you to think of the bad memory we'll be working with. Pick out the worst moment from the memory, maybe the part that you think about when you don't want to. Do you have something like that?

Child: (nods).

Therapist: Do you want to tell me what it is, or just think it?

Child: Just think it.

Therapist: Okay. Now, when you have this picture, what are you saying, what are you telling yourself?

Child: I'm scared.

Therapist: And when you have this memory, what does it make you believe about yourself right now?

Child: What do you mean?

Therapist: Well, here are some things that other girls might be thinking in your situation. Tell me if any of these fits for you, or what would feel most true. Some might say, "It was my fault," or "I'm not safe," or "There's something wrong with me," or maybe something else. What would be most true for you?

Child: I'm not safe, I'm afraid to go anywhere by myself anymore.

Therapist: And when you have this picture, and the "I'm not safe," the feeling that goes with that, you said scared?

Child: (nods).

Therapist: Where do you feel that, where in your body?

Child: In my chest and throat, it feels kind of closed in, tight.

Therapist: On a scale of 0 to 10, with 10 the worst possible feeling, and 0 being no bad feeling at all, how strong is the bad feeling now?

Child: Nine or 10.

Therapist: Pretty bad then. Now remember, when you do the eye movements, you have two jobs. One is to concentrate on this as well as you can, or if something comes up, just concentrate on that. There's no right or wrong, whatever happens is okay. The other job is to be an observer, like you're watching it on the VCR. Okay?

Child: (nods).

Therapist: So now get back the picture—"I'm not safe . . . scared"—that feeling in your chest and throat (eye movements). Good. Take a deep breath, relax. Now, what was that like, what did you notice?

Child: Nothing.

Therapist: Did the picture get stronger or weaker or change or stay the same?

Child: A little stronger.

Therapist: Okay. What about the scared feeling: more, less, different, the same?

Child: More.

Therapist: Concentrate on that (eye movements). What came up this time?

Child: A little less scared now.

Therapist: Okay, stay with that (eye movements). What did you notice this time?

Child: Less scared, more relaxed up here (taps chest).

Therapist: Stay with that (eye movements). What did you notice now?

Child: Now I'm really mad!

This proceeded for about forty-five minutes, with Shirley moving through various disturbing aspects of the memory, along with various feelings: fear, anger, sadness, a sense of acceptance, and the idea that she could become stronger from the experience. Along the way there were several periods of intense emotion, which in each instance dissipated over several minutes. If we had gotten stuck along the way—meaning no apparent progress or change after a couple of sets of eye movements—I would have had Shirley imagine bringing her tiger in to protect her. However, this was not necessary. I don't know if starting out with the tiger actually facilitated the session, or if she would have been fine anyway. My habit is to help the client access this type of resource up front, so if we do need it later, it's handy.

Many children and adolescents start out by saying that they would rather "just think it" and not tell me about their target image. Usually, as the session moves along, they do disclose many details, and being able to talk about it seems to be part of the healing. In Shirley's case, she kept the details to herself. I respected this and knew that she was able to talk to her own therapist about these details if she wanted to. But it made for an odd experience for me, not knowing the details of what we were actually working on for much of the session.

When we ended the session, Shirley had made a lot of progress but had not completely worked through the distressing aspects of the memory. She reported an ending SUDS of 3, which indicated substantial resolution as well as an unspecified amount left to process. (The SUDS ratings are not always entirely accurate; someone can think something is a 3 and then get into the memory and find that it's really much higher.) In the last few minutes of the session, we focused on positives to help Shirley consolidate the gains she made in the session, and to regain her composure. During eye movements, I had her concentrate on the tiger and say, "I'm safe." I also guided her in a deep breathing relaxation exercise. She seemed reasonably comfortable and composed when she left. I told her that sometimes "waves of feelings" or other unpredictable reactions may follow a session, and that if she was concerned she should call her therapist.

My colleague told me a week, and again a month, later that Shirley's bad dreams and intrusive memories were no longer a problem. The fears were still present but not so pervasive. I explained that the EMDR should be continued until the memory was completely processed (e.g., SUDS rating of 0), and that there might also be unidentified prior memories feeding the symptoms. I had no follow-up session with Shirley. She and the therapist were both apparently quite satisfied that EMDR had helped Shirley get over the "hump," and chose to go back to doing the rest of the treatment their own way.

2

Latency-Aged Boys with Disruptive Behavior Disorders

Many clinicians now consider EMDR the treatment of choice for obvious trauma cases such as those described in the previous chapter. EMDR is also useful in a much wider range of applications, including many types of cases that have not traditionally been identified as trauma based. But many children's mental health and behavioral problems actually are trauma based (see Appendix B), even if we have been slow to recognize this. Also, even when there has not been an extreme trauma as defined by the *Diagnostic and Statistical Manual* (*DSM-IV*), children's problems often develop from upsetting experiences such as family breakup, school frustrations, peer rejection, or major loss. EMDR's accelerated information processing effect seems to work regardless of the severity of the upsetting memory.

The Accelerated Information Processing Effect

Shapiro (1995) has proposed accelerated information processing as a way to account for EMDR's effect. Trauma can lead to symptoms not simply because it was so upsetting, but because the person does not get over it. Instead of gradually processing upsetting material—or "information"—to integration, something gets stuck. EMDR seems not only to restart the integration process, but also to facilitate a much more rapid processing of such material than we have seen in other forms of therapy. The accelerated information processing effect can also account for EMDR's apparent enhancement of learning, performance, visualization, and other positive-focused applications.

I tend to conceptualize cases by extending trauma theory to account for the notion that children's problems come, at least in part, from upsetting past experiences (see Appendix B). Most children referred for treatment have experienced significant trauma or loss, which either predisposed to vulnerability or directly precipitated the presenting problem. My awareness of the trauma's (broadly defined) contribution to children's problems has become a guiding principle for case formulation and treatment planning. This orientation does not replace other ways of understanding child problems (e.g., systems, psychodynamic, behavioral); rather, it provides a framework for organizing the various perspectives that may apply.

THE TREATMENT APPROACH

This chapter is about using EMDR in the context of a comprehensive trauma-informed treatment approach for problems that may not seem to be trauma related. EMDR represents only a small portion of the overall treatment approach, which also includes family therapy as well as other interventions as needed. The approach will be demonstrated with the example of latency-aged boys with disruptive behavior disorders.

Disruptive behavior disorder implies an impulse control problem, which in turn implies strong underlying impulses as well as poor self-control. This comprehensive approach targets the underlying anger, sadness, and fear as well as the behavior itself. The same approach may often be used, with only slight modification, for treatment of children with a variety of presenting problems such as depression or anxiety. In each case, the trauma-based case formulation leads to efforts to make the environment more supportive and secure, to resolve upsetting memories that may drive the symptoms, and to develop more adaptive behaviors.

This treatment approach has been developed and used primarily with boys who present with school-related behavior problems. Commonly identified concerns include low frustration tolerance, poor coping skills, quick temper, and disruptive and/or aggressive acting out. Most have been previously diagnosed with attention deficit/hyperactive disorder (AD/HD), but not always accurately (some posttraumatic reactions mimic symptoms of AD/HD). Some have additional specific learning disabilities. Nearly all of these children also present behavior problems at home. By the time these children are finally referred, the child, parents, and teacher have often become mired in a cycle of increasing frustration and anger.

Because chronic disruptive behavior is typically supported by a number of factors, it merits a comprehensive treatment approach. The first step is a careful evaluation, so that an accurate case formulation can be presented to the family. This formulation should help all concerned to achieve a shift in perspective, from viewing the child as bad to seeing him as sad, scared, or angry. Once adults have this understanding, they are in a better position to implement the suggested interventions: consistent discipline, a supportive attitude, and a focus on positive behaviors. The individual portion of the treatment typically begins with EMDR for trauma and loss, followed by EMDR-enhanced skill development for self-control and other desired behaviors related to doing well in school and socially. Some cases also warrant medication and/or a formal behavior modification program.

ASSESSMENT

The assessment process is important in its own right, but also because it is the beginning of the clinical intervention and of the therapist's relationship with the child and the caregiving adults. The assessment of an acting-out child benefits from the information provided by multiple sources, including the teacher, parent, and child, as well as from firsthand observation.

The Teacher

The best way to work with teachers is to show respect for their competence. Elementary school teachers generally feel that they know their students well. They also tend to feel that the student is the problem. The therapist can develop a good working relationship with the teacher by conveying a positive view of her. Start by asking about the child, what he does well, when and how he gets in trouble, and how the teacher then responds. Ask also how the teacher handles other challenging students with whom she may be more successful. When the teacher feels that you regard her as competent, she will be less likely to be defensive and more likely to lay out her problem with the child and ask for help. Later, the therapist can provide advice on implementing a more therapeutic classroom environment for the child, perhaps involving a quicker disciplinary response, focusing on positive behaviors, and/or a behavioral program. Teachers, like parents, are clients as well as collaborators in the child's treatment, and need to be treated with care and consideration.

The Parents

Although meeting with the family as a whole is important, it can also be worthwhile to spend some time with the parents alone.

One of the main goals of therapy is often for the parents to gain greater authority in the family, which requires role differentiation. Meeting alone with the parents, and discussing things that could not be discussed with the child present, helps to establish this sense of role differentiation. In families where nothing is kept from the children, the parents' meetings are particularly important as opportunities to make the point that children should not be exposed to "grown-up" talk. Also, if the parents have an opportunity to talk about the child's problems without the child there, they are less likely to embarrass the child by saying those things in front of him or her.

The assessment routine with parents is straightforward. The therapist asks for the child's developmental history and a comprehensive description of the problem including antecedents, behaviors, and consequences. It is worthwhile to ask the parents for their theory about why the child has the problem. Sometimes they will give an insightful answer that can be helpful; an answer reflecting lack of insight is also noteworthy.

I start by drawing a genogram, which is a map of the family members and their relationships to one another. Most families appreciate a therapist who will make an effort to learn "normal" things about them ("What kind of work do you do?" "When were you married?" "What do you do together as a family?") prior to focusing on the problems. It is important to gain and convey a positive impression of the family early in the interview, and, conversely, for the family to gain a positive impression of the therapist. The following issues should also be addressed in the interview:

- Evidence of possible physiological causes of AD/HD-like traits: prenatal exposure to alcohol or drugs, other prenatal or perinatal insult, a hyperactive temperament from infancy on, seizures, high fevers, and head injuries.
- Attachment history, including parent–infant bonding, family relationships, and friendships.

- Reasons for difficulty in school, including AD/HD, low IQ, and specific learning disabilities. Sometimes high IQ also leads to difficulty if the child becomes bored.
- Method of discipline in the family. Rather than asking, "Do you hit your child?" which may make a parent defensive, the therapist asks, "When the kids break a rule, how do you set them straight? Scold, spank, time-out, ground, what do you do?" Discipline is a critical issue. Do both parents use the same approach? Every time? Do parents give in, change their minds, get angry? If physical discipline is used, is it administered in a rule-bound and systematic manner (e.g., an automatic spanking for lying), or do the parents simply strike when angry?
- History of the problem, with as much detail as necessary for the therapist to get the picture. When did it start? When did it get worse? How does it look at home, at school, with peers? What are the contexts and consequences in each setting?
- The child's trauma and loss history, including cumulative trauma, broadly defined, such as repeated school failure experiences, a pattern of harsh treatment by a family member, or a pattern of social rejection. The therapist may preface this inquiry by commenting, "Unfortunately, no matter how hard parents try, most kids end up facing some hard times." The therapist can give a "menu" of examples of potentially upsetting experiences—"a car accident, a house fire, a hurricane, the death of a friend or someone in the family, physical or sexual abuse, getting hurt, seeing someone else get hurt, seeing parents yelling or throwing things . . ."—to orient the parents to the type of material that may be pertinent. This list can be tailored to include items that the therapist may suspect were upsetting for the child, for example, divorce. Parents often underestimate the impact that a given event may have had on their child.

- Trauma symptoms, such as nightmares, bed-wetting, night fears, anger, irritability, anxiety, or withdrawal. Objectively scored parent-report trauma symptom scales can be helpful (see Appendices A and B). Even if parents had not previously connected an event with the child's presenting problem, they may be able to tie the onset of some trauma symptoms to a particular upsetting event.
- The child's good points: "What do you like most about your child?" Intentionally posed after the description of discipline and the trauma history, which may already be leading to a preliminary understanding of the child's problems, this question builds the parents' sympathy for the child, perhaps beginning a shift from the usual anger and frustration.

Throughout the interview I ask questions and make comments, share impressions, and test hypotheses. At the end I present my overall impressions, tentative conclusions, and recommendations. This gives the parents the opportunity to nip any of my misconceptions in the bud, and their responses give me new information. This exposure to my ideas helps parents know what to expect at the treatment planning meeting. Some parents have the initiative to act on my ideas and report progress by our next session.

The Child

Most children who meet with mental health professionals are not really sure why they are there or what to expect, in part because their parents are not sure themselves, and so don't know how to explain it. I start by asking the child if he knows why he is meeting with me and what he was told. I rarely get a good answer. I explain: "Your mom and dad and your teacher told me they want you to do better in school instead of just getting in trouble the way you do. They asked me to get to know you bet-

ter, so maybe I can help figure out how you can do better in
school." Since most children would also like to do better, this
introduction is generally sufficient to elicit cooperation.

The next task is to make the child comfortable in disclos-
ing important information. One approach is to start by asking
easy questions to get the child used to responding before asking about personal and potentially painful material. Another
strategy is to give the child overt control over the choice to disclose. It is important to avoid going into too much depth at this
point, lest the child leave the session in distress, which would
be bad for the child and bad for the therapy relationship. After
introducing the purpose of the assessment, I typically proceed
as follows:

> *Therapist:* My first job is to get to know a lot about you, so
> I'll be asking you a lot of questions. But what if I ask
> you a question that you don't want to answer, maybe
> you don't know me well enough to talk about some-
> thing, or maybe it would hurt your feelings to talk
> about it. What could you do?
>
> *Child:* (shrugs shoulders).
>
> *Therapist:* Well, what could you say if you don't want to talk
> about something?
>
> *Child:* I don't want to talk about it?
>
> *Therapist:* Sure, that would work. Try saying that again.
>
> *Child:* I don't want to talk about it.
>
> *Therapist:* I think that'll work. Let's try it. I'll ask you a ques-
> tion that you don't want to answer. What's the capital
> of Guatemala?
>
> *Child:* I don't want to talk about that (smiles).
>
> *Therapist:* Good. Now what if you forget how to use words,
> let's have a hand signal, too. How does a cop stop cars
> with his hand?
>
> *Child:* (holds hand out facing forward).
>
> *Therapist:* So that can be a signal, too. Let's try it out.
> What's 26 times 491?

Child: (holds hand out again).

Therapist: Okay, that works, too. So here come the questions. Ready? What's your favorite color?

The interview can proceed from favorite color to favorite food, favorite activities, school likes and dislikes, and whatever digressions follow naturally. Asking a child what he likes to do or what he's good at can help him feel more comfortable and more positively viewed. This is a refreshing change for a child who is used to eliciting anger and scoldings from adults, and a good way to further the therapy alliance. The child should also be asked about family relationships and discipline, about friendships, and about his own view of the presenting problem. Many children believe that they only act out when provoked; however, they may also acknowledge that they overreact.

Projective interviewing can help to identify potential sources of motivation as well as themes of concern. I typically ask for a future goal ("When you're older and done with school, what do you think you want to be doing?"), a favorite animal they would like to be ("If you could be any animal, what would you be?"), three wishes, and the "magic wand" question ("If you could just wave a magic wand and make things better in your life, what would be different?"). Some of these questions may need follow-up to clarify the child's intent:

Therapist: So you might want to be a policeman, or maybe build houses? What would be good about being a policeman? What does a policeman do?

Child: Well, he catches the bad guys and locks them up in jail. The police, they have this special radar stuff to find out where the bad guys are, where the crimes are gonna happen, they have it in their police cars.

Therapist: That would help a lot. And what would be good about building houses?

Child: My uncle, he builds houses, he lets me help him sometimes when I'm on vacation. It's fun, and he says it's good money, too. I could build my own house someday.

Finally, ascertaining the history and symptoms of trauma is both critical and highly sensitive. (This information should be obtained from both the parents and the child, since either may omit important data.) The therapist should provide a lot of guidance in this part of the interview, to help the child feel safe and to orient him to the types of responses that are called for.

Therapist: Now I'm going to ask some questions that might be hard to answer. Do you remember what to do if you don't want to answer a question?

Child: Say "I don't want to talk about it."

Therapist: Right. Say that again, just for practice.

Child: I don't want to talk about it.

Therapist: Good. Now I'm going to ask you to tell me about the worst things that ever happened to you. Things that maybe scared you, or hurt your feelings inside. Can you think of some, or should I tell you what other kids say?

Child: Other kids.

Therapist: Well, what other kids might say is if they had been in a car accident, or a house fire, or a hurricane . . .

Child: I was in a hurricane, we had to hide in the bathroom. Then after, we had to move, the house was all wrecked.

Therapist: Okay, that's a good example. Let's see, what else do other kids say? Some kids had their feelings hurt when they were beat up, or if someone made them do sex things, or if they saw something really bad, like someone getting hurt, or their parents fighting, or if someone died.

Child: My parents used to fight pretty bad before they broke up. We used to hide behind the stairs.

Therapist: Okay, so the hurricane, and when your parents would fight. Anything else?

Child: When my grandma died.
Therapist: Did you know your grandma much?
Child: Yeah, we used to stay with her all summer.
Therapist: Oh, that's sad that she died. How old were you then?

The therapist is trying to get the basic information in a reasonably sensitive manner, without, however, inviting the child to open up the wounds at this point. If the parents have mentioned additional events not volunteered by the child, the therapist can ask about them as well. It is worthwhile to get a SUDS rating on each event, as well as the approximate age at which it happened. However, the therapist should not be fooled if the child denies any current distress regarding the things that actually bother him most.

It is particularly useful to identify possible trauma symptoms, not only to validate the therapist's hypothesis, but also because these symptoms may be distressing and thus provide motivation for treatment. An objectively scored measure of trauma symptoms can be useful. The "menu" approach is also useful here, in that children seem to find it easier to select from the menu than to initiate disclosure of such socially unacceptable things as bed-wetting or not having friends. Of course, while such problems may indeed reflect trauma effects, other causes or contributing factors should not be ruled out.

Therapist: Let me tell you some of the things that other kids wish could be better for them, and you can tell me if you wish any of these things. Some kids wish they didn't wet their bed anymore . . .
Child: I don't wet my bed.
Therapist: Oh, good for you. Some kids wish they didn't have bad dreams so much, or weren't afraid at night . . .
Child: I have bad dreams a lot.
Therapist: A lot like every night, or once a week, or once a month?

Child: Some nights, like not every night but a lot.
Therapist: Is that something you wish you didn't have?
Child: Yes.
Therapist: Okay. Some kids wish they had more friends, or got along better with kids . . .
Child: I just hate it when I get into fights.
Therapist. Okay. And some kids wish they didn't get into so much trouble, or wish they could do better in school.
Child: I wish all that.

Here is where the therapist can begin to suggest a trauma-based case formulation to the child. One purpose is to help the child to see himself in a more positive light, as someone who is trying to do well but is thwarted. Another purpose is to build motivation for treatment activities.

Therapist: I'm getting a little confused here. Before, you told me that you don't really pay attention much in school, that you don't try as hard as you should. Now you're saying that you really want to do well. Is that true, you want to do better?
Child: Yeah. Sometimes I try but then I mess up anyway.
Therapist: I have an idea why that might be happening. Should I tell you my idea?
Child: Yeah.
Therapist: Sometimes, when bad things happen to kids, the bad feelings get stuck inside and don't go away. Those bad feelings can stay stuck for a long time, even from as long ago as when you used to see your parents fight, or from the hurricane. Then later, maybe you're in school, and something goes a little wrong for you, those bad feelings come up and it's so strong that you mess up. Do you think that could be happening with you?
Child: I think so, maybe.

Therapist: Do you think that if those bad feelings got smaller, you could be more in charge of how well you do in school?

Child: Yeah.

TREATMENT

Developing the Treatment Contract

Although treatment has been occurring since first contact, the more formal phase of treatment begins following the evaluation, when the findings and recommendations are presented to the family. My own preference is for giving each party a sneak preview so that they are prepared to take the next step together. This trauma-based case formulation defines trauma broadly to include loss as well as any pattern of cumulatively damaging experiences. Connecting a problem behavior to specific experiences helps to exonerate the child somewhat; it's not that he was born bad or that he wants to be bad, he is just stuck with some bad feelings from past experience, and doesn't know what else to do. This view of the problem allows for sympathy as well as expectation of change, and it sets the stage nicely for both the individual and the family interventions.

Therapist: Let me tell you what I've learned about your child, and what I think can be done for him. Then we can talk about it and you can decide what you want to do. One thing I've found out is that everyone I talk to really likes him! He watches out for his little sister, helps around the house sometimes, wants to do well at school, and has friends who like to play with him. But I know he has a lot of trouble with his reading, and that makes schoolwork hard to do. And the reason you're talking with me is because he also gets into a lot of trouble at school, not doing his work, making noise, and getting into fights. And you told me that sometimes at home he doesn't listen, either. So let me tell you why I think he is the way he is.

Any kid who has this much trouble reading is bound to have a hard time in school. When he sees the other kids doing stuff he can't do, he probably wonders if he's stupid, even though he's really not. It's got to be pretty frustrating to hit that wall again and again. And when it's hard to read, it's hard to do almost any subject in school. Even math has word problems this year. So one thing I think is happening is that he's so sick of getting frustrated that sometimes he'd rather not even try, so he doesn't have to get frustrated again. And then when he does try and something is hard, it reminds him of all those other times, and so he decides right away he can't do it, and just gives up. It's like all the years of frustration are piled up on him.

Parent: Yeah, that's true, reading's in everything. And he gives up more and more now, sometimes he won't even try anymore.

Therapist: And there's something else that's made it even harder for him. When something really upsetting happens to kids, like seeing their parents in a bad fight, or like the hurricane, the bad feelings can get stuck inside. And when something happens that reminds him of the bad things, even if it's a little thing, all those old feelings kick in and his reaction can be really strong. I think that's why he gets into so much trouble, because he's reacting with all the old feelings too, not just what's going on at the time.

Nearly all parents can understand the idea of a pileup of stress due to cumulative negative experiences. They can also generally understand the concept of a trigger activating the stuck feelings. However, bringing up specific behavioral examples can be useful to illustrate the point if a parent is struggling. Once this case formulation has been accepted, recommendations can be made. At this stage parents almost always accept the formulation and embrace the plan. The critical element at this point is to insist on the importance of the parents' role, so they don't think that they can just leave all the work to the therapist.

> *Therapist:* There are several things that we usually do for kids in your son's situation. The first, of course, is to give the special help in reading that he's getting at school. Then there are things that you can do at home that can help him to feel more secure and less worried. That will help him to calm down. Also, I can work with him one on one to help him get over the old bad feelings that he still carries around. Down the line, we might want to do a behavior chart, but we might not need it.
>
> *Parent:* That sounds good. I really think he needs that individual counseling, to have someone to talk to.
>
> *Therapist:* Yes, I think it should help. But the biggest job will be yours. If you can make him feel more secure at home, then my job will go much better and I can get a lot more done. You're much more important than I am. I'm just some guy he talks to once in a while. You're his mom.
>
> *Parent:* So what should I be doing?
>
> *Therapist:* There are a few things, we talked a little about them before. When you told me that your husband is kind of hard on the kids, and you give in to them a lot? That kind of makes a kid feel insecure, because the rules are always changing. Also you said that sometimes you get really mad and end up yelling at him, or making some big punishment you know you won't keep, later. So you kind of lose control, doing things

you don't really want to do. When you lose control, that also can make him feel insecure. He really needs you to be in charge, so you can protect him and keep him safe and under control.

Parent: It's not easy with these kids. They do make me mad sometimes.

Therapist: I know it's not easy. I can give you some things to try, and you can see how they work for you. Where there are problems, I'll help you figure it out. It's a lot of work for you, but most parents find that once they get into it, their kids really do calm down and things are better.

Some parents may already feel like failures because they couldn't handle the child's problem on their own. When the therapist sets the parents up as active partners in the child's treatment, the parents are likely to become more confident and effective. The therapist should also be vigilant in pointing out the parents' contributions at every opportunity. Even when the child responds dramatically to an individual session, the therapist can accurately say that the parental support made it possible. The therapist's goal is not to get the glory but to help the family.

Therapist: So if your child skins his knee, gets a cut, what do you do?

Parent: Wash it up, put on a Band-Aid.

Therapist: Okay. What if he breaks his leg, do you put on a splint, or what?

Parent: No, take him to the emergency room, to the hospital.

Therapist: Of course you do. The everyday things you can handle yourself, but sometimes a problem gets too big, and you go to a professional for help. This is the same thing. This is what good parents do when it gets too big to handle on their own.

The last part of the agenda for the treatment contracting session is to have the parents give the child explicit permission to engage in treatment, and to make progress. Parental support can be conveyed simply by reviewing the child's goals, for example, doing better in school and getting in less trouble, and encouraging the child to cooperate with the therapist. Feared negative outcomes associated with progress should be addressed as needed (see Chapter 10).

> *Therapist:* Your mom and dad were telling me that they want you to learn to control yourself better, so you can do better in school and not get in so much trouble. You were saying you wanted that too, when we talked last week, remember? So you and I are going to work together to help you get better at controlling yourself. Do you think that when you're older, more strong, you can control yourself better?
>
> *Child:* Yeah, when I'm older.
>
> *Therapist:* So what we'll be working on is helping you get older and stronger so that you can handle things better, things that are hard now like when someone gets you mad. Okay?
>
> *Child:* Okay.
>
> *Therapist:* So here's what we'll be doing. Your parents told me that they might be getting more strict at home, to help you learn to do what you're supposed to do. And you and I will meet once a week, I can kind of coach you in some tricks to help you control yourself better. Also, remember what we talked about, how those bad feelings could be stuck inside from old things that happened, from the hurricane and from seeing your parents fight?
>
> *Child:* Yeah.
>
> *Therapist:* Another thing we can do is talk about those old things, and try to make the bad feelings be smaller so they don't mess you up so much.

The main goal at this point is simply to let the child know, in the parents' presence and with their participation and support, that he will be meeting with you in treatment to accomplish goals set by himself and his parents. The specifics of the individual treatment will be worked out in subsequent sessions.

Parent/Family Therapy

Stabilizing the home environment can make a very strong contribution to the child's treatment. My focus with parents is child centered, and boils down to helping them to implement consistent, supportive discipline: "Remember, discipline is about keeping your child safe, it's about helping him to become a good person. Remember, discipline comes from love, not anger." In some families, other factors such as overly variable daily routines, intense parental conflict, and unreliable visits with noncustodial parents can also contribute to the child's sense of insecurity, and should be addressed accordingly. However, discipline is typically the primary focus of this portion of the treatment.

There are a number of common obstacles to effective discipline with which parents may require special assistance. Parents may confuse discipline with being harsh or cruel, and so they attempt to avoid it. Parents, especially single mothers, may feel guilty that their children have been exposed to hard times previously, and so attempt to compensate by indulging them. Parents may find themselves compensating for each other, with one parent becoming harsher the more the other is lax, and vice versa; this is especially common with stepfamilies. Parents may be worn out and lack the energy to follow through, even when they make the attempt to take a stand with the child. Of course, ineffective disciplinary approaches facilitate acting out, which causes the parents to get angry and then to make an even more ineffective response. This cycle tends to reinforce the parents' misconception that discipline is about anger and punishment. Furthermore, many parents—like their children—are quite reactive, and can get more angry at their child than the situation warrants.

I use the trauma-based formulation to emphasize the need for consistent discipline. I rely on a parenting skills handout (see Appendix A) and typically take a full session just to go over the concepts and details. By the end of that session, parents should understand that their consistent and supportive discipline can serve as the foundation for their child's sense of security, which is in turn a precursor of the success of the individual portion of treatment. Parents should have sufficient opportunity to discuss and rehearse this discipline approach in the session so that they feel prepared to implement it at home. A caution against overly high expectations can help parents to feel successful with even small progress.

> *Therapist:* Habits take time to change. What I would like you to do is try this out, do your best, and then come back and tell me which parts worked and which parts didn't. Then we can solve the problems and you can do even better after that. So we're not expecting any dramatic changes right now. We're just getting started.

The following repertoire of interventions can help parents to understand the issues involved, overcome the obstacles, and acquire the specific behaviors necessary for effective discipline. The therapist will have to judge which interventions to use and which to skip, according to the demands of each case.

Keep Your Promises

One of the most important concepts for parents to understand is that routines and rules are like the parents' promises to the child. This helps the parents to realize how much their own behavior has been compromising the child's sense of security. It can be introduced gently, however, by conveying the assumption that the parent has positive intent but just didn't know better.

> *Therapist:* Let me ask you something. If you tell your son, "If you clean up this mess, I'll give you some ice cream," and then he cleans up, are you going to say, "Oh, I was just kidding about that ice cream" or would you come through with it?
>
> *Parent:* Oh, I would never do that, of course I would give him the ice cream like I said.
>
> *Therapist:* I thought so. You make a promise, you wouldn't let him down. But what about this: What if he doesn't do what you say, some little thing, and finally you get so mad that you say, "Okay, you can't go to the park tomorrow." And then tomorrow comes and you're not mad anymore, and you realize that the punishment was too big, and it's a nice day . . .
>
> *Parent:* Oh, I let him go. Usually I do give in later on.
>
> *Therapist:* So you do break your promise in that situation?
>
> *Parent:* I guess so. I never thought of it that way.
>
> *Therapist:* When you don't do what you say, you let him down. A lot of parents don't realize that. But when you say what's going to happen, he's counting on you to make it happen. He needs you to be a rock that he can always count on. You know how it is when you can't count on someone? It feels pretty shaky. Also, you have rules for good reasons, right?
>
> *Parent:* I like to think so.
>
> *Therapist:* So let's say that he's not allowed to play in the street, and . . .
>
> *Parent:* That's a good example. There are a lot of fast cars that go by our house.
>
> *Therapist:* So let's say you tell him, "Don't play in the street or you'll have to come inside." And then he plays in the street, and you let him stay out. What will he be thinking about that?

Parent: He'll be happy he can keep on playing. He'll think
   he got away with it.

Therapist: Part of him might be happy, but part of him is
   going to wonder, going to feel all shaky and nervous
   inside . . .

Parent: Oh, like maybe I don't care about him.

Therapist: That's exactly right. Like maybe you don't care if
   he's safe or not. If you have a rule to keep him safe, to
   help him learn to be a good person, whatever, you show
   you care by keeping your rules. And by doing what you
   say, so he knows he can always count on you. That will
   help him feel safer and he can start to calm down.

Slot Machine

The importance of keeping one's word consistently can be il-
lustrated with the slot-machine metaphor.

Therapist: So you understand now that whatever you say is
   like a promise to your child. In the same way, it's really important to stick with what you say. You know how
   at the checkout counter at the store, there's always
   some kid who says, "Please, Mommy, please please
   please?"

Parent: Right, and she finally says, "Okay, here, just shut up
   already!"

Therapist: The funny thing is, that parent is actually training her kid to be a pest, to act that way.

Parent: What do you mean?

Therapist: Well, I'm gonna tell you how Las Vegas works, why
   they make so much money, because it's the same principle, and it's something you can use at home. Let's say
   I'm putting quarters in a machine, and every time I put
   a quarter in, I get a dollar back. What am I gonna do?

Parent: Keep putting quarters in.

Therapist: That's right. And then what happens if I put in a quarter, and nothing comes back?

Parent: You quit.

Therapist: Soon I quit. First, though, maybe I put in a bunch more quarters, saying, "What's wrong with this machine?" maybe bang it a couple of times. But you're right, soon I say, "I guess this machine just doesn't work anymore" and I quit, go try some other game. But what about this: What if I'm putting quarters in a machine, and mostly nothing happens, but every once in a while I get a jackpot?

Parent: That's like the slot machines.

Therapist: That's right. The real ones, they work this way for a reason. Because what's going to happen if I put in a quarter and nothing comes back?

Parent: You keep on trying.

Therapist: That's right. Maybe I'd put in ten more quarters, maybe a hundred, and each time, I'm saying to myself, "Keep trying, the next one could be the jackpot."

Parent: And then you're a millionaire and you quit your job.

Therapist: And that's just the same thing that that kid at the checkout counter is doing, when he says "Please, Mommy?" and she says "No" and it's "Please? No. Please? No. Please? No." ten times. He's saying to himself, "Keep trying, the next one could be the jackpot."

Parent: So when he bugs me and I give in . . .

Therapist: That's right. Jackpot.

Parent: I see what you're saying.

Therapist: So the trick is to just remember that yes means yes and no means no. Once you say it, just stick with it. Otherwise, you're training him to keep on bugging you, to go for that jackpot.

Parent: I've got it.

Therapist: I want to warn you, though, that this might get harder at first. Remember what happens when the machine doesn't work anymore?

Parent: He might try harder.

Therapist: Right, he might put in all those extra quarters, or hit the machine, which means that he might really try to push you, see if he really can count on you now, or if you're just kidding. And what happens if you just get tired, finally give in?

Parent: Jackpot.

Therapist: Right. So if you're going to make this work, you really have to stick with it. Once he learns, though, that you mean what you say, well, why bother putting in all those quarters? He'll have to find a different game.

Stop a Problem Quickly

This strategy serves multiple functions. It provides parents with practical steps with which to implement effective discipline. It helps parents to keep their promises, by using such small punishments that follow-through is less problematic. And it helps parents to avoid losing their temper, by intervening before a problem situation gets out of hand. When parents can learn to intervene very quickly, with very small consequences, the child is reassured without having to escalate, and the discipline problem becomes much smaller.

Therapist: One of the biggest problems parents have in keeping their promises is that they get so angry that they make punishments that seem too big later, when they're not mad anymore.

Parent: Yes, I do that.

Therapist: One way to fix this is to decide ahead of time what punishments you will use, so you don't have to think up something when you're mad.

Parent: That makes sense.

Therapist: Do you ever use time-out?

Parent: Yes, sometimes I send him to his room if I get mad and don't want him around. He can come back later, maybe in half an hour, if he wants to be good.

Therapist: I want to teach you a kind of time-out that you can use. You just pick a spot wherever you are, like in a chair or against the wall in the room you're in. And when he's in a time-out he can't talk, or play with anything, or kick the wall, or really do much of anything. And the time-out should last a minute.

Parent: A minute? That doesn't seem like much.

Therapist: Maybe it should be even shorter. I'm looking for a consequence that's so small that it won't break your heart to follow through on it. Can you stand it to keep him in a time-out for a minute?

Parent: (laughs) That won't be a problem.

Therapist: Good. Because now I'm going to tell you to do this every chance you get, and to look for chances. You know how we were talking about one of the problems is that he can get you mad?

Parent: That's for sure.

Therapist: Do you get mad right away, or only after a long time?

Parent: No, it's just when I tell him and he keeps on doing it. He won't stop, won't listen, and finally I get frustrated with him.

Therapist: That's what I thought. So here's what I want you to do: Tell him the first time. Then if he doesn't do it, tell him one more time, and count to 3, not 1, 2, 2½, 2¾, just a straight 1, 2, 3. Then pow! It's time-out, one minute. Then he still has to do what you say. No arguing, that's just the way it is.

Parent: That's it? That seems simple enough.

Therapist: The trick to this is that you don't have a chance to get angry, because you're not letting it drag on and on. And you can keep your punishment small because he hasn't done much. And the time-out isn't really even a punishment, it's just like, well, you don't follow the rules, you're on the bench a little while, then you can come out and try again.

Parent: I think I can do that.

Therapist: This week I want you to practice every chance you get. If you're not sure, go for it. And if you ever catch yourself starting to get frustrated or angry, you've probably let it go too far already, but you can still give a time-out right away. The funny thing about this is, the more strict you try to be, the less you end up giving those really big punishments.

If the child is present, or can be brought into the session, I like to role-play the time-out procedure several times, first with me playing the parent, then with the parent playing herself. Sometimes the child likes to have a crack at the parent role as well. There are several benefits to this exercise. First, the parent gets to observe and then practice under observation. The child has a positive, even playful, first experience of this intervention, perhaps making it feel nonpunitive. Second, by role-playing obedient and disobedient behavior, the child may develop a stronger sense of control over his symptomatic behavior. Third, the therapist can put a therapeutic spin on the whole enterprise.

Therapist: Your mom and I were talking, and she decided that she's going to be in charge more, so that you can feel safer at home. So now we want to practice something. Will you help us?

Child: Okay.

Therapist: Okay, I'm going to tell you to put away the toys, but you keep playing with them. Ready? Put those toys away.

Child: (keeps playing).

Therapist: I told you to put those toys away: 1, 2, 3. Now you have to do a time-out. Stand up over there in that corner, right over there. No, you can't play with that during a time-out. Here, I'll hold it for you. Okay, good, just stand there. I'll time you for a minute and tell you when you're done. . . . That's good, you're done now. Good job! This time it's your Mom's turn. Do you think she can do that like I did? Will you help her practice it?

The "Damn-Shit-Fuck" Progression

If the principle of early intervention needs to be further emphasized, this should do the trick. The dramatic language can help parents remember the point. Also, it ties the child's misbehavior to his insecurity, which should elict the parents' desire to reassure, rather than their aversion to punish. Of course, these words should only be used with parents for whom it would not be too uncomfortable, and the child should not be present.

Therapist: When your child does something wrong, I think he's asking for help. He's asking you to set him straight so that he feels safe. When he feels out of control, he needs you to help him, until he can control himself again. But if he messes up and you just let it go, he gets more and more nervous. Then what do you think happens?

Parent: Well, he just keeps going.

Therapist: That's right. There's something I call the "Damn-Shit-Fuck Progression" which I think happens with your child. When he says "Damn" and nothing happens, he gets more nervous, and asks for help even louder. Then he tries "Shit" to see if you'll help him. If you don't come through then, he'll go to the next step.

Parent: I've seen that before, he just gets out of hand.

Therapist: When he's nervous, he really needs you to take
charge, to show him that you're in control. When you
give the time-out, he's reassured, and he can calm
down. Otherwise, he'll just go to the next level, until
you come through.

Physical Restraint

Occasionally, a parent will say, "But he won't stay in the time-
out." Then the therapist simply says, "Make him stay. You're in
charge." Then the "how" must be addressed in some detail. In
most cases, the parent can simply insist, or even stand in front
of the child to block escape. Sometimes I have had to teach
physical restraint techniques, which requires being able to trust
the parent to implement this complex intervention effectively
and safely. The parent must be able to proceed in a caring,
authoritative, and nonreactive manner, so the child feels safe
rather than attacked.

Alternate Time-Out System (Dutton 1996)

The standard approach to time-out described above may be too
hard for some reactive parents. When the parents can't help
becoming visibly upset at every minor offense, the time-out procedure may become simply one more arena in which the parents' negative attention reinforces the child's disobedience. The
following time-out system offers parents increased physical control of the child, while keeping them away from the child so they
do not reinforce the negative behavior.

The parents must designate a time-out room, such as the
child's bedroom, in which there is nothing, including the walls
and the furniture, that the parents are not willing to risk. The
room should probably not contain a TV, but toys are okay. If
the child does not go immediately when given the time-out, he

is physically transported by the parent. If he does not stay in the room voluntarily, the closed door forces him to do so. The child completes this time-out by being quiet for the specified period, perhaps five minutes, or one minute for each year of his age.

During a time-out, the parents go about their business, regardless of what happens in the room. The child may be screaming and destroying everything within reach for minutes or even hours; the parents must ignore him. Only after the child has been quiet for the designated period do the parents make contact. Then the parents are to praise the child for behaving well for the past few minutes and thus completing the designated time-out. Note that the child is not required to sit silent and motionless, but merely to occupy himself quietly in his room.

This system relies on the principle that the child will do whatever is reinforced by the parents' attention. When the child misbehaves, the parents immediately send him to the time-out room so that no reinforcement is available. When the child behaves properly by successfully completing the time-out, the parents reinforce the positive behavior. Negative behavior diminishes when the child learns that it will not be reinforced. If the parents can stick it out, this system can be effective even with very challenging children.

Beyond Time-Out: Natural Consequences

Beyond time-out for annoying or disobedient behavior, the therapist can help the parents apply the principles of trauma treatment to the variety of discipline challenges that may arise. The goal is to support the child's sense of safety and security while providing appropriate limits as well as learning opportunities. These principles include:

- Keep your promises—be willing to follow through on the consequences you select.

- Avoid retaliation or revenge, which represents parental loss of control.
- Avoid depriving the child of meals, sleep, school, and (if possible) other worthwhile activities.
- Use consequences that are fair, make sense, and offer opportunities for a positive outcome.

These principles can guide parents in evaluating disciplinary options. For example, physical discipline (e.g., spanking) is generally problematic because it represents retaliation—loss of control—by the parents, and because it gives the child something else to be afraid about. The restitution approach has the advantage of being rehabilitative rather than punitive; it is clearly fair, and the child may actually make up for his misdeed, thereby repairing damaged relationships as well as self-esteem.

The concept of "natural consequences" helps many parents to grasp the constructive intent of this approach to discipline. The parents' role is not exactly to punish, but to ensure that the child has an opportunity to learn from his mistakes by taking responsibility for them. Examples of natural consequences include:

- "Make a mess—clean it up."
- "Break something—fix it or replace it." Replacement can be done with cash or labor (e.g., extra chores).
- "Break my trust—you lose it until you earn it back." For example: "You didn't come back home by dark tonight, so you can't go out after dinner tomorrow. And I lost half an hour worrying while you were late, so you owe me a half an hour of chores."
- "Work before play," especially if the work isn't getting done. Poor grades? "No TV until your homework's done."

Although such consequences are often necessary, a positive emphasis is a preferable means of eliciting wanted behavior. If parents seem to be getting bogged down around a particular problem behavior, the therapist can suggest a focused incentive program to encourage the child to do better. Sometimes the carrot-and-stick approach—having both positive and negative consequences around the same events—works. For example, if the child doesn't get ready for school on time, he may have to go to bed fifteen minutes early that night. On the other hand, if he is ready every morning, he may get a treat Friday after school.

One of the important components in either a formal behavioral program or a more general approach to discipline is the parents' attitude of supportive neutrality. When the child is facing known consequences for a behavioral choice, the parents can help him to see that he has chosen the consequence with his actions. This takes the parents off the hook and helps them feel less mean. When the parents can see the child as struggling with the consequences of his own choices, they are in a position to be less personally reactive, and more able to focus on the child's needs.

> *Therapist:* So when he tells you that you're mean because he has to go to bed early, how do you react to that?
> *Parent:* I get mad. I feel like I am mean, and I'm sick of him grumbling.
> *Therapist:* Try saying this: "You told me you wanted to go to bed early, you told me this morning with your actions. It's not my choice, it's yours." Say that.
> *Parent:* "You chose that yourself, you were late this morning and that was the deal."
> *Therapist:* How does it feel when you say that?
> *Parent:* Like it's not my problem.
> *Therapist:* That's right. You're being a good parent. You're keeping your promises, and you're letting him learn from his mistakes so he can do better.
> *Parent:* But I know him. He'll just grumble some more.
> *Therapist:* That's not your problem either! In fact, it's his job to grumble, he's trying to find out if he can really

count on you or not. He'll push your buttons—what are they, the "guilt" button, the "mean" button, what else?

Parent: Oh, he knows them all.

Therapist: So your first job is to come through, keep your promise. Then you can help him learn by telling him that it's his choice, and he can be happier if he makes better choices. And if he still is grumbling, if you want you can help him with his feelings. Try saying this: "You don't sound very happy about going to bed early."

Parent: "You don't sound happy about going to bed early."

Therapist: That's it. You can help him learn to handle things he doesn't like. But it's not your problem.

You're in Charge

Parents must understand that out-of-control children need someone else to be in control, and to help contain them, until they can control themselves again. This concept can be conveyed in many ways, and is a recurring theme in the parenting sessions. First, the parents must grasp that the child's sense of security rests on the adult being in charge. Then parents must learn to identify specific situations in which they may be relinquishing their authority, and learn how to recover it.

Therapist: We talked before about how your child feels scared inside, how every time some little thing makes him nervous, all those old scared feelings kick in.

Parent: Right, you said, from the hurricane, I didn't realize that before. And the fighting. I know he didn't like that, but I didn't know it was still bothering him.

Therapist: Sometimes it's hard to know what kids are thinking. What happens with kids is that those old feelings can get stuck inside, and now any little thing can make him start feeling scared again. But you know how you can tell when he's scared?

Parent: No, he never talks about that stuff.

Therapist: Kids don't know much about how to talk about stuff. He shows you he's scared, he shows you by doing something he's not supposed to do. Then when you put him in his place, he feels safe because you're in charge, he can count on you.

Parent: Right, we talked about that, the time-outs.

Therapist: But there's more to it. If you argue with him, or if you yell, you've lost control, and that can spoil the help you're giving him.

Parent: Just from yelling at him?

Therapist: Sure. When you're in charge, acting like the parent, what you say goes, no fuss about it. But if he can get you going, get you to argue with him, negotiate points, then you're just like another kid, just like him, instead of in charge. Or if he can push your buttons, get you mad, you've given him control again. He's gotten you to yell and fight with him. Just like you were another kid. When you're the parent, you don't have to do that. When he's out of control, he needs you to be the parent, to be in control.

Parents may have difficulty maintaining their own self-control and avoiding the arguing, yelling, or hitting that may have become habitual. The following strategies can contribute to success in this effort:

- Simply viewing the child's misbehavior as reflecting fear can help the parents feel sympathy for the child instead of feeling personally affronted.
- Using the quick, small punishments can preclude opportunities for parental frustration.
- The "not my problem" approach can further depersonalize parent–child conflict.

When this child-focused approach is insufficient for parental self-control, individual work with the parents may be required. Some of the anger-management techniques described in the next chapter for adolescents with conduct problems can be helpful. Another approach is to view the child's misbehavior as triggering a traumatic memory for the parent, and to use EMDR to help the parent resolve the source memory.

The Stepfamily Trap

In many families, one parent, typically the father, plays the role of the overly harsh disciplinarian, while the other parent, typically the mother, plays the overindulgent role. (This is most common after divorce, when the mother has custody of her children and she has remarried, however, many intact families have a similar dynamic.) The problem is, the more the father disciplines harshly, the more indulgent and protective the mother becomes, and the more the mother neglects to discipline, the more the father feels obliged to. This creates a cycle of increasing polarization, resulting in considerable family tension. And when the father is punitive and the mother indulgent, the child cannot really count on either parent for appropriate guidance and support.

The therapist can simply explain these dynamics to the parents, and tell them they can resolve it by having the mother (or the one who has been "soft") take the lead as the disciplinarian. Her relationship with her children will not be damaged by exerting her authority—it will actually be strengthened. Her becoming the primary disciplinarian gives her husband the opportunity to back off and to develop a more positive relationship with the children.

Focus on the Positive

Parents can be encouraged to give frequent praise for their children's positive behavior, rather than only giving attention in response to misbehavior. In some situations the parents can learn to ignore the child's negative behaviors and focus instead on positive behaviors of other children, perhaps thereby encouraging the problem child to join in. The therapist can also suggest that the parent regularly devotes some time to doing an enjoyable activity with the child. In conjunction with the effective discipline approach, this can help to shift the family's energy to more positive interactions. Also, as noted above, specific behaviors can be developed and encouraged through the use of incentives.

Individual Child Therapy

The individual portion of this treatment approach typically involves rapport-building, trauma work, resource development, and skill building.

Rapport

Rapport is that mysterious relationship element that allows for continued collaboration, as opposed to the child's just clamming up on you. Rapport with a child is enhanced by demonstrating teamwork with the parents, responding to the child's own concerns, making disclosure and difficult processing feel reasonably safe, and helping the child to have positive—even fun—experiences in the therapy session. Of course, positive results from therapy activities can't hurt.

Teamwork with Parents

Teamwork with parents has already been demonstrated in the treatment planning and family therapy phases. The therapist can reinforce this alliance by referring to conversations with the parents and by showing respect for their authority.

Responding to the Child's Concerns

Asking the child about his own treatment goals and inviting him to prioritize them conveys the message that his concerns are guiding the choice of treatment activities. The treatment will probably be about the same regardless, but the child doesn't know that.

Making It Safe

Confidentiality is a component of safety that should be discussed early on, typically in fairly simple terms: "My rule is that I don't talk about what you say to any other kids. But if I'm afraid someone might be getting hurt, I have to do something about it." The mandated reporting law contributes to treatment in that a specific mechanism for ensuring safety has been specified. Whenever kids ask about other kids they know in treatment, the therapist has a chance to demonstrate and reiterate the confidentiality policy.

The therapist can also support the child's sense of safety by maintaining the therapeutic frame (starting and ending on time, avoiding self-focusing self-disclosure, etc.) and by providing overt opportunities for the child to maintain control of the discussion of difficult material. The therapist need not merely wait until the child brings something up; a structured, active, directive approach works well as long as the child feels supported and retains the prerogative to say no.

Check-in

The therapist can establish a routine of disclosure to begin each session; for example, "Tell me about the best thing and the worst thing that happened since we met last." Structuring a ritual is itself reassuring. The check-in encourages the child to reveal what is most pressing on his mind, thus supplying prime raw material for other interventions. Anticipating the check-in ritual may increase the child's awareness of therapy-relevant incidents as they occur between sessions.

Children who are uncomfortable with disclosure may deny having anything to report. The therapist can generally elicit a response by lowering the stakes: "Just try to think of a time when you felt good (or bad) for a minute. It doesn't have to be any big deal." Early, relatively innocuous responses may pave the way for subsequent, more substantive ones. The ritualized nature of this routine—"This is how we start every time"—can help to break the ice.

Naturally, as therapy progresses, more information may be requested at check-in. The therapist may follow-up on previously addressed issues: "Did the nightmare come back? Did you practice that self-control trick this week?" Check-in is also an occasion to ask about other events that may be significant for the child. Incidentally, since many children are inadvertently poor reporters, regular contact with a parent is welcome.

Fun

Although the goals of treatment are serious and the child should understand that there is work to be done, incorporating elements of fun can boost the child's level of cooperation. The therapist can offer to play a game of the child's choice for the last portion of the session after the child cooperates with other therapy activities for the first portion. Of course, the play itself can be a part of treatment, perhaps as a time to focus on the child's sportsmanship or frustration tolerance. Fun can also be incorporated by challenging the child to perform the given therapy activities, for example, disclosure, hand-slapping (for eye movements), focus on a disturbing memory, or push-ups. Even the end of the session can be turned into a contest or a game: "How many seconds will it take to put the toys away?" "Race you back to class, but no running." Some children look forward to these bits of fun so much that they are willing to put up with the rest of the treatment.

Getting Stronger

Since most children want to feel bigger and stronger, the metaphor can be used as leverage for therapy activities. The therapist can encourage the confusion of physical and inner strength, which children seem to readily accept. Then the child's sense of physical strength can give him the confidence to face difficult emotional material. The therapist can help the child to build up his sense of strength and confidence in a number of ways. EMDR is integrated into most of these interventions.

> *Therapist:* We were talking about your getting stronger. How strong are you? Make a muscle, let me see.
> *Child:* (makes a muscle).
> *Therapist:* Oh, you're already pretty strong. How many push-ups can you do?
> *Child:* Maybe five.
> *Therapist:* Let's see. Go ahead.
> *Child:* (does eight push-ups while therapist counts out loud).
> *Therapist:* Eight! And I bet you that next time we meet, you can do ten. What kinds of things do you do to make yourself strong?
> *Child:* I don't lift weights or anything.
> *Therapist:* Do you eat good meals? (Child nods.) Well, eating helps you grow. Do you ride your bike?
> *Child:* I ride my bike a lot, with my friend.
> *Therapist:* Well, exercise makes you get stronger. Do you walk much, or get any other exercise?
> *Child:* I play tag at recess, and play some basketball in the park.

Therapist: Good, so you do a lot of things to make yourself strong. No wonder you can already do so many push-ups. The more exercise you get, the stronger you get. Now I'm going to see if you can do something that might be hard, see if it's too hard or if you can do it. Ready?

Child: (nods).

Therapist: I'm going to move my hand back and forth, see if you can watch with your eyes, without moving your head. (Therapist moves hand from side to side for a few seconds, child follows with eyes.) Oh, you did it! Was that easy or hard?

Child: Easy.

Therapist: Well, let me try to make it harder, then. Okay, when you think of yourself getting stronger, what is the picture you have?

Child: Me lifting up a house.

Therapist: So this time, I'm going to ask you to do two things at once, see if you can do it. Think of yourself lifting up a house, you have the picture now? Good, think of that picture, and move your eyes (therapist moves hand again). All right, you did it! Was that easy, or is it hard now?

Child: Easy.

Therapist: Well, let me try to make it even harder. Think of that picture again, of lifting up a house, and say to yourself, "I'm getting stronger," and now move your eyes (therapist moves hand). How did that go, were you able to concentrate on all that?

Child: Yes.

Therapist: Wow, you did that, too. No matter how hard I make it, you can do it. What were those things you do to make yourself stronger?

Child: Eating, riding my bike, playing basketball.

Therapist: Which one of those do you want to think about?

Child: Riding my bike.

Therapist: Okay, think of that now, and say to yourself, "I'm getting stronger" (moves hand). Okay. Now say that again, out loud: "I'm getting stronger."

Child: I'm getting stronger.

Therapist: Does that feel more true, or more not true?

Child: More true.

The child thus has an experience of mastering challenges and impressing the therapist, while the content is simultaneously focused on boosting self-image and confidence. As the child makes progress in treatment, he is likely to attribute it to his own efforts, which increases confidence as well as cooperation.

Installations involving strength and strength-building may be repeated on various occasions throughout the treatment. The therapist can regularly assign strength-building homework exercises, ask for reports indicating increased strength (tolerance of difficult emotion) during challenging situations, and ask for demonstrations of physical strength in session. If the child is losing in a game, the therapist can invoke the child's strength to encourage sportsmanship. Later in treatment—and perhaps not much later—the therapist can build on this pattern of having the child overcoming challenge through strength when trauma work is introduced.

Trauma Work

The baggage of unprocessed trauma weakens the child and makes coping efforts less likely to succeed. Following trauma resolution, some of the presenting problems may fade away; others should be more amenable to other effective interventions.

Trauma work typically begins within the first three individual sessions. The therapist should have a list of trauma and loss memories, including age and SUDS level, from the evaluation phase of the treatment. All things being equal, it is generally best to work through each traumatic memory with EMDR in chronological order, or in chronological order within a given theme, if appropriate. However, things are not always equal. The pressure of being asked to do this trauma work so quickly can be balanced by giving the child some control over the pacing.

> *Therapist:* We talked before about what we'll be doing, talking about some of those things you told me about that still hurt inside. Some kids like to start right out on the worst thing, so that they can feel better from it quicker. But some kids like to start out on something smaller so they can see how it goes. Which way do you want to do it?
>
> *Child:* Something smaller.
>
> *Therapist:* Okay. What's good about starting with something smaller?
>
> *Child:* I can try it, see what it's like.
>
> *Therapist:* Okay. You told me that the worst thing to think about is when your grandma died, and the least bad thing was the hurricane. So we'll start with the hurricane. Before we do that, though, let's practice that stop signal again. Make me stop my hand (therapist moves hand until child gives the stop signal). Good. Let's make sure you remember how to do that with your other hand.

Before starting on the first major traumatic memory, a safe place, strength image, or other safety device should be installed. This will substantially reduce the child's need to interrupt EMDR, which can occur when negative affect overwhelms the child, causing him to reject the therapy activity. This installation can also lead right into the processing itself, thus sliding by another common obstacle: getting started.

> *Therapist:* What was the worst part of the hurricane, was it during the storm, or after, what was happening?

Child: The worst part was when the glass was breaking from the windows.

Therapist: Before we get started, I'm going to ask you something different. I know this really happened, but just imagine that it was a bad dream, and you had to go back into that dream again. What would you need to be safe in that dream?

Child: Huh?

Therapist: What would help you to feel safe? Maybe being stronger or bigger, or something to protect you, or being with a certain person . . .

Child: A house made all of bricks.

Therapist: Good idea. I want you to think about that house, what it looks like, what it's like, who would be in there with you, how safe it feels in there (eye movements). Do you feel more safe, or less safe, or about the same?

Child: More safe. The hurricane can't tear down bricks.

Therapist: Let's do that again, think about being in that brick house (eye movements). What was it like that time?

Child: Still safe. You can hear the wind, but nothing happens to the house.

Therapist: All right. Now we're going to practice, see how fast you can think of that place. I'm going to ask you to think of something else, and then when I say "Switch," see how fast you can think of being in the brick house. When you have it, tell me. Ready? Okay, now think of elephants (eye movements). Switch.

Child: Did it.

Therapist: Wow, that was fast, about three seconds. Let's try it again. Okay, think of pineapples (eye movements). Switch.

Child: Did it.

Therapist: Only one second! You're fast! Should we practice one more time, or are you already pretty good at this?

Child: I'm already good enough.

Therapist: Okay, I'm glad. Because you know what you can do, if the memory of the hurricane gets too hard, hurts your feelings too much? You can switch, think about being safe in the brick house. Okay?

Child: Okay.

Therapist: So now think of when the glass was breaking. Ready? (eye movements)

In this phase of treatment, the therapist simply proceeds with trauma and loss processing with EMDR until it's all done. Of course, this is generally much simpler in the case of discrete events than with chronic exposure to trauma. The therapist also continues the parenting/family work to ensure that the home environment is as consistent and supportive as possible. Following the initial assessment and treatment planning, the individual and family components of treatment coincide.

Sleep-Related Problems

Children tend to be highly motivated to eliminate bed-wetting, nightmares, and night fears, so these problems can serve as good motivators for trauma work. If such problems remain following trauma work, they can be further addressed directly with EMDR. (The bed-wetting treatment is more complex; see Chapter 11.) Nightmares can be recalled and processed, along with installation of safety devices ("What would you need in that dream to be safe?"). Once subjected to EMDR, a particular nightmare is unlikely to recur. Others may surface, however, unless the trauma work is completed. Night fears can also be addressed with EMDR, both by having the child face the fear directly, and by installing resources sufficient to master the fear (using the safety devices as above).

These problems tend to respond to this treatment approach rather quickly, and the success can help the therapist gain credibility while reducing family stress. When such problems do not resolve as expected, it generally indicates either additional unresolved trauma or an ongoing situational source of distress that precludes resolution.

Self-Control Skills Training

Training in self-control skills, the final component of this treatment approach, may include relaxation, self-talk, thinking about choices and consequences, and problem solving, depending on the therapist's repertoire, available role models, and the child's specific problem areas. Typical problem areas are academic challenges, feeling slighted or put down, losing in a game, and not having one's way. The interventions described below use EMDR primarily to enhance the learning of control skills. However, the trauma-related triggers, which induce the child to overreact in challenging situations, may also get desensitized along the way.

Because the child clearly does need to control himself better, many parents and teachers believe that the control-skills component represents the core of the treatment approach. While the therapist can accept improved control as a primary goal, it is important to stick to the game plan. Latency-aged children generally have the best chance of mastering these skills only following resolution of traumatic memories; premature skills training can lead to failure in the face of overwhelming trauma-based reactivity.

Choices Have Consequences

This intervention serves to desensitize the child to common situational triggers while raising his awareness that his impulsive responses are actually behavioral choices, and that he can do better. Imaginal rehearsal of alternative, more effective behavioral choices is built in. The goal is to transfer this learning to challenging situations, so that the child's reactivity is reduced and his sense of control and choice increased. (A more sophisticated and complex version of this intervention is described in Chapter 3.)

The first step is to identify a typical challenging situation as well as a positive behavioral alternative to the child's habitual impulsive acting-out response, based on the evaluation and treatment planning sessions, contact with the parents (and possibly the teacher), and the check-in reports at the beginning of the session. The therapist can help the child to come up with appropriate strategies, potentially including imagery, self-talk, and behaviors, and can devise role plays and cognitive reframes to help develop the positive behavioral alternatives.

> *Therapist:* You told me that you had to miss recess yesterday because you got in a fight with Ryan. What happened exactly?
>
> *Child:* He pushed me.
>
> *Therapist:* He pushed you. How come? What happened first?
>
> *Child:* He called me a name, so I called him a name back. Then he pushed me.
>
> *Therapist:* And then what did you do after that? How come you got in trouble, too?
>
> *Child:* Well, then I pushed him back, and the teacher made us both stay in for recess.
>
> *Therapist:* Is that how you wanted it to happen, that you end up missing recess?
>
> *Child:* No, I hate to miss recess.
>
> *Therapist:* What do you wish happened instead? How do you wish it came out?
>
> *Child:* I wish he was nice to me and would be my friend.
>
> *Therapist:* But if he calls you that name again—what did he say to you?

Child: He used the "F" word.

Therapist: Oh. Well if he does that again, and you wanted to end up going out to recess instead of getting into a fight, what could you do?

Child: I could ignore him?

Therapist: What would happen if you did that?

Child: Nothing.

Therapist: So would you end up in a fight, or end up going out for recess?

Child: Going out for recess.

This setup provides specific required material including the negative and positive behavioral alternatives along with the likely outcome associated with each choice. The crux of the intervention is to have the child concentrate on the typical challenging situation, and imaginally view a "movie" of it during eye movements. The movie is viewed first along with the child's typical impulsive, acting-out response, and paired with a typical bad outcome. Then the movie is viewed with a more effective behavioral choice, and ending with a more desired outcome. Finally, the child is given the behavioral choice in the movie, but instructed as follows: "Bad choice, bad ending; good choice, good ending."

Therapist: You know how I had you concentrate on a picture from the hurricane before, while you moved your eyes? Today I'm going to ask you to concentrate on a movie of what happened with Ryan, like you're watching it on the VCR. First, in the movie, he's going to call you that name. Then you're going to get mad and do what you did, and the ending will be that you have to stay in for recess. So start at the beginning, when he called you that name, and when you're all the way to the end, let me know. Ready? (eye movements) What happened, how did the movie go?

Child: Well, he called me the name, I got mad, called him
a name, he pushed me, I pushed him, had to miss
recess.

Therapist: Okay. This time the movie starts the same way:
he calls you that name, you feel mad. But this time
we're going to go for the good ending, you getting to
go out for recess. So what can you do to get to the
good ending?

Child: Ignore him, walk away.

Therapist: Okay, let's go for the good ending. Start at the
beginning, ready?

The Choices Have Consequences intervention can be applied to variants of the same situation, as well as to other situations such as getting frustrated during a school task. This can
also be combined with elements of other interventions. For example, the child can visualize himself (during eye movements)
becoming stronger, then enacting the desired behavior, then
achieving the desired outcome.

Tease-Proofing

Many children are highly reactive to provocation by their peers,
who in turn deliberately provoke to elicit the reaction. The first
step in reducing the reactivity is to help the child understand
the dynamics of teasing so he no longer takes it personally.
Sometimes role-playing different responses to teasing can teach
the child that his angry response just encourages the provoker.
The goal is to help the child be able to erect a boundary between himself and the provoker, so that he does not get hurt
or triggered by the provocation. (A more sophisticated and complex version of this intervention is described in Chapter 3.)

Therapist: Do you know why Ryan calls you names?

Child: No. Sometimes he's my friend.

Therapist: Well, does he say bad things to you because you're a bad person, or because he has some bad feelings he wants to get out?

Child: He has some bad feelings.

Therapist: So you're not a bad person?

Child: No.

Therapist: Think about that (eye movements). You're not a bad person?

Child: No.

Therapist: So they're his bad feelings, not yours?

Child: Yes.

Therapist: (eye movements) But sometimes he can get you really mad. Is that because his bad feelings can get inside you, when he calls you a name?

Child: I guess so.

Therapist: I'm going to show you a trick you can try, to keep his bad feelings from getting inside you. What if you could put up a wall to keep those bad feelings from getting through? What would the wall be made out of?

Child: Steel.

Therapist: Think about that steel wall, how high it is, how wide it is. You're going to need to put it up right away, in just about no time, how will you do that?

Child: I'll just press a button.

Therapist: Okay, good. Now think about him calling you a name, and you put up that wall, see what happens (eye movements). What happened?

Child: Well, he said the "F" word, I put up the wall, and it just bounced off and hit him.

Therapist: So the bad feelings didn't get inside you?

Child: No.

This approach can be repeated with variations on the same theme, and with other challenges featuring teasing or provocation. It can also be incorporated as a preferred strategy in the Choices Have Consequences exercise.

Other Considerations

While preadolescents may not be oriented toward compliance, securing their commitment to treatment goals is critical. It is often helpful to offer choices as much as possible within the treatment framework, and to use methods that include client control of the process. For example, the child may enjoy slapping the therapist's hands to effect the eye movements, or may prefer placing small objects on the wall for use as alternate foci.

Traumatized children in this age range often have trouble remembering back in time. They may need to begin EMDR with the most recent trauma or manifestation, which they experience not only as more accessible but also more relevant. Jumping too quickly to a more remote traumatic memory may lead to refusal.

Distrustful, reluctant children in this age range may require considerable familiarity with the therapist and therapy before they can address their traumatic memories. Using the check-in routine described above as an introduction to EMDR may be relatively nonthreatening, as follows: "We start with a check-in before we play. Think of the best feeling you've had all week, and what were you doing then, what was happening?" (Get a target image, with associated feeling, and install with eye movements.) "Now think of the worst feeling you've had all week." (Get a target and process with EMDR. End with reinstallation of the positive.) Over time, increased familiarity with this low-pressure EMDR may lead to greater trust and willingness to cooperate.

Many children in this age group only identify problems outside themselves, claiming, for example, that others give them trouble. Sutton (1994) recommends an outside-inside-outside approach, as follows: (1) start with the identified external problem, for example, getting in trouble in school yesterday; (2) use EMDR to process the memory, which may include images, feelings, and insights; and (3) use EMDR to rehearse (install) behavioral alternatives likely to lead to more desirable outcomes.

This approach has the advantage of meeting children on their own terms, helping them to get over residual upset from the incident, and leaving them with practical solutions.

CONCLUSION

The trauma orientation to working with latency-aged children with disruptive behavior disorders organizes interventions on both the individual and family levels, and can incorporate pharmacological and behavior modification approaches as needed. In this chapter I presented typical as well as innovative applications of EMDR within this comprehensive treatment approach, for a presenting problem that is perhaps not overtly trauma related. Like any other approach, it requires good clinical judgment and flexible, responsive use.

3

Adolescents with Conduct Disorder

Although it was developed for use with incarcerated adolescent males, the following treatment approach adapts well to outpatient work with adolescents (and others) with impulsive and antisocial behaviors (Greenwald 1997c). Adolescents with conduct problems are notoriously difficult to help, or even to engage in treatment. They typically have little concern for the future, poor impulse control and coping skills (often complicated by AD/HD), and a driving anger born of trauma and/or loss. Treatment can be enhanced by systematically addressing the motivation, self-management, and trauma/loss components.

Although other factors may come into play, every conduct disorder symptom might also represent a trauma symptom (Greenwald 1998c), including impaired empathy, disregard for the future, anger, aggression, impulsivity, substance abuse, risk-seeking behavior, reactivity, and avoidance of negative affect. While general principles of trauma treatment apply, they must be adapted to this population. This protocol begins by attempting to foster the adolescent's investment in the future and thus his participation in treatment. The self-control training is intended to promote the client's sense of safety—better self-control means a more predictable and favorable environment—generally a prerequisite to trauma resolution work. This protocol combines some standard components of conduct disorder treatment with other more unique elements, sequenced to compose a systematic individual treatment for trauma. (See Greenwald 1998c for the empirical basis for this approach.)

This protocol uses a weekly individual therapy hour, and does not rely on integration with other elements, such as residential program, school, or home environment, although such integration is certainly preferable. However, it helps if the client is compelled to attend the sessions! The protocol is structured, directive, and relatively brief (about two to six months). It consists of three overlapping phases—motivation, skill building, and trauma resolution work—each of which incorporates EMDR. Of course, treatment does not always proceed in this orderly manner; individual differences in therapists, clients, and situations dictate variations in many cases.

MOTIVATION

The treatment goals in the motivation phase include developing rapport, helping the client identify personal goals and care about achieving them, developing a case formulation and a treatment plan that makes sense to the client, and obtaining the client's commitment to fully participate in the treatment.

Rapport

Being straightforward with the client is important, and his point of view must be acknowledged and respected. For example, he may more readily identify impulsive acting out as a problem not because his actions hurt others, but because he gets in trouble. An adolescent who feels recognized and respected will be less likely to dismiss the therapist as irrelevant.

The client should have as much overt power in the relationship as possible, within the limits the therapist must set to maintain the therapeutic frame. The client should have the right to choose whether to disclose or not, whether to buy into any given treatment goal, even whether to speak at all. Giving clients permission to stop the treatment activity actually seems to encourage and advance their movement.

Since many adolescents are not particularly articulate, the "menu" is a useful technique for generating information. For example, in asking for a trauma/loss history, sometimes it is sufficient to ask, "What are the worst things that ever happened to you?" However, it is often better to specify the possibilities: "Have you ever been in a car accident, or a house fire, or was there some other time when you thought you might get hurt or die? Have you ever seen someone else get hurt badly? Did someone important to you ever die, like someone in your family or a good friend?" This menu technique can also be used to enhance self-observation: "When you get mad, what do you notice first? Some kids get shaky, or tense, or hot, or their hands sweat, or they have bad words in their head." The trick here is to avoid leading the client, while orienting him to the information that he already has. This not only helps the therapist to elicit the necessary information, but keeps the client from getting into a habit of coming up with nothing, which frustrates both parties.

Sometimes the therapist can get good results from reading the questions off a form. For some reason, the mystique of a form allows people to answer questions they might not otherwise be willing to respond to. The therapist can also depersonalize the procedure this way, for example, by saying, "This paperwork, it's part of my job."

The best way to contribute to the development of the therapeutic alliance is by producing results. The client's positive experiences in the therapy session, and the corresponding benefits outside, will be key to his willingness to take the next steps in treatment. The various stages of the protocol are organized with this principle in mind, and the stages should be reorganized accordingly for the needs of each individual. For example, if the client is so angry that he is liable to leave the session and do something he will later regret, the time is probably right to teach a calming exercise or do EMDR on the current issue, even if the protocol does not indicate its use. If a client is preoccupied with his out-of-control response to a provocative peer, this is a good time to introduce the tease-proofing exercises. The whole protocol should be viewed as a model, and used with judgment and flexibility.

Initial Interview

The first meeting is very important in establishing a productive working relationship, especially given the time constraints of many treatment contexts. The goal of the first session or two is to develop rapport, to begin with the case formulation and treatment plan, and to enlist the client's commitment to treatment. This approach can be described as a variant of motivational interviewing.

The Basics

One important ground rule to discuss is confidentiality and its limits. The therapist must distinguish between merely breaking the law and actual danger. I might quiz a client by saying, "What if you told me that you stole some cigarettes from the store? Would I have to tell or not? Why? What if you told me that you stole a knife?"

Explain to the client the kinds of things that can be worked on in treatment, and what the process might be like. Acknowledge the client's power: nothing will happen unless he chooses to work on something. Once this is understood, it's easier to ask the client to give it a try, at least for a couple of sessions, before writing it off. I might introduce therapy as follows:

Some people don't want to talk to a counselor, even though they have to come. But if you decide to get something out of it, there are a lot of different ways to use your time with me. Some kids just come and talk about what's bothering them and let off steam, because they know I won't tell anyone else what they say. Some kids want to get stronger in some way, like maybe controlling their anger better, and I know a lot about that, so they use me like a coach for that. And some kids hurt inside, even from something that might have happened a long time ago, so we work on getting that bad feeling to get smaller. Sometimes kids are trying to figure something out, like how to handle a problem, and they talk to me to get another opinion. I don't help everyone, even though I try, but a lot of kids do say they were glad they came, after all.

Here's what I'd like to do. My first job is to get to know a whole lot about you, so that I can get an idea of what might be most helpful for us to work on. You'll also be checking me out at the same time. By the end of our next meeting, or maybe sooner, I'll tell you what I've learned about you, and what I think we should do. But remember, we won't work on anything unless you decide that it's important. That's why one of the things I'll be asking you, later, is what you care about. And even now, while I'm asking you questions, you don't have to say anything you don't want to.

It is worthwhile to ask about prior experiences with counselors (very few adolescents use the word *therapist*), and to try to learn, together, from those experiences. Occasionally there will be an acknowledged positive experience, and the therapist can ask what was good about it, what the client liked about his counselor, and how the present experience might be the same or different. More often, the client will complain that past counselors didn't help, and even did bad things such as show disrespect or violate confidentiality. Then the therapist and client can discuss in detail how to recognize and handle similar problems should they arise. For example:

Therapist: How would you know if I went and told someone what you said?

Client: Well, I'd hear about it from the teachers or something.

Therapist: Do you think I might do something like that?

Client: I don't know. Maybe.

Therapist: Well, how can you figure it out, without putting yourself in a bad spot?

Client: Just not say anything to you.

Therapist: I guess that would work. But what if it turns out you really could trust me?

Client: Well, I guess I could tell you a small thing, and see what happens.

Therapist: You also said that a lot of times, grownups say they want to help, but they just say things that make you mad. I wouldn't say something disrespectful on purpose, but I might do it by accident. How would I be able to tell if that was happening?

Client: I'd be mad.

Therapist: And if I'm watching you, what would I see?

Client: I don't know. I'd just be heated.

Therapist: Like, would you start yelling and swearing, or would you walk away, or would you get quiet? What would it be?

Client: Oh, I just don't say anything and I look down like you're not there anymore.

Therapist: Okay, so if I see you getting quiet and not looking at me, that might be a sign that I've said something you don't like?

Client: Yeah, I guess so.

Therapist: I know you can ignore me and protect yourself, like you do with your teachers. But I'm hoping that if I make a mistake with you, I can find out about it and try to fix it.

A reasonably thorough developmental history should be obtained in the first session, including details of family relations, activities/behaviors relating to the present problem, a loss and trauma history, and a history of successes of any kind, including school, work, social, athletic, and even criminal (a good car thief or drug dealer has talents and skills that are transferable). This information constitutes the raw material for many later interventions.

Selectively sharing impressions with the client throughout the interview, rather than holding back until the end, can make him feel safe. Many disturbed adolescents have grown up in unpredictable environments in which "reading" others is a survival skill. The therapist's transparency in this potentially threatening situation is reassuring and allows the client to lower his guard. When the client is invited to respond to the therapist's impressions, he can play a more active role in the case formulation. (Of course, the therapist will also be learning from the way in which the client responds.) When the therapist formally presents the case formulation to the client, it can include the client's own words, which can have more impact.

Future Movies

After the basics are covered, including therapy ground rules, history, life situation, and rapport, the therapist should have a fairly detailed preliminary understanding of the client's character, strengths, and problems—perhaps enough to offer a case formulation and treatment plan. But the therapist should wait, because now it is only the therapist's formulation and plan. With a little more work, it can also become the client's. The "Future Movies" intervention can make the difference. It starts with the "good movie," a positive vision of the client's future.

> *Therapist:* I've asked all I can think of about your past. Now I want to know about your future. Let's say that ten

years from now—How old will you be, 25?—I stop at the video store on my way home, and pick up a movie called *The [client's name] Story*. It starts out kind of bad. There's this kid, seems like a good kid but a lot of things go wrong for him, he does a lot of bad stuff, and I'm saying to myself, "This is a bummer. I used to work with kids like this. Looks like another good one going down the drain." But then things start to change. First one good thing, then another, then another . . . till finally, by the end of the movie, when the credits are rolling, I'm saying, "Way to go—you made it!" So, tell me what happens in this movie? What happens first?

Client: You mean if this was me?

Therapist: Yes, if this was your story, the way you're hoping it would happen.

Client: Well, I wouldn't get in trouble anymore.

Therapist: Okay. What would you do?

Client: First I'd do good in school and graduate and make my mom proud.

Therapist: So what do you have to do to do good in school?

Client: Have to go every day, pay attention, do my homework.

Therapist: And after you graduate, do you see yourself getting a job, joining the service, going to college, what?

Client: I'll probably work with my uncle, cleaning up cars, and go to college at night. Then learn about computers, there's good money in computers.

Therapist: Okay, and when the movie's ending in ten years, where do you think you'll be living? In the neighborhood you're in now, or someplace else in the city, or where? Your own house or an apartment? By yourself, with a buddy, with a girlfriend? Maybe married by then? Will you have your own car? What kind? What color? What kind of sound system?

The point of this questioning is to help the client envision a detailed, step-by-step plan for how to move toward a positive future, and to develop a detailed picture of that future. This is not always a smooth process, as many such clients will initially deny having any goals, and will struggle against identifying positive prospects. However, almost everyone is able to do this with sufficient prodding. The final image is particularly important, and should be invested with full detail, including emotion, sensation, and cognition:

> *Therapist:* So when the credits are rolling, what is the picture on the screen?
> *Client:* I'm in front of my house with my wife and my kid.
> *Therapist:* When you have this picture, what kind of feeling goes with it?
> *Client:* Good, happy.
> *Therapist:* Where do you feel that, where in your body?
> *Client:* All over.
> *Therapist:* And what do you say to yourself? Something like, "I can do it," or "I'm gonna make it"?
> *Client:* "Go for it."

The final image is installed with eye movements. Since most clients have not yet tried eye movements, it is often simpler to have them imaginally view the image first with eyes closed, and then again while moving the eyes. Then the entire "good movie" is installed, including the various steps along the way (e.g., doing homework, graduating high school), and ending with the final image. After explaining the movie, the therapist says, "Tell me when it's done," and initiates the eye movements until the client gives the signal. Then the therapist asks, "How did it go? What happened in the movie?" If all components were not included, the movie is repeated, e.g., "Don't forget to say, 'Go for it' when you get to the end this time."

At this point it is not necessary to formally introduce EMDR, since there is very little risk associated with this type of installation. If the client wants an explanation for the eye movement request, I might just say, "This helps drill it in better."

At the end of treatment, many of my clients have told me that this exercise was their favorite part. Many had given little thought or credence to a possibly positive future, and found that this exercise generated hope for them. It is also possible that they appreciated the opportunity to share this with an adult who is not focused on telling them how bad they are.

After the good movie has been developed and installed at least once, it is time to do the same with a bad movie, that is, a negative vision of the future. The therapist asks, "What if it doesn't go the good way we've been talking about? What if you keep on doing the same old stuff, things keep going bad?" A detailed bad-ending image should be developed, with associated emotion, sensation, and cognition. The therapist tentatively provides a specific cognition, as follows:

> *Therapist:* Okay, so in the bad ending you see yourself behind bars?
> *Client:* Yeah. In a concrete room, like at the lockup.
> *Therapist:* And what kind of feeling goes with this picture?
> *Client:* Bad. Sad.
> *Therapist:* Where do you feel that?
> *Client:* In my mind.
> *Therapist:* With this picture, would it fit to say to yourself, "It wasn't worth it"?
> *Client:* It's not worth it. That's for sure.

The bad-ending image, with associated emotion and cognition, is then installed. The cognition, "It's not worth it" should be presented and used in all cases unless rejected by the client. (Many clients, when asked for a cognition, simply berate themselves, but "I'm stupid" will not be useful in this context.) This bad-ending image should be practiced with eye movements at least a couple of times.

These good- and bad-ending pictures will be used again later for cognitive-behavioral training. Right now, though, their function is to orient the client to the notion that he can choose his own path. Next, he is asked to declare an investment in the positive outcome. Having completed the good-future movie, the client is already moving in that direction.

Strengths and Obstacles

Next, with the client's input, the therapist lists client attributes that would contribute to the good future. Typically, the client will be fairly inarticulate on this matter, so it will be up to the therapist to generate the bulk of the items on the list. Client strengths might include intelligence (adequate to meet the stated goals), specific talents (mechanical, artistic, business, persuasiveness), track record of specific past successes showing ability in a related area, ability to persevere, family and/or social support, ability to form supportive relationships, and the desire to achieve the goals. The list does not have to be exhaustive.

> *Therapist:* It's not easy to get to that good future, but maybe it's possible. What is there about you that might help you get there?
>
> *Client:* What do you mean? I'll just do it, try my best.
>
> *Therapist:* Well, you said you want to graduate high school and then get a basketball scholarship to college. Are you a good basketball player?
>
> *Client:* Yes, I was the best one in my high school before I got kicked off the team.
>
> *Therapist:* Okay, I'll write down "good basketball player." See, that's something that will help you get to your goals. What else is there?
>
> *Client:* If I decide to do something, I don't give up.
>
> *Therapist:* Okay, I'll write that down too. Also, you tell me that you have a close family?

Client: Yeah, we'll do anything for each other.

Therapist: I'll write down, "close family," because it's easier to get to your goal when your family is behind you. What else?

Then a list should be made of the attributes that might prevent the client from achieving his goals. The therapist can ask, "What could stop you from getting to your goals? What could get in your way?" This is where the client, having already identified and endorsed positive goals, now identifies his problem behavior as a personal obstacle. A client will typically respond by saying, "My attitude," "My temper," or "Getting in trouble." This is often the first point at which the client will identify personal responsibility for his problems. The obstacle list should also contain some specificity: "When something is hard at school, I give up," or "I get in too many fights."

Percent Motivation

The therapist asks the client to declare what percent he is motivated toward the good future, and what percent toward the bad future (i.e., toward "doing the same old stuff"). Many adolescents don't understand the concept of percentages, so I often find myself giving a little math lesson, by running through the following questions:

Therapist: If I tell you I'm with you one hundred percent, what do I mean?

Client: That you're with me all the way.

Therapist: Right. And if we're partners fifty-fifty, what does that mean?

Client: That we split the profits down the middle.

Therapist: Right. And if I have three quarters, how much is that worth?

Client: Seventy-five cents.

Therapist: Right. See, percent is just how much of a hundred, like how many cents out of a dollar. So out of a hundred percent, how much of you really wants to work toward that good future we were talking about? And how much of you wants to just keep getting in trouble?

Most clients will declare at least 50 percent toward the positive future, many going much higher. It is important to try to get a reasonably accurate estimate of the client's conflicting motivations. If a client is unrealistically high (e.g., 100 percent), I might explain that even if most of him wants that, there must be a part that does not. For example:

Therapist: Okay, listen. When I was a kid I used to steal from stores. Now I don't do that, and I haven't for a long time. But still, when I go to a store, there's a part of me that thinks about stealing. So for me, I would say maybe 10 percent still feels like stealing—even though the rest of me makes sure it doesn't happen. How much would there be for you?

Client: I want to be a hundred percent but there's a part of me, too, sometimes I just don't care about anything, maybe about a quarter, 25 percent.

Therapist: So 75 percent for the good future and 25 percent for the bad future?

Client: That's about right.

If motivation is not expressed here, it is probably best to go very slowly, working more with rapport and contemporaneous concerns. Until personal goals are endorsed as important, commitment to engaging in uncomfortable or boring treatment activities is unlikely. Occasionally a client will simply refuse to buy into the motivational approach described above. There can be several reasons for this, including inadequate rapport, prior negative experiences with therapists, client mistrust, or lack of interest in the therapy and/or the positive future. For some of the clients who continue to deny motivation, the following intervention may be helpful.

Wearing a Sign

Sometimes a client feels particularly victimized by peers or authority figures, and resists taking personal responsibility for his own contribution to this pattern of interactions. "The teacher always picks on me, the kids lie about me, the other one starts it and I get in trouble . . ." Despite some exploration, the client may continue to resist insight regarding his own role. Alternately, the client may glory in his role as provocateur/hero, blaming others and claiming not to care about the consequences. This intervention involves labeling the client's role as intentional, by using a metaphor that is both graphic and humorous.

> *Therapist:* I hear you had a rough day yesterday.
> *Client:* You should have seen me! I told them what I thought of them. I'm not scared of them, they took away my privileges again but I don't care.
> *Therapist:* I thought you told me you didn't want to miss any more movies.
> *Client:* I don't care. They can't get to me.
> *Therapist:* So what happened?
> *Client:* (long story of incidents leading to confrontation and punishment) But no matter how it starts or who starts it, it's always me that gets in trouble, no one else. They have it in for me.
> *Therapist:* You know why, don't you?
> *Client:* I think they're prejudiced or something.
> *Therapist:* Do they treat the other (client's race) kids like that?
> *Client:* No, not really, mainly me.
> *Therapist:* Should I tell you?

Client: Yeah, tell me.

Therapist: It's that sign you wear.

Client: What are you talking about? I don't have a sign.

Therapist: That sign you always wear, it says, "Mess with me."

Client: (laughs).

Therapist: You wear that sign everywhere you go?

Client: Yup. Just about everywhere.

Therapist: Well, that's how people know—they just read the sign. How long have you been wearing that sign for?

Client: Oh, couple of years, anyway.

Therapist: Well, it must be good to wear it.

Client: Why do you say that, good to wear it?

Therapist: Otherwise, I figure you'd rather go to the movies like the other kids. But since you don't, I figure it must be good to wear that sign. Mess with me.

This type of metaphor can be worked repeatedly, often in a casual or joking manner, from session to session. The client can likewise be accused of liking the consequences of his behavior, including the punishments as well as the confrontations leading up to them. This paradoxical intervention should be done in an accepting, positive manner, leaving the client to reject the negative behavior on his own. The metaphor can be continued even as progress is being made, for example, "I hope you get into at least a little trouble this week. I hate to think of you missing out on all those arguments you used to have." Sometimes, the client will come around to requesting help in working on specific issues.

Commitment to Treatment

In most cases, the motivational interviewing will proceed reasonably smoothly, and the client will declare a more-than-half-hearted desire for the positive future. Now it is time to formally engage the client in the treatment process. He has just acknowledged caring about achieving positive goals, and has identified certain problems as obstacles in his path. The therapist can now offer treatment in the service of the client's goals. For example:

> *Therapist:* So 80 percent of you wants to stay out of jail, get your GED [general equivalency diploma], and join the army, but the 20 percent of you that doesn't care gets you into trouble. So far, that 20 percent has been in charge. If you want, we can work on some things to help that 80 percent to get stronger, to be in charge more of the time.
>
> *Client:* Like what would we do?
>
> *Therapist:* Different kinds of things, I have a bag of tricks. It's like twenty-eight flavors of ice cream, you won't like all of them, but we keep trying until we find a few you like, the ones that work for you. I would explain each thing before we do it, you won't have to do anything you don't want to do. But it will be a lot of work to get stronger, it can be hard, and it can be boring. Do you remember learning how to [shoot a basket, ride a bike . . .]? How at first it was clumsy but you practice practice practice until it's like second nature? We can practice things that can help you control yourself. You'll still have to do all the work, but I can help you practice the skills.
>
> *Client:* Okay, let's start.

At this point the therapist might try a "not too fast" approach. The client can be told that the work may be an ordeal, may be boring, may be hard, and won't be effective right away. The therapist can also ask questions to reconfirm that this plan does indeed support the client's own goals. This paradoxical approach sets the client up to insist on the treatment, which increases commitment. In general, this commitment to treatment can be obtained by the first or second session. Then, in most cases, the skill building portion of the protocol can be implemented.

SKILL BUILDING

The skill building portion of this approach is roughly equivalent to the parent training portion of the approach described in the previous chapter: it serves to establish the sense of safety preliminary to the trauma-resolution work. With younger children, parents may play a larger role in establishing this safety. Also, younger children tend to be a bit more compliant, and are therefore more likely to simply cooperate when the therapist suggests targeting traumatic memories with EMDR. With conduct-disordered adolescents, the sense of control gained from these skill-building activities is often required before they are willing to proceed with EMDR for trauma resolution. Of course, there are exceptions in all directions, so this should only be viewed as a model.

Preparation

For many adolescents with disruptive behavior problems, this portion of the treatment plan has the most face validity; the client may readily state that he needs to control his temper. Since the skill-building work is relatively nonthreatening and can be effective, it is often a good place to start.

However, the therapist should also warn the client that the effectiveness of the skill-building work may be limited due to internal pressures related to prior trauma and loss. This can be done as part of the case formulation used to justify proposed treatment activities. Since most clients acknowledge poor self-control or anger-management skills, the skill-building portion of the treatment is self-evident. The effect of past trauma or loss can be effectively explained in terms of a stress buildup, giving examples to which the client can relate.

> *Therapist:* Let's say this is my boiling point (holds hand at neck). Now maybe when you're a baby, no stress piled up yet, you start out down here (holds hand at ankles). But me, maybe when I was little my dog died, got some stress piled up from that (holds hand at knee), maybe I got beat up some, pile up some more stress (holds hand halfway up thigh), maybe my favorite cousin dies, now I'm up to here (hold's hand at waist), so maybe now I walk around like this. You with me so far?
>
> *Client:* Yes, I know what you mean, I have a lot of stress like that, too, too stressed.
>
> *Therapist:* So let's say I have a bad day. Alarm clock didn't work, so I wake up late and I have to hurry (brings hand up a few inches). Then I pour milk into my cereal and it's sour (brings hand up higher). Then I get stuck at some red lights (brings hand up higher), and some jerk cuts me off in traffic and almost makes me crash (brings hand up higher), and then I'm late for work and get stink-eye from my boss (hand up to neck). One little thing goes wrong, you know what could happen?
>
> *Client:* You could go off, lose it.
>
> *Therapist:* That's right. So maybe I better do a little something to bring it back down, maybe tell some jokes, or take a walk to let off steam, or something. Lucky for me I start way down here (hand at waist) so I can take a lot of buildup before I reach that boiling point. But you, the way you go off all the time, I think maybe you're walking around like this (holds hand almost up to neck), so just a little bit of extra stress and there you go.

The therapist can suggest examples from the client's past as possible sources of the trauma buildup, and even obtain SUDS ratings for each event. Once this model is accepted by the client, he may have a new appreciation for why he is so reactive, and why he might need more training in coping skills than someone who has less of a stress buildup. This discussion can also serve, later, as a basis for understanding the limitations of the skill-building and as entree to trauma work.

> *Therapist:* We'll start out working on these self-control skills. They can help. But they can only help so much, when you're walking around like this all the time (hand at neck), ready to blow. Later, maybe we can do something to bring this (stress level) down lower.

The therapist should start by learning in detail about the problem behavior, including typical triggers as well as responses and consequences. Alternative coping methods can be reviewed. Most people already utilize some strategies for self-control, with varying degrees of effectiveness. When possible, it is best to build on appropriate preexisting strategies. This makes the intervention seem less foreign, and the client can feel that he is already partway there. There are many effective non-EMDR methods for enhancing self-control, including time-out, deep breathing, and letting off steam by doing a high-energy or relaxing activity such as walking, playing sports, or listening to music. Talking it out can also be helpful, and may be practiced during the therapy session.

This protocol includes three cognitive-behavioral interventions that incorporate EMDR: (1) the *Early Warning System* focuses on increasing awareness of the steps in the escalation toward acting out, so that the client can interrupt the process earlier, before losing control; (2) *Choices Have Consequences* is used to reduce impulsivity by increasing the client's awareness, in the moment, of the consequences of any given behavioral choice; and (3) *Tease-Proofing* is used to help clients become resistant to provocation. Although these can be used in any combination, they are designed to follow the good and bad movies presented above, and are presented in order with the later interventions building on the earlier ones.

Early Warning System

This intervention is particularly useful for those adolescents who experience their anger and impulsiveness as a surprise or as an explosion. They are not aware of the various steps leading up to their problem behaviors. By the time they realize they are headed for trouble, they are often past the point of no return. The Early Warning System helps them to identify the various steps leading to that explosion, so they will be able to recognize earlier points at which they can more easily interrupt the process.

> *Therapist:* You know how in the movies, the attacker can sneak right up to the house, maybe even sneak inside, before anyone even knows he's there? And then he's got you! But the really rich people have these early warning systems, you know, the guard at the gate, the motion detectors, the video cameras, the dogs . . . So by the time the attacker gets anywhere close, they're ready and waiting. So what you need is one of those early warning systems for your own temper, so you can catch it early, before it gets the jump on you.

The client is asked to focus on a typical problem event, perhaps a recent one, in detail. First he is asked to describe the situation in terms of the provocation and then his response. Then he is asked to examine his response in more detail, to discern intervening events that he may have skipped in his first description. The therapist can help by offering a menu of possible responses, and by having patience as the client struggles to see himself in a new way.

> *Therapist:* So he's talking trash to you and the next thing you know, you punch him out?
>
> *Client:* That's about it.
>
> *Therapist:* Now I want you to concentrate on when he's talking trash to you, close your eyes if it helps to concentrate just on that moment. What's going on inside you?
>
> *Client:* I'm getting heated. No one can talk to me that way.
>
> *Therapist:* Good. How can you tell you're getting heated? What lets you know?
>
> *Client:* I just know.
>
> *Therapist:* Well, what's happening with your body? Is it hot or cold, is it loose or tense or shaky, is it dry or sweaty?
>
> *Client:* I get it. Well, I can't see nothin' but the guy, and my whole body tenses up, and my heart's beating fast, and my hands are in fists.
>
> *Therapist:* Good, that's what we're looking for. And what are you thinking, what words are in your head?
>
> *Client:* "Kill him."
>
> *Therapist:* Okay, what happens first? When he's talking trash to you, what's your first sign that something's going wrong?
>
> *Client:* Well, he's dissing me. I don't like that.
>
> *Therapist:* Good, so first you notice what he's doing, and what you think about it. What happens next?
>
> *Client:* It just all happens at once.
>
> *Therapist:* Let's look at it very carefully, like a movie in slow motion. Close your eyes and start with him talking trash, and right away freeze the frame and see what you notice.

This process is continued until both therapist and client are satisfied that a reliable sequence has been identified, for example, (1) provocation, (2) don't like being disrespected, (3) heart races, (4) anger and swearing, (5) hitting. The point here is not to attain insight about the reasons for the client's reactivity, but to help him to notice, and learn to recognize, the details of his own behavioral patterns.

The final exercise in the Early Warning System is to imaginally view a movie in which each step along the escalation is ordered and discrete, during eye movements. This should be done several times, and the client questioned after each viewing to ensure that each discrete step was noticed. This should help the client to increase awareness of the various steps involved. (There may also be some incidental desensitization of the provoking stimulus.)

The Early Warning System is not always essential to this protocol. If the client's acting out is not of the sudden, explosive variety, and he can become aware of the various components of escalation without too much difficulty, it may be skipped. Then the awareness of the various steps is simply included more informally in the next intervention. This is not generally recommended as a stand-alone intervention, and should be followed by Choices Have Consequences as soon as possible. However, if a session ends with the Early Warning System, the client might be assigned to write a brief nightly journal entry about the most upsetting event of the day, including all aspects of his response. This can further increase insight as well as awareness in the moment.

Choices Have Consequences

This is the real workhorse of the cognitive-behavioral training component of the protocol. It builds on the future movies and on the early warning system. The goal here is to train the client to understand that choices have consequences, and to maintain that awareness even at challenging moments.

The client is asked to describe a typical challenging situation (typically some type of provocation or temptation) that is present in his current life circumstances. This should be a situation in which the client frequently responds in the problematic way previously identified. Together the therapist and the client come up with at least one positive alternative behavioral choice with which the client might respond to the challenge. Then the therapist explains the rationale of this exercise: that bad choices lead to bad endings (consequences) and vice versa. By practicing imaginal movies that demonstrate this principle, the client should become better at making choices that will help him toward his goals.

The client is asked to prepare a movie including the following components, in this order:

1. The provocation, or the challenging situation
2. The client's internal response (i.e., the early warning system)
3. The acting out, or "bad" behavioral choice
4. The bad-ending image, along with the words, "It's not worth it."

The movie is then viewed imaginally during eye movements. As with other movie techniques, the client is asked to indicate when it's over.

The therapist then asks the client what happened, to ensure that all components were included. Often, clients fill in missing pieces to help the story fit together, especially between the bad choice and the bad ending. Then the client is asked to view another movie (also during eye movements) that starts the same way but replaces the bad choice and bad ending with the good choice and good ending. Different good-ending images can be used on different occasions, representing a range of goals. The client can include a cognition with the good-ending image, such as, "It's worth it," or "I can do it." Again the therapist asks what happened, and if all components were not included, insists on a corrected repeat effort. Often clients generate effective coping strategies during this exercise, for example, "I just said to myself, 'He's not my friend, I don't care what he says,' and I walked away."

For the third movie, the client is told to start the same way (steps 1 and 2) but to just see what happens next. The client is instructed, however, that a bad choice must lead to a bad ending, and a good choice to a good ending. Usually, the client will spontaneously choose a good choice and ending. However, if the bad choice and ending are chosen, the therapist accepts that, and simply asks the client to do it again: "Start the same way, and see what happens, and remember: bad choice, bad ending; good choice, good ending." The client will almost certainly spontaneously choose the good choice and ending the next time. The movie can be repeated once more with the same instructions.

This procedure should be repeated to cover a variety of similar situations, starting with relatively less challenging situations and building up. For example, if the issue is fighting versus walking away, this can be played out in a series of situations involving different provoking peers and authority figures. It can also progress from contemporaneous challenges to anticipated future challenges, thus resembling a relapse prevention approach.

Choices Have Consequences has a number of effects. In addition to pairing choices with consequences, it is reinforcing the client's investment in the positive future, by giving him practice imagining not only the good ending but practical steps to achieve it. Covert sensitization may make the bad choice less appealing. The client is also continuing to practice the awareness of the Early Warning System, and possibly to desensitize to the target situations. However, the latter effect may be minimal, since the situational triggers are being targeted prior to the reprocessing of the source events.

This intervention can be practiced with many targets, and over many sessions. It is important to emphasize to the client that practice only develops a skill, but it will still be up to the client to use the skill and make the choices. Since this tool is in the hands of a reactive client, it may still be difficult to use it successfully, especially at first. Some who gain confidence from this exercise may expect dramatic progress and be disappointed. Therefore, it is important that the client does not expect instant change, so that even minor or sporadic progress can represent positive momentum.

Tease-Proofing

The tease-proofing interventions are designed for those who are particularly reactive to provocation by others, and for whom this is an identified problem. Sometimes the client is very clear that it is a problem: "I hate it when the kids tease me. I just get so mad and I lose it and I'm the one that gets in trouble." However, others are more confused, perhaps believing that they are right to stand up for themselves, regardless of the consequences—yet not liking the consequences. (Of course, there are legitimate examples of self-defense, but these are much rarer than most clients suppose.) Therefore, before addressing the problem of the client's vulnerability to provocation, it is sometimes necessary to convince the client that it is indeed a problem. This can be done with one or more of the following cognitive reframes.

Who's in Charge of You?

Since most teens who are reactive to provocation feel that they are standing up for themselves, it can be rather alarming to consider that their reactivity makes them a slave to their enemies. The following discussion can convert the client in a matter of minutes from insisting on being reactive to insisting on controlling the reaction.

> *Therapist:* So why would someone say bad things about your mother, anyway? Does that kid even know your mother?
>
> *Client:* No, he doesn't know my mom. He just has an attitude or something, you know, he wants to get something going, thinks he can push me around.
>
> *Therapist:* So let's say I'm some kid having a bad day. And let's say that I don't like feeling bad inside me, so I want to get my feelings out on someone else, maybe I'll feel a little better if I can make someone else feel bad. So I want some action, I want to really get someone going. So I walk into the room and I see you. Are you the kind of guy I can get going?
>
> *Client:* No, not unless you're disrespectful about my family.
>
> *Therapist:* So if I want to get you going, all I have to do is say something bad about your mother?
>
> *Client:* That's right. No one gets away with that.
>
> *Therapist:* So it's just like pushing a button. I just push the right button and there you go.
>
> *Client:* I guess you could say that.
>
> *Therapist:* So you're there minding your own business, and anyone having a bad day can make you get all heated and get yourself in trouble.
>
> *Client:* Well, no one can talk about my mother like that.
>
> *Therapist:* So that kid who said that stuff yesterday, what's his name?
>
> *Client:* Jerry.
>
> *Therapist:* Yeah, Jerry. I didn't realize you liked Jerry so much.
>
> *Client:* What are you talking about, I hate his guts!
>
> *Therapist:* Yeah, I didn't realize you liked him so much. Yesterday, you let him decide when you would get angry, you let him decide for you when you would get in trouble.

Client: I don't like him.

Therapist: How come you put him in charge of how you act? You let him run you. All he has to do is press the button and you go off. You must really look up to him.

Client: He's not in charge of me, I'm in charge of me.

Therapist: Then who decides how you act? Some jerk having a bad day, or you?

This point can also be demonstrated by role play, with the therapist asking the client to say something insulting, and the therapist first responding in a reactive manner and then in a controlled manner. Or the roles can be reversed. It can also be important for the client to figure out that those provoking him are simply acting out their own problems, which the client need not take personally: "Is he saying that because you're really a bad person, or just because he has some bad feelings that he wants to take out on someone?"

The client may emerge from this discussion with a particularly useful cognition, such as "I'm in charge of myself," or "It's not my problem." Such cognitions can be paired with positive behavioral choices in the Choices Have Consequences activity as well as the interventions described below. Once the client is clear that his reactivity is a problem, the following interventions can lead to very rapid changes.

"Play Therapy"

This is essentially an imagination plus EMDR version of play therapy, in which the client can learn to master what was previously overwhelming. The client is instructed to select a typical provocation event, including a peer or authority figure with whom the client tends to be reactive. He is then introduced to a fantasy context, such as a comic book or a dream, and instructed to devise a resolution to the problem. Then this sequence is viewed as a movie during eye movements, including the provocation and the resolution.

> *Therapist:* So Mrs. C. is going to tell you you lost a point, and you notice that you're getting heated, feel like going off. Now let's just make believe for a minute, this is happening in a comic book and you're the artist. How are you going to handle this?
>
> *Client:* Erase her from the page.
>
> *Therapist:* Okay, let's try that. Start with her saying that, and then erase her from the page. Ready? (Does eye movements until the client indicates that the movie is over.) What happened?
>
> *Client:* Just what I said. Erased her, she was gone.
>
> *Therapist:* Okay, same situation, you're the artist again. What's another way to handle it?
>
> *Client:* Turn her into a bug and step on her.
>
> *Therapist:* Try that.

This procedure can be repeated with a variety of creative resolutions and with a variety of target images (provoking people and situations). This is a good ice-breaker for the other tease-proofing techniques, as it can be humorous while increasing confidence in the possibility that such provocation can indeed be mastered. Some clients try to discount this intervention by saying that they can't use these strategies in real life. The therapist can answer, "We're just fooling around, it's okay," so that not too much is expected.

Walls

This intervention teaches the client, metaphorically, to create a boundary between himself and the provoker. As in "Play Therapy," the client is instructed to select a typical provocation event, including a peer or authority figure with whom the client tends to be reactive. This time, the therapist tells the client to imagine a barrier preventing the provoker from having access to the client. The client is asked to imagine this barrier in every detail. Then, as above, a movie is viewed with eye movements, in which the provocation is followed by the implementation of this barrier. In other words, a coping strategy is being installed.

> *Therapist:* This time, you're going to put up a wall between you. Think of what the wall is made of, what it looks like, ar d how you're going to put it up in a split-second.
>
> *Client:* It's a high brick wall. I just snap my fingers and there it is.
>
> *Therapist:* So we'll start that movie the same way, but this time, you put that wall up. Ready? Tell me when you're done (eye movements). What happened this time?
>
> *Client:* I put that wall up, and he kept on talking trash, but I couldn't hear him anymore and it didn't bother me. I just laughed and walked away.

This procedure can be tried with various types of barriers, including other walls, doors, and even force fields. It can be repeated with other provoking peers and authority figures, in increasingly challenging situations. It can also be integrated with Choices Have Consequences, simply by instructing the client to include a good ending to the movie, if he has made a good behavioral choice. In the above vignette, for example, the client might end by saying, "And he got in trouble and I didn't."

Role Model

Here the client integrates a role model's more adaptive approach to handling provocation. The role model may be previously identified (from the initial interview) or may be generated specifically for this intervention. The role model may be a peer, relative, community member, or pop culture figure. The client is asked to describe how the role model would handle this type of situation. (Curiously enough, role models usually handle provocations with humor; sometimes also by both ignoring the provoker and outperforming him.) Then, with eye movements, the client is asked to observe an imaginal movie of the role model handling the target situation. Next, the client is asked to "become" the role model (as in the example below) and imagine, during eye movements, handling the target situation. Finally, the client is asked to try the role model's strategy independently of the role model, again with the movie and eye movements.

> *Therapist:* Who can you think of that can handle this kind of thing really well?
>
> *Client:* My friend Joe.
>
> *Therapist:* What does Joe do when someone says something like that to him?
>
> *Client:* He just laughs it off, makes a joke out of it.
>
> *Therapist:* So do people give him a lot of trouble, try to get him going the way they do with you?
>
> *Client:* No, he gets along good with everyone.
>
> *Therapist:* I want you to imagine someone saying something bad to Joe, and how he'll take care of it. Tell me when you're done (eye movements). What happened?
>
> *Client:* Some guy says, "Your sister's a dog," and Joe just says, "She still turns *you* down," and everyone laughs, and that's the end of it.
>
> *Therapist:* Now I want you to imagine this. There's Joe, you sneak up close to him, so close you can hear his breathing. Now you sneak up right inside him, feel what it feels like to be him. Now the guy will say "Your sister's a dog," and you're inside Joe, while he handles it (eye movements). What happened this time?
>
> *Client:* It felt kind of weird but I did it. Same thing happened.

Therapist: This time, just be yourself, and see how you
  handle it (eye movements). What happened this time?
Client: He said my sister was a dog, and I said, "Yeah, it runs
  in the family" and I start barking at him, everyone busts
  out laughing and no one's mad any more.

Sometimes the client will anticipate by visualizing himself
using the role model's strategy during an earlier step in the procedure. In that case, it's okay to skip the intervening steps. This
procedure can be tried with several challenging situations, but
it may not be necessary. The Role Model activity can also be integrated with Choices Have Consequences, by adding a good
ending onto the movie provided that the good behavioral choice
is made.

The entire tease-proofing package can generally be accomplished in a single session. As noted above, several of the procedures can be expanded to incorporate the Choices Have Consequences activity. Self-talk can also be incorporated, if the client
has generated useful cognitions such as "It's not worth it," or
"I'm in charge of myself." Later, when practicing Choices Have
Consequences, the tease-proofing strategies can be among the
options for positive behavioral choices. Quite frequently, the
client will be enthusiastic about learning these powerful new
coping skills, and many report immediate and lasting success
following the tease-proofing session.

The skill-building phase of treatment may take several sessions, and some elements may continue to be worked into subsequent sessions. If it becomes boring for the client, he can be
reminded that achieving his goals will take some hard work. The
therapist can ask the client to report at each session on successes
and setbacks, which in either case should be taken in stride.
Setbacks can be viewed as learning experiences, while successes
should be treated with caution; setbacks may still occur. The
therapist's attitude can help to keep the client from expecting
too much too soon and becoming discouraged.

These coping strategies can help the client to be more successful and in control, enhancing the sense of safety that is so critical to trauma treatment. However, overwhelming internal pressures may continue to make the client's reactivity too strong to manage on some occasions. It may be time to suggest trauma work.

TRAUMA WORK

EMDR for major trauma and loss can be a critical component of treatment for this population; enhancement of coping skills may be insufficient if reactivity is overwhelming. However, many clients are extremely reluctant to try EMDR on even relatively minor upsetting memories. Chief concerns are the risk of being overwhelmed by affect, leading to violent or self-destructive behavior; the client's fear of being overwhelmed; and a premature EMDR attempt leading to refusal to continue or reattempt. These are fairly typical concerns, and more so in a population defined by limited coping skills and habitual acting out. It is therefore especially important to proceed with caution and to establish a strong foundation in terms of the therapeutic relationship as well as the client's coping skills, before proceeding with work on major trauma or loss.

The client is likely to gain trust when the therapist has successfully presented the treatment plan as a reflection of the client's goals, and when the client has made some progress toward his goals by working with the therapist. This track record is very important, because many clients will be skeptical about the need for trauma work, or acknowledge the need and then later deny it. Also, working with upsetting memories can be scary. Use of EMDR on relatively minor upsetting memories may help the client to establish his own track record with EMDR, making it easier to move into the more difficult work.

EMDR for minor upsetting memories is most easily introduced in response to a contemporaneous event. For example, the client may be very angry at a peer or a teacher because of an incident that occurred the day before the therapy meeting. Some clients will readily discuss this type of incident with the therapist. With others, who seem to have little to report from one meeting to the next, it can be helpful to ask about the best and the worst moments since the previous meeting. This gets the client in a routine of disclosure to the therapist, which can also build skills in articulating feelings. And, of course, the high and low points of the previous week provide useful material for the session.

When an upsetting recent event is identified and described, the therapist can frame the ongoing negative affect (e.g., anger) as a current problem, in that it increases the risk for overreacting on subsequent contact with the same person. The therapist can also refer to the previous discussion of stress buildup: the higher the stress level, the more risk of losing control. Then the therapist asks the client if he is willing to try to think about this incident while using EMDR, even though the feelings might get strong for a little while. Detailed information about EMDR may not be necessary at this point, since there seems to be little risk of other memories emerging at this time, and the client is already familiar with eye movements.

Clients frequently resist using EMDR, even for relatively minor recent events, because they are afraid that they will just get more upset by bringing it up again, and perhaps act out. This fear should be explicitly discussed before proceeding. After listening to the client's concerns, the therapist can refer to her own experience with other, similar cases, in which the clients have generally felt more calm afterward, and can promise that the client can stay in the session until he feels calm enough to return safely to his environment, "even if we're here till midnight." The client should also be told that he can change his mind at any point, if it becomes too difficult for him. Fortunately, many view that last comment as a challenge and become more willing to try it, once the safety concerns have been addressed.

If EMDR for a specific memory is discussed but not pursued in the same session, the memory should be put back away in an installed "container," after which a relaxation exercise such as deep breathing should be done. This precaution will minimize the risk the client has already taken by simply discussing the memory. It will also give the client a track record of being able to bring up the memory in session and still emerge in good shape.

> *Therapist:* I want you to think of some kind of container that can hold that memory for you until you need to get to it again. Do you have one in mind?
>
> *Client:* A steel safe.
>
> *Therapist:* I'm going to ask you to imagine putting every bit of that memory into the safe, and when it's all packed in and closed up, you tell me. Ready? (Eye movements.) Is it all packed away now?

The EMDR procedure for a recent upsetting event in this context is fairly simple. After obtaining a SUDS on the worst image, the incident is processed in "movie" form (with eye movements), from beginning to end, only focusing on particularly upsetting moments as necessary. It is important to keep moving at this sensitive phase in the treatment, so the process can be completed and relief achieved as quickly as possible. This is also not the time to look for source memories. The main purpose of using EMDR on recent events is to introduce the client to EMDR for trauma work in a safe, limited, and positive way. In most cases the SUDS will be eliminated, and the client will spontaneously produce a useful cognition. Following EMDR with a recent incident, it is often useful to practice Choices Have Consequences (or Tease-Proofing if appropriate) to rehearse effective coping for a similar type of event.

This selective use of EMDR for recent upsetting events can be applied once or a number of times over several sessions. Although the results may not be profound or lasting, this type of experience goes a long way toward building the client's trust in the therapist, as well as in his own ability to face and work through difficult material. The insights gained through reprocessing the minor events can help the client to recognize that he is habitually overreacting, so that the therapist's explanation of the stress buildup will come to make more sense. Ultimately, these experiences can be used as a stepping stone to using EMDR for the source memories, those underlying the reactivity.

EMDR for major trauma and loss can be very effective with this population, and the adult protocol can be used with only minor modifications. For example, the therapist should not insist too strongly on the production of negative and positive cognitions; if they are not readily provided, the client could simply get frustrated. The cognitions will normally be generated during the processing anyway.

Cognitions in the EMDR Protocol

Cognitions are considered an essential component of the standard (adult) EMDR protocol. The initially targeted distressing image carries a negative cognition or self-referencing belief with ongoing felt validity, such as, "It was my fault," or "I'm not safe." The client is also asked to select a positive cognition with a preferred statement, such as "I did the best I could," or "I'm safe now." The negative cognition becomes part of the image that is targeted for processing, whereas the positive cognition becomes part of the adaptive perspective to which the client aspires. With adolescents, including these cognitions can be very useful as long as the process of identifying them does not become too confusing or frustrating.

The therapist should be particularly vigilant on the client's behalf and not allow him to try EMDR on major trauma prematurely. Some clients will declare themselves ready to face the most difficult of their memories right now. The usual informed consent procedures may have little cautionary effect, as the client overestimates his capacity to tolerate the difficult experience. Therefore, the therapist must consider exercising restraint on behalf of a client who has poor judgment and little history of successful stress tolerance and may be unlikely to persevere in a potentially overwhelming EMDR session.

On the other hand, sometimes the therapist and the client can more or less agree on the potential benefits of EMDR for trauma work, and the therapist may believe that the client can be successful, but the client continues to resist. Particularly in time-limited treatment, the therapist may need to look for creative ways to encourage the client to proceed with this potentially life-changing experience, before the opportunity is lost. There are many ways to help the client overcome this resistance. The therapist can ask the client to trust the therapist, and just give it a try. The therapist can challenge the client by paradoxically withholding the treatment, saying it may be too difficult for the client. Incentives can also be very effective. For example, the client can earn a prized activity or treat by completing a session to the therapist's satisfaction. I have even gambled with skeptical clients: "If you try this for an hour and you feel better, then you win for feeling better. If you try it for an hour and you don't feel better, I'll buy you a burger. If you don't try it for the full hour, the bet's off." Of course, the latter strategy must be used selectively, as there is a potential for a reverse incentive.

CONCLUSION

This approach to the individual treatment of acting-out adolescents should be used in a flexible manner, with other interventions incorporated as appropriate. It would be ideal to coordinate this treatment with other efforts being made on the client's behalf, possibly including a behavior modification program, group treatment, family treatment, and support for educational and employment placements. For example, efforts should be made to enhance safety as well as opportunities for success in the adolescent's daily environment. The trauma orientation can effectively guide the choice and sequence of interventions within a multifaceted approach to treatment for adolescents, even for problems, such as conduct disorder, that are not typically viewed as trauma based. Because EMDR works so well in trauma-resolution work and can enhance other processes such as visualization and learning, it can play a central role in the individual treatment of adolescents with conduct problems.

PART II

THE TECHNICAL REPERTOIRE

4

EMDR: A Review of the Standard Protocol

To use EMDR effectively with children requires sufficient background both in child therapy and in EMDR. Here is a quick review of the basic EMDR theory and protocol, as used with adults. This chapter is adapted from Shapiro (1995), with added comments and illustrative material. For more detail, please refer to the original source as well as formal, supervised training. Thorough familiarity with this material serves as the foundation for using EMDR with children.

ACCELERATED INFORMATION PROCESSING THEORY

Shapiro (1995) proposed the accelerated information processing theory, which is roughly consistent with extant trauma processing theories, to account for the effects seen with EMDR. According to this view, humans are designed to heal naturally from emotional wounds, just as from physical wounds. This healing involves a process of progressive integration of the upsetting memory aspects, through activities such as talking, thinking, feeling, and dreaming, until the memory has been completely worked through (metabolized, digested). The memory then becomes neutralized, merely another past experience. Processed memories are the basis of growth and maturity.

However, if an experience is so overwhelming that it shocks the system, the healing process may become blocked, and the disturbing information does not get integrated. Then the memory is locked in raw, unprocessed form, and disturbing features of the memory may emerge as posttraumatic symptoms, perhaps triggered by a current stimulus. A traumatic memory can thus be disturbing for an indefinite period, until the memory is unlocked and worked through to full integration, that is, until the natural healing processes can proceed (Shapiro 1995).

The role of EMDR is to help the client access and metabolize this memory, and transform it from the locked, state-specific form to the neutral and healthier integrated form. This is a central goal of many therapeutic approaches to trauma. EMDR is distinguished by the accelerated information processing effect, which apparently condenses the natural healing process into a very brief period.

To target a memory for reprocessing, it may not be sufficient to target just the most prominent feature or most disturbing part of the memory. Additional aspects of the memory must also be pursued for maximum effect, including the associated imagery, thoughts, feelings, and physical sensations. This is important because aspects of the trauma may be stored in state-specific forms represented by an apparently obscure part of the memory. Also, memories are not isolated and discrete, but connect along numerous associative chains. Therefore, other thematically related memories may also require processing for maximum effect. Finally, other stimuli or experiences may have become associated with the memory subsequently, and may also require processing with EMDR.

BASIC COMPONENTS
OF EMDR

The EMDR protocol is designed to access and reprocess all the elements of a traumatic memory that may be stored in the pathology-inducing manner described above. This protocol includes a number of component tools that assist in focusing on the memory, facilitating the memory reprocessing, and tracking progress. I will describe the protocol after introducing these components.

It is important for the clinician to be sensitive to the client's feelings during the process, and to avoid making the client feel frustrated or inadequate for not giving the "right" answers. This risk can be minimized by using plain language rather than jargon, by taking personal responsibility for misunderstandings ("I guess I didn't explain that right"), and by responding with flexibility and acceptance even when the answer is wrong. It can also be helpful for the therapist to be prepared with concrete examples to orient the client to the type of information that is being requested. For example, the therapist may ask for a self-evaluation and instead get a feeling, and handle it as follows:

> *Therapist:* When you bring this memory up, what are you saying to yourself right now?
> *Client:* That I'm sad.
> *Therapist:* Oh, you got ahead of me, I was going to ask you about the feeling, too. When you have the picture of the memory, and the sad feeling, what does this make you believe about yourself?
> *Client:* What do you mean?
> *Therapist:* Well, I'm not good at explaining this part. Look at this list [of self-referenced belief statements]. See if any of these statements feel true for you, to go with the memory.

Imagery

The client is instructed to choose an image representing the quintessential moment from the memory, perhaps the most disturbing or intrusive image or one that best captures its negative impact on the client. The therapist may say, "Is there an image that stands out for you? Which part bothers you the most now, when you bring it up?" If this is not sufficient to elicit the desired image, the therapist may say, "If this were a movie and you needed a picture for the poster to show how bad the story feels, what would the picture be? What would go on the poster?"

Negative Cognition

The client is instructed to describe the negative self-statement, or belief about the self, that arises from the memory. As with the other elements of the memory, it may not be objectively accurate or broadly representative, but may be prominent within the state-specific memory itself. This negative cognition should be an interpretation or view of the self, not merely a description of the event. For example, "I was helpless" may be an accurate description; what is wanted here is the interpretation, "I am a helpless person," or whatever feels true for the person. Common negative cognitions include "I'm a bad person" and "It was my fault." Such beliefs often persist after the trauma, and infect the client's life with apathy, self-blame, and other crippling attitudes. A list of common negative cognitions can be shown to clients to orient them to possibly useful responses.

The negative cognition is typically the most difficult component to elicit from the client, who generally doesn't understand what the therapist is asking for. It may be helpful for the therapist to ask, once the target image has been identified, "What does that make you believe about yourself?" or "When you bring that picture up, what are you saying to yourself about it right now?" If the client makes a statement that does not meet format requirements, the therapist may reinterpret to make the statement more suitable. Even so, it's important to avoid putting words into the client's mouth, so choices should be offered neutrally.

> *Therapist:* What does that make you believe about yourself?
> *Client:* I feel lonely.
> *Therapist:* Would it feel true to say, "I'm alone in the world," or "I'm not worth caring about," or something else?
> *Client:* Yes.
> *Therapist:* Does one of those fit the picture best, or would it be something else?
> *Client:* I can't count on anyone, no one will help me.
> *Therapist:* And what does that make you believe about yourself?
> *Client:* I'm not important enough, I'm nobody.

Positive Cognition

The client is then instructed to choose a more positive, adaptive self-statement, even if it does not feel completely true prior to reprocessing. Again, this should not be descriptive—for example, "I wish it never happened" will not be useful here—but interpretive. Common positive cognitions include "It's over," "I'm a good person," "I'm safe now," and "I can take care of myself." The positive cognition represents one formulation of the goal of the treatment: how the client hopes to view herself afterward. The therapist may elicit the positive cognition by saying, "What would you rather be saying to yourself next time you remember this event?" or "What do you wish you could believe about yourself, instead of that [negative cognition]?"

Validity of Cognition (VoC) Scale

The client is asked to rate the positive cognition on a 1 to 7 scale, from 1 as completely false, to 7 as completely true. The rating should reflect the "felt truth" rather than what the client may know intellectually but not fully believe. The VoC (Validity of Cognition scale) allows both the therapist and the client to track progress during and after the EMDR session. The therapist may ask, "On a scale of 1 to 7, 7 is all the way true, and 1 is a lie, it's false. Say that [positive cognition] again and tell me how true it feels right now from 1 to 7, how true it feels in your gut."

Emotion

The client is instructed to report on his current affective reaction to the selected memory image. It is important to focus on emotion itself, not a restatement of another component of the memory. "I feel like I was stupid" should be transformed either to a negative cognition—"I am stupid"—or an emotion—"I feel ashamed." Common emotions include fear, anger, and sadness. The emotion is elicited by asking, "What feeling goes with this picture [the image from the memory]? How does it make you react right now?"

Subjective Units of Disturbance Scale (SUDS)

The client is asked to rate the current intensity of the negative emotion on a 0 to 10 scale, from 0 as no disturbance to 10 as the most intense disturbance possible. The SUDS allows both the therapist and the client to track progress during and after the EMDR session. It is important to remember that the SUDS may rise and fall as the client progresses through the memory and different emotions arise. To elicit the SUDS, the therapist asks,

"On a scale from 0 to 10, with 10 being the worst possible feeling and 0 being no bad feeling at all, how strong is it right now?"

Even though the client may have just named a specific emotion such as fear or anger, it's best for the therapist to avoid repeating that emotion word when requesting the SUDS rating, because there may be multiple emotions contributing to the sense of feeling bad, even if the client has named only one. Therefore, it's best to simply ask how bad the feeling is, without naming it.

Physical Sensation

The client is instructed to report the location of any physical sensation that may accompany her current reaction to this focus on the traumatic memory. This is considered an element of the memory, as state-specific aspects of the memory may be stored in the body. Common sensations include localized tension, nausea, and tiredness. Like the VoC and SUDS, physical sensation is also used as a process measure, during and after the session. There is often, but not always, considerable overlap between these three indicators, which is why it is important to track each one. To elicit the physical sensation, the therapist asks, "Where do you feel it [the emotion] in your body?"

Eye Movements

Rapid bilateral eye movements are used to facilitate the accessing, reprocessing, and integration of the target memory. The therapist induces eye movements by having the client visually track the therapist's moving fingers (or other object such as a pen or pointer). This is typically done at the rate of about one back-and-forth per second, twenty to thirty times, about 1 to 2 feet from the client's face. However, there is much variation in terms of speed, distance, direction of movements, and duration.

Other types of alternating stimulation (e.g., using sound or touch) may also be used if eye movements are contraindicated. In general, the eye movements or other alternating stimulus should last until just after the client has worked through a discrete portion of the memory, and achieved a new plateau of understanding. At first, the therapist guesses at the stopping point by observing the client's body language; later on, the client may develop a sense of when to stop.

The role of eye movements, or other alternating stimulus, is not yet clearly understood, and there is even controversy about whether such stimulus is an essential component of EMDR. However, until there is proof to the contrary, it seems that the alternating stimulus should be considered essential, as it has been present in the majority of studies documenting EMDR's effectiveness. For similar reasons, eye movements are preferable to alternatives, although within the clinical community there is some disagreement on this count. In this book, I use the term *eye movement* to refer to any type of alternating stimulus, unless otherwise specified.

THE EMDR PROTOCOL: THE EIGHT PHASES
OF TREATMENT

Shapiro (1995) summarizes the basic EMDR protocol as follows:

> EMDR treatment consists of eight essential phases. The number of sessions devoted to each phase and the number of phases included in each session vary greatly from client to client. . . . The first phase involves taking a client history and planning the treatment. This is followed by the preparation phase, in which the clinician introduces the client to EMDR procedures, explains EMDR theory, establishes expectations about treatment effects, and prepares the client for possible between-session disturbance. The third phase, assessment, includes determining the target and baseline response using

the SUD and VOC Scales. The fourth phase, desensitization, addresses the client's disturbing emotions. The fifth, or installation, phase focuses on the cognitive restructuring. The sixth phase, which evaluates and addresses residual body tension, is the body scan. Next comes closure, a phase that includes debriefing and is essential for maintaining client equilibrium between sessions. The eighth and final phase is termed reevaluation.

While each phase focuses on different aspects of treatment, it may be useful to remember that many of their effects—an increase in self-efficacy, desensitization of negative affect, shifting of body tension, and a cognitive restructuring—occur simultaneously as the dysfunctional information is processed. [pp. 67–68]

Phase 1: Client History and Treatment Planning

This phase includes the initial intake and assessment. The client is screened for contraindications such as limited physical capacity for stress, emotional instability (likelihood of acting out under stress), and other risk factors. If EMDR is deemed appropriate, a fuller clinical picture is obtained, including the parameters of the problem, trauma history, and other information necessary to formulate an appropriate treatment plan and identify targets for reprocessing.

Phase 2: Preparation

This phase includes an explanation of EMDR and possible effects of treatment. In addition to obtaining informed consent for EMDR, potential obstacles such as fears or secondary gains are explored and worked through. This phase also involves ensuring that the client is able to cope effectively with a high level of stress, and may involve teaching relaxation or other self-soothing skills.

Phase 3: Assessment

This phase involves a detailed assessment of the targeted
memory, including, in this order, the selected image, the negative cognition, the positive cognition and VoC, the emotion and
SUDS, and the physical sensation. This provides a baseline measurement of the client's response to the memory, while focusing the client on the memory to be reprocessed.

Phase 4: Desensitization

In this phase the eye movements are combined with concentration on the targeted memory, as the client works through the
various aspects of the memory, often in a progressive manner.
For the first set of eye movements, the client is asked to concentrate on the multiple aspects of the targeted memory as elicited above. After this and subsequent sets, the client is asked,
"What came up?" The client simply reports what she noticed
during the set, perhaps involving imagery, cognition, emotion,
or sensation (all are common). For example, the client may
report, "I don't feel so scared now, but I'm more angry." Then
the therapist instructs the client, "Concentrate on that now," or
"Stay with that," and the client focuses accordingly during the
next set of eye movements. This is continued until every aspect
of the memory is completely neutralized, as indicated by no
change with additional eye movements, a 0 (or 1) on the SUDS,
a "clean" body scan (phase 6), and a 7 (or 6) on the VoC for
the installation.

  Targets involving memories of recent events (within the past
2 to 3 months) often require an additional variant of this procedure. It seems that more recent memories entail more diffuse
storage of distressing elements, so the standard protocol may not
be sufficient to access all relevant memory aspects. Therefore,
once the standard protocol has been completed, targeting the
most distressing segments of the memory, the recent-memory

protocol is used. This involves having the client concentrate sequentially on the entire series of target-related events, "like you're watching the whole thing happen in a movie," during eye movements. This seems to pick up additional distressing elements, which can then be processed to completion.

Phase 5: Installation

In this phase, the positive cognition is "installed" by concentrating on it during eye movements. This is continued until it feels completely true, measuring 7 (or 6) on the VoC. This cognition may be the one initially selected, or another more germane cognition that has emerged spontaneously during phase 4. The cognition is first installed in isolation, then while paired with the targeted memory. When installation does not lead to maximum VoC ratings, this may reveal a memory aspect that has not been fully desensitized. When maximum ratings are achieved, this indicates that the client has come to a healthier, more adaptive perspective.

Phase 6: Body Scan

While focusing on the target memory and the positive cognition, the client scans his body for any remaining tension or discomfort. If any is found, the client focuses on the sensation while performing eye movements. If this discomfort represents an unresolved aspect of the memory, the memory is reopened for further desensitization. However, often the discomfort simply dissipates with eye movements.

Phase 7: Closure

In this phase, the therapist helps the client to regain composure prior to leaving the session. Closure activities may include visualization, relaxation, and calming exercises, especially if the reprocessing was not completed. The client is also prepared for the possibility of additional effects between sessions, including possible emergence of additional disturbing memories, images, thoughts, feelings, or sensations. The client is instructed to keep a log of effects noticed in between sessions, and additional coping strategies may also be discussed.

Phase 8: Reevaluation

At the beginning of any session after EMDR has been performed, a reevaluation is conducted to track the effects of treatment, and to determine the next focus or course of action. The client is asked to note current responses to the treated memory, to see if any aspect of the memory is still disturbing. The log is reviewed for possible additional treatment targets, such as situational triggers or related memories. Also, the client's status and life situation are reviewed in light of the treatment progress, to determine if additional issues must be addressed.

ADVANCED APPLICATIONS

So far, the general approach to training EMDR practitioners has been to provide the basic training, allow a couple of months for supervised practice, and then to provide the more advanced training. One advantage to this approach is that it gives those newly trained in EMDR a chance to get used to "getting out of the way" and following the client's lead during the EMDR processing. For those therapists accustomed to intervening by providing interpretations, confrontation, reassurance, or other input, the EMDR protocol does take some getting used to. When a session is going smoothly, the therapist may simply ask, "What came up?" following a set of eye movements, and then respond to the client's report by saying, "Stay with that," and doing another set of eye movements. When a session goes smoothly, this type of strategy may frequently be sufficient to get through much of the processing of a single traumatic memory.

However, the session does not always go smoothly. Furthermore, there are a number of applications of EMDR that are much more complex than treatment of a discrete traumatic memory. EMDR has been used for complex/chronic trauma, anxiety, depression, psychological aspects of medical disorders, and other problems. Therefore, there are a number of specialized approaches, protocols, and specific interventions that are part of the advanced EMDR repertoire.

For example, in treating an anxiety disorder, it is recognized that past episodes of panic attacks or traumatic triggers leading to flashbacks may constitute the psychological equivalent of additional traumatic memories, and so these must be addressed along with memories of possibly precipitating events. Furthermore, specific situations or other stimuli may be identified that have become contaminated by their association with such events, and these must also be addressed. Finally, anticipated situations or other triggers are addressed by using a variant of the standard EMDR protocol while imagining potentially challenging future events.

There are a number of EMDR-based protocols now available to address a variety of problems, including dissociative identity disorder, substance abuse, chronic pain, specific phobia, chronic depression, and performance anxiety. The core principles remain consistent, including respect for the client's spontaneous responses as the source and impetus for the healing process, resolution of obstacles to the healing process, relentless pursuit of unprocessed target-related material, and reliance on the accelerated information processing effect to promote both resolution of upsetting material and enhanced learning of adaptive behaviors.

One of the most interesting and important of the advanced interventions is the cognitive interweave, which is essentially a premature installation, in that adaptive material is installed prior to the complete reduction of memory-related distress. This is generally a fall-back intervention to be used when the processing is stuck, for example, when repeated sets of eye movements fail to lead to any change in the target material. The therapist then offers a comment or question that may help the client to continue moving through the processing:

> *Therapist:* What do you notice this time?
> *Client:* It's still the same, an 8 [a SUDS rating indicating a high level of distress]. I just can't get it out of my head that I should have known what to do, I could have saved her.
> *Therapist:* How old were you then, 5?
> *Client:* Yeah, 5.
> *Therapist:* Do you know any other 5-year-olds that would know what to do in that situation?
> *Client:* No, I guess not.
> *Therapist:* Think about that (eye movements). What do you notice this time?
> *Client:* I couldn't have known what to do, I was just a little kid. It's not my fault.
> *Therapist:* Stay with that (eye movements).

In the above example, the cognitive interweave runs counter to the general procedure, and is only used in specific situations to solve a problem, so that the normal procedure can resume. However, another variant of the cognitive interweave has become part of the standard protocol: namely, the "safe place" installation. This entails imagining being in a special and protected place, which often elicits a strong sense of safety and security. This type of installation (discussed in detail in Chapters 5 and 7) is now routinely used prior to beginning work on a traumatic memory. It seems to help many clients to feel more prepared to face the trauma, less afraid of going through the process.

Other types of imagery may be used in a similar manner to help the client access additional psychological resources (Greenwald 1993a). Although the cognitive interweave came first historically, it is now probably more correctly viewed as one variant of the larger class of resource installations (Leeds 1997).

Thus, there are two opposing, but not necessarily incompatible, trends within the practice of EMDR. On the one hand, the therapist follows the client's lead, and guides the client to stay on his own track until the distressing material has been processed to completion. On the other hand, carefully timed resource installation applications continue to proliferate, to help the standard procedure go more smoothly, and to facilitate EMDR's use with an ever-wider range of challenging populations. The client-centered processing and the resource installation approaches both take advantage of the hypothesized accelerated information processing effect. Whether the focus is on working through a distressing aspect of the memory or on enhancing a psychological resource, the eye movements seem to enhance both the speed and the depth of processing.

The various advanced applications, and the resource installation approach in particular, are widely used and adapted in this text, often without reference to the adult variant. Although full knowledge of the advanced repertoire is not required to read this text, it is essential to using many of the techniques described. The following chapters provide detailed information on adapting the adult protocol to use with children and adolescents.

5

Overview: Using EMDR with Children

Some aspects of using EMDR with children are typical of any child therapy: the need for parental cooperation and support for treatment; the problem of motivating a child who did not request treatment; and the tendency of many children to be uninterested in therapy, have short attention spans, or not be verbally oriented. There are some EMDR-specific innovations to the management of these issues, as well as a heavy reliance on established approaches. Many child therapists find themselves creatively integrating EMDR with the other modalities they employ.

As with other individual child therapy modalities, it is important to exercise clinical judgment regarding the context of treatment and the range of treatment needs. Physical discomfort, unsafe or inadequate living conditions, inappropriate educational placement, secondary gains, and family pressures may interfere with a child's ability to participate in treatment or benefit from it. For example, some clinicians consider an EMDR failure, given child cooperation, to be diagnostic of the problem's embeddedness, or function, in the family dynamic. Thorough assessment of the child, including history and psychosocial context, is still the essential first step in planning treatment.

The standard EMDR procedure is used with children, often with modifications. The therapist may take more initiative in target selection and in stimulating motivation for treatment. Work with children tends to be more concrete and imagery based, and less focused on articulation of cognition, emotion, or sensation. A greater repertoire of techniques is required to ensure that the client can perform the eye movements. Some steps of the procedure may be omitted or shortened, and completion of processing is sometimes quite rapid. In general, it is important to keep things moving, to incorporate an element of play, and to be flexible, responsive, and resourceful.

There is a consensus among clinicians that EMDR with children is most effective when discrete targets are available. Such targets may include memories of traumatic events, images of a feared person, bad dreams, physical symptoms or sensations, specific anxieties or fears, and positive goals that can be represented by specific imagery. EMDR should generally not be initiated until a specific target can be identified. With some children, EMDR is initially used only with positive installations, which may be less threatening and easier to negotiate.

The main problem that clinicians have occasionally reported is that some children do not cooperate with EMDR; some will not begin, and others start but refuse to continue. Also, occasional physical discomfort may develop during processing, such as dizziness, fatigue, or headache, but as with adults, this tends to pass quickly. As with other therapy modalities, sometimes EMDR leads to increased disturbance between sessions. Although this reportedly happens much less often with EMDR, as processing may be completed in a single session, it still may occur, especially if the processing is stopped prematurely (i.e., prior to complete SUDS reduction). Clinicians have consistently reported that overall, negative therapy effects are decreased by using EMDR (Greenwald 1993c, Lipke 1994).

Perhaps the trickiest aspect of doing EMDR with children, once the techniques are mastered, is deciding when to introduce the use of EMDR in therapy. It is tempting, and often effective, to begin using EMDR in the first or second session. However, even when EMDR is clearly the treatment of choice, there is a risk of crippling the therapeutic alliance by moving into sensitive material so rapidly that the child becomes afraid and refuses to continue. On the other hand, it would be unfortunate to withhold EMDR treatment for many weeks, using slower methods instead, for a child who could heal much more rapidly. Fortunately, there are now many techniques available to help a child engage in EMDR with both safety and reasonable speed.

There is no simple formula for knowing when to start using EMDR with a particular child. To say that the therapeutic relationship must be able to support this work would be an oversimplification. Many children can work successfully with a stranger with five minutes of introduction. This decision might more reliably be based on the child's own level of trust, and her capacity for tolerating pain, anxiety and fear. A child who has functioned well prior to a trauma, or who still functions well in most ways, may have an innate capacity for doing EMDR soon after meeting a therapist who seems generally trustworthy. On the other hand, a child who has a poor attachment history and has not successfully developed basic trust, or who has been traumatized so extensively that trust has been badly damaged, may require extensive relationship support in therapy prior to directly facing sensitive material with EMDR. Similarly, a child who is very young or very anxious will require more relationship support than one who is older, has more perspective on the need for momentary discomfort, and more capacity to tolerate it. At present, a good rule of thumb is that the therapeutic relationship must compensate for any deficiencies in the child's innate level of trust and capacity for tolerating distress, prior to beginning the use of EMDR on potentially upsetting targets (Greenwald 1994d). Of course, the child's motivation is also a factor.

There is also no simple formula for selection from among the numerous standard and modified interventions available for using EMDR with children. In general, deviation from the standard adult protocol increases with increasing problem complexity and with decreasing age or mental capacity. However, even the guidelines provided for working with a specific problem or population may not quite fit an individual member of that group. Therefore, it is important to be familiar with a good repertoire of alternatives if the intervention initially selected does not perform as expected.

SAFETY FIRST

In therapy, the client's sense of safety must be constantly supported. The use of EMDR in child therapy may constitute a philosophical challenge for those therapists who are accustomed to following the client's lead and pacing. The EMDR-trained therapist may appropriately consider early use of EMDR for the benefit of the child, though the child, with limited information, perspective, and judgment, may have naturally selected a slower pace. Therefore, the therapist should be sure to introduce EMDR in a manner that allows the child to continue to feel safe and in control.

There is a repertoire of safety-promoting interventions. While perfect foresight is preferable, this repertoire is also a good reference for reparative strategies if the therapy is not progressing and/or the relationship has been damaged.

Alliance with Parents

If the parents have not expressed concrete, active support for treatment, this problem must be addressed and resolved. The therapist can build this alliance by showing respect for the parents' values and by responding to their concerns. It is also helpful to give the parents a role in the treatment, while avoiding blaming them for the problem. A number of specific parent-focused interventions are discussed in the problem-focused chapters.

Child Access to Parent

Some children will feel more secure if they have ready access to the accompanying parent. This access can be demonstrated graphically in a number of ways: by having the parent present, or nearby, during the session; having the very young child sit on the parent's lap for EMDR; or having the child visit the parent in the waiting room during the session. Younger children often benefit from a presession ritual of walking to the spot at which the parent will be waiting, and/or walking the parent to the therapy location.

Demonstration

Have the parent or older sibling demonstrate EMDR procedures for the client, to show that it is safe. Also, the child and therapist may reverse roles for a demonstration, with the child initiating eye movements in the therapist. Often the child will join in on the demonstration, while the focus is on an older family member.

> *Therapist* (to client): I want you to watch your sister try something that you might be doing. Then you tell me if you think that you can do it, too. (To sister): Will you help us?
>
> *Sister:* Okay.
>
> *Therapist:* I'm going to move my hand back and forth like this. See if you can move your eyes back and forth to follow my hand—but don't move your head, just your eyes (moves hand). That's it, you've got it. Was that easy or hard?

Sister: Easy.

Therapist: Well, I'd better make it harder. What's your favorite food?

Sister: Ice cream.

Therapist: This time, think about having some ice cream. Now at the same time, move your eyes again (moves hand). You did it again. Were you able to think about ice cream at the same time?

Sister: Yes.

Therapist (to client): I noticed that you were moving your eyes, too. What were you thinking about?

Client: Ice cream.

Therapist: Was that easy, or hard?

Client: Easy.

Rapport

A child who is uncomfortable with the therapist will not easily cooperate with structured treatment activities such as EMDR. It is important for the therapist to develop rapport with the child. This can be done in many ways, including joining the child in play, conveying warmth and acceptance, and handing out goodies. However, games and stickers are not necessary with every child. What is necessary is that the child feels cared for and understood. The therapist can convey this by responding to the child's priorities and concerns.

Therapist: Your mom said you didn't want to come today. I don't blame you. What would you be doing if you weren't here?

Child: I'd be out playing with my friends.

Therapist: That sounds like more fun. Problem is, your mom told me that you'll probably have to come here every week for a while, until things get better. Do you know what things she's talking about?

Child: She probably thinks I have a bad attitude, that's what she tells me.

Therapist: What do you think?

Child: There's never a problem with me until someone makes a problem.

Therapist: Like who would make a problem? What would they do?

Child: Like today when Mom wanted me to take out the garbage, she won't just ask me once and let me get around to it, she has to keep on bugging me and yelling at me.

Therapist: That doesn't sound like much fun. I hear you've been getting in a lot of trouble, too.

Child: I'm sick of it. Every time I turn around, they're grounding me again.

Therapist: Wow. Sounds like you've got some people really on your case.

Child: You said it.

Therapist: Well, your mom did tell me you were stuck coming here for a while. I told you that my job is to try and help people feel better about how their life is going. While you're coming here, do you think that's something we should work on, how to get people off your case?

Child: How?

Therapeutic Relationship

The therapeutic relationship may require further development beyond rapport. Consider a screaming child, who may tolerate having a cut washed with soap only on the strength of the relationship with his mother. For a younger child, or one who has a low distress tolerance, doing EMDR may be like having a cut washed with soap. The therapeutic relationship is built by developing a track record of trust and results. Children test therapists repeatedly to see if they can be trusted. Therapists pass these tests by not laughing at the child, not rejecting the child, perhaps by not allowing the child to cheat in a game, and even by simply showing up for the scheduled appointment. It is also important for the child to learn, through experience, that participation in therapy activities can lead to feeling better.

Baby Steps

Some children may appreciate, or require, a more gradual introduction to EMDR, rather than abruptly facing the most upsetting memory. For example, EMDR can be tried first on a low SUDS target. Alternately, EMDR can be used first with a positive installation, either as a lead-in to trauma processing, or with no connection to trauma work. For children with limited tolerance, or for whom trauma work is not a current focus, EMDR use may be limited to positive installations.

Positive Installations

Many types of positive installations may be used during or prior to the processing of potentially distressing material. The most popular ones follow. Such installations can enable the child to access a positive resource state, which facilitates the mastery of the challenges inherent in trauma resolution work (see Phase 5: Installation in Chapter 7).

Safety Device

Install a "safety device" (Greenwald 1993b) before approaching a high SUDS target. If the child is being asked to face a monster, at least she deserves to carry a laser sword in her hand. In other words, the positive installation may be done before, as well as after, reducing the SUDS level. If EMDR is under way and the SUDS is not moving, installing a safety device is a fairly reliable way of facilitating continued progress.

> *Therapist:* If you had to go back in that dream again, with the wolf chasing you, what would you need so that you could be safe?
>
> *Child:* A knife.
>
> *Therapist:* I want you to think about that knife now: what size is it, what color, what's it made of, is it smooth or rough, heavy or light, how it feels to hold it. Now concentrate on that (moves hand for eye movements). Good. What was that like?
>
> *Child:* I was holding the knife and I felt safer.
>
> *Therapist:* Okay. Concentrate on holding the knife again. . . .

Sometimes the child will spontaneously bring the safety device into the previously difficult scene, such as, in the above example, by saying, "This time I showed the knife to the wolf and he ran away." Sometimes the child will simply feel safer or stronger, and then be able to proceed through difficult material with no further reference to the safety device. There is no one right way for this to be used. If, however, following installation of a safety device, the client is not using it and is failing to make progress, the therapist can suggest that the safety device be brought into the difficult scene: "This time, when the wolf is chasing you, why don't you use that knife and see what happens."

Although this intervention was initially developed for use with dream-related targets, it can be adapted to memory targets as well, by using the "dream question": "If everything that happened was a bad dream, and you had to go back into that dream, what would you need to be safe [or okay]?"

There are many types of safety devices in addition to weapons. Sometimes a helper can be called in, such as a parent, a guardian angel, or a superhero. Often, what is needed is a certain quality, such as being bigger or stronger. The goal is to help the child access inner resources sufficient to face and work through the difficult material. As long as the image is internally generated (i.e., by the child) and embodied through detail, it should work with a wide range of content. However, the therapist must often be quite creative to successfully elicit an image that can represent the desired resource.

> *Therapist:* If you had to go back into that dream, what would you need to be okay?
>
> *Child:* Would need to be stronger.
>
> *Therapist:* Of all the animals, what's the strongest one you can think of?
>
> *Child:* A bear.
>
> *Therapist:* There's a bear that's going to be your friend. I want you to think of that bear, how big it is, what it looks like, what color, how strong it is, what it does (eye movements). Okay, what was that like?
>
> *Child:* The bear stayed near me and no one could bother me anymore.
>
> *Therapist:* Good. This time we're going to do something a little different. Concentrate on that bear again, now imagine that you're behind it, sneaking up, getting closer and closer, until you're so close that you can hear it breathing. Now imagine sneaking right inside it, so you can feel what it's like to be that bear (eye movements). What was that like?
>
> *Child:* I was the bear. Grr!

Once a safety device has been installed, it is part of the child's repertoire and may be used flexibly. For example, following the above installation, the child may choose to bring the bear into the targeted memory, or to be the bear. If a safety device has contributed to successful processing, it may certainly be used as a final installation as well. In fact, the 9-year-old girl in the vignette above enjoyed this installation so much that she bear-walked out of my office on all fours, growling and smiling. (I don't remember what I said to her mother!)

Safe Place

This installation is commonly used prior to working on difficult material, with adults as well as children. The child is asked to visualize, describe, or draw a special place characterized by comfort, safety, or other desired features. This is installed.

> *Therapist:* Can you think of a place where you always feel good? It could be a real place, or someplace that you make up. Someplace where you're always safe, and comfortable, and nothing bad can happen there.
>
> *Child:* At my auntie's house.
>
> *Therapist:* Tell me about your auntie's house.
>
> *Child:* Well, I go there after school if no one's home at my house, and my auntie gives me a snack and lets me watch TV there.
>
> *Therapist:* You told me before that you go there at night, too, if your parents are fighting.
>
> *Child:* Yeah, if my parents are yelling a lot, my auntie comes and gets me.
>
> *Therapist:* So where is it in your auntie's house that you feel the best? In the kitchen, watching TV, somewhere else?
>
> *Child:* In the kitchen when I first go there and she gives me a snack and sits with me.
>
> *Therapist:* Think of being in the kitchen with her. What kind of feeling goes with that?
>
> *Child:* Good.
>
> *Therapist:* Would it feel true to say "I'm safe" there?
>
> *Child:* Yes.

> *Therapist:* Concentrate on being there, having a snack with
>   your auntie. Notice that good feeling, and say to your-
>   self, "I'm safe" (eye movements). How did that go?
> *Child:* Good.
> *Therapist:* Were you able to concentrate on everything and
>   say "I'm safe," too?
> *Child:* Yes.

Although the fantasy option is consistently offered, younger
children tend to select a safe place with which they are familiar,
whereas older children and adolescents will occasionally select
a mountaintop, beach, or other imaginary scene. The important
thing is that the safe place is unspoiled, meaning that there are
no elements that undo its purpose. For example, if the child selects playing football in the park, and then during installation
finds himself visualizing getting teased by other boys, this is not
a safe enough place. If the safe place is spoiled, simply select
another one. To maintain functionality, it is generally preferable
for the child to either be alone in the safe place (e.g., his bedroom) or with protectors such as positive adult family members.
This is not an "anything goes" installation; the therapist must
guide target selection to avoid spoilage. If no previously experienced places are completely safe, the therapist may help the
child develop a fantasy location.

> *Therapist:* What if you could make up a place where you
>   could always feel good, and where nothing bad would
>   happen? Would it be inside, or outside?
> *Child:* Inside.
> *Therapist:* What kind of a place is it? Would it be a room,
>   or a house, or something else?
> *Child:* It would be my own house, and there's a 'fridgerator,
>   and a TV, and big locks on the doors so no one can
>   come in unless I let them.
> *Therapist:* And where in this house would you feel the saf-
>   est? . . .

Once a safe place has been selected and installed, it can be used in various ways. It provides a positive, "feel-good" introduction to eye movements, while helping the child to access additional emotional resources prior to doing trauma work. The safe place can also be used to train the child in self-soothing, for example by having her take three deep breaths and imagine herself in the safe place. A variant of this approach is to practice "going" to the safe place during eye movements. Then the child is told that she can go to the safe place anytime the traumatic material becomes too difficult. Later, if the processing is getting bogged down, the therapist can remind the child to use the safe place.

Although, and perhaps because, the safe place is useful, versatile, and relatively easy to implement, it is probably overused in current clinical practice. There is no basis to assume that this particular installation is the best option for accessing those resources the child may need to process the trauma. In contrast, the advantage of the safety device is that the child is specifically asked to generate exactly the resource that would be most helpful. The safe place is most appropriately used when no other safety device can be generated, and/or when the child can benefit from learning an additional self-soothing method.

Resources or Solutions

Other positive installations are also available for use prior to beginning EMDR, or to jump-start a stalled session. Resource installation is limited only by the therapist's creativity. For example, the child can be asked to visualize, describe, or draw the solution to the problem, or the resources, skills, or behaviors needed to address the problem. Alternately, the therapist may suggest a solution, or a series of possible ones. Solutions can be fantasy based—"What if you make the bad guy shrink?"—or realistic— "This time, imagine yourself doing it the way you wish you would." Although the therapist may make suggestions and provide considerable guidance, it is generally preferable to elicit the actual material from the client. Then the material is likely to be more personally meaningful and potent.

Stop Means Stop

The child is told that he can stop the process at will, and he can practice with hand or verbal "stop" signals.

> *Therapist:* I'm going to move my fingers like this. Now you say stop, and let's see what happens. Go ahead, say stop.
> *Child:* Stop.
> *Therapist:* Well, my hand stopped moving.

This is both reassuring and amusing to children, and may contribute to a sense of control as well as playfulness. Sometimes simply knowing that stop means stop can allow the child to continue with nearly intolerable processing. This can be reinforced by simply having the child stop the therapist's moving hand a number of times in a row, perhaps adding challenges such as, "What if you forget how to talk, can you stop it with your hand, like a cop stops traffic? What if you forget how to use your hand, how can you stop it?"

Pain Means Stop

The therapist should consider stopping if the child feels physical discomfort. Even if EMDR would normally continue with an adult, doing so with a child may make her feel unsafe with the therapist and the process. The child will be impressed by the manner in which the therapist responds to her physical pain. One option is to eliminate the unpleasant sensation in another manner, for example by visualizing the sensation leaving the body with exhalation, and once this is accomplished, continuing with EMDR. Another alternative is to install a visualization to eliminate the sensation (e.g., healing white light, or being soothed by a comforting adult). The therapist may also simply discuss the situation with the child, recommend continuation as with adults, but also offer other options, such as discontinuation, a break, or attempts at relief.

The general principle is to help children feel as safe as possible, and in as much control of the process as possible, within appropriate limits. The child's behavior or expressed preference can be used as a guide for technique selection. Attention to these safety issues can mean the difference between treatment impasse and success.

6

Basic Components of EMDR for Children and Adolescents

This chapter, following the format set out by Shapiro (1995), introduces age-appropriate variations on the basic components of EMDR. Many of the suggestions apply to specific age groups. For the purposes of this text, "adolescents" refers to ages 13 and over, "children" to ages 12 and under, "older children" to ages 9 to 12, "younger children" to ages 8 and under, and "very young children" to ages 5 and under. These should be considered rough guidelines only, and not a replacement for clinical judgment.

The "menu" technique can be very useful when asking children or adolescents to produce information in a specific format, such as occurs during the assessment phase of EMDR. The therapist offers a menu of potentially appropriate choices, thus orienting the client to what kind of answer the therapist is looking for. The goal here is to reduce the potential for pointless frustration and confrontation—the "I don't know" syndrome—while still allowing the client to generate internally valid responses.

IMAGERY

The imagery component is virtually always used with children, in about the same way as with adults. The child is asked, "Is there a part of this memory that stands out, seems like the worst part to you?" If the child isn't sure how to respond, the therapist can ask, "If this memory were a movie and you had to make a poster to show how bad it was, what picture would you choose?" If symptoms include intrusive imagery or nightmares, a useful image may already be identified.

When a child has difficulty generating an appropriate response, the menu technique (described above) can be tried. To do this, it helps if the therapist has done a thorough assessment and is familiar with the specifics of this particular event as well as typical responses to such an event. If, for example, the target trauma is a car accident, the therapist may say, "Tell me which of these times has the worst bad feeling when you remember it now: Would it be when you saw the other car coming toward you? When the crash happened? When you were in the hospital? Was some other time the worst?" The therapist is showing the child what kind of response is wanted, while still leaving it sufficiently open for the child to either choose from the menu or generate an original response.

NEGATIVE COGNITION

The negative cognition is often a sticking point with adults, and can be very difficult to elicit from adolescents and children. It is important to keep moving. Once eye movements are started with the image (and possibly the emotion), the negative cognition often emerges spontaneously. However, even if the cognitions are omitted during the assessment phase, they can be important later on. And even if the child has not spontaneously noted negative cognitions during the reprocessing, the therapist can raise likely negative cognitions during the "cleanup" (challenge) phase, to make sure the client has not retained residual negative effects from the memory.

To minimize confusion or frustration and clarify what is expected, any of the following questions may be useful in eliciting the appropriate response. "When you remember this now, what do you tell yourself?" "When you think of this now, what are you saying to yourself?" "What does this make you believe about yourself?" The menu can also be used here (and anywhere). For example, the therapist may say, "I know other kids who have been through this kind of thing. Let me tell you what some of them have said, and you tell me if any of these fit for you. Other kids have said, 'There's something wrong with me,' or 'It was my fault,' or 'I'm not good enough.' Is it anything like that for you?"

POSITIVE COGNITION

The positive cognition can be obtained creatively, using drawings or other symbolic expression, perhaps by asking the child, "Show me how it would be if it was better." It's important to keep the client engaged rather than to get every bit of detail. When it's time for a positive installation, there will often be one available. If not, then the therapist can generate one, by asking, "What are you saying to yourself about this now?" or "What does this make you believe about yourself now?" If that isn't sufficient, the menu can be used, for example, by asking, "Would it feel more true now to say, 'I'm safe now,' or 'I'm okay,' or 'I'm a good person,' or something else?"

VALIDITY OF COGNITION (VoC) SCALE

The VoC is often modified as well, especially with children. However, if the negative and positive cognitions have already been elicited as per the adult protocol, the VoC is easy enough to use. Although most adolescents and older children have little trouble with the 1 to 7 scale, younger children may prefer a less abstract format. Popular options include variations of the hand spread (described below), and variations of graphical scales such as a line of faces ranging from sad to happy or a color bar (see below).

EMOTION

The emotion component is normally included unless there is some reason not to—for example, with very young children it may be skipped. The advantage of getting a specific emotion named is that it helps the therapist to track the child's status and progress, as well as focusing the child in preparation for the desensitization phase. Normally, it is enough to ask, "What kind of feeling goes with that?" If the child answers, "I don't know" or "Bad," the therapist can show pictures of "feelings faces" (these come in very handy) and say, "Is it any of these?" This procedure helps to keep the session moving along without unnecessary delay or discomfort, while the child incidentally learns to articulate feelings more explicitly. The therapist also has the opportunity to introduce the notion that the child may have more than one feeling at a time, by giving the child the option of selecting more than one from the graphic display.

SUBJECTIVE UNITS OF DISTURBANCE SCALE (SUDS)

The SUDS is always used in some form, except with very young and inarticulate children, and is considered one of the primary means of tracking the client's progress. Most adolescents and some older children can use the numerical adult format with reasonable ease. There are a number of less abstract options for other children.

The most common and low-tech child SUDS measurement is the hand spread. The therapist says, "When you think of that, how bad is the feeling? This would be like the worst feeling in the world [holds out hands as wide as possible], this would be pretty bad [moves hands to halfway out], and this would be just a little bad [moves hands to a few inches apart]. You show me how bad the feeling is, with your hands." Children may need to be reminded of this method once or twice in subsequent sets, but they generally understand it and can use it readily. A child may report an "11" by gesturing wider than his own hand spread, to the room around him; he will report a "0" by closing his hands together (and smiling).

One variation involves tracing the child's feet onto a large piece of paper, which is universally experienced as a treat. When it comes time to ask for SUDS, the child is given a marker and told, "Draw a circle for how bad this feeling is, the bigger the circle, the worse the feeling." As the EMDR progresses, the circles will move from covering the entire paper, surrounding the feet, to becoming a small dot in between the feet. Children often enjoy this activity, and like to have a visual record of their progress. This SUDS variation adds fun, and children may request EMDR for the opportunity to have their feet traced.

Any variation that works is acceptable. The therapist can ask if the child feels a little better than before, a little worse, or about the same. One retarded boy could only manage reporting that he felt a large, medium, or small amount of "bad."

Despite the therapist's best efforts and explanations, occasionally a child will use SUDS in an idiosyncratic manner that is difficult to interpret, or that appears to be the correct use while actually intended to convey some other meaning. Other children will more clearly demonstrate that their use of SUDS is nonstandard and perhaps meaningless. In short, children cannot always be relied on to communicate effectively on the therapist's terms. Especially when SUDS is not clearly valid, the therapist must use clinical observation to monitor progress and treatment effects. The activity immediately subsequent to EMDR often dramatizes the child's recent achievement and current concerns. Feedback over the course of the week, especially from the parent, is also informative.

PHYSICAL SENSATION

The sensation component is used in the same manner with children as with adults. Some clinicians prefer to inquire about sensation immediately following the naming of the emotion, whereas most prefer to obtain the SUDS prior to sensation. Either way, children often respond well to the question, "Where do you feel that in your body?" Any unusual sensation can be elicited and then focused on during eye movements, which can lead to extension of positive effects as well.

EYE MOVEMENTS

Most normal adolescents and older children can move their eyes to the same motion used with adults. The sets of eye movements can be shorter; children sometimes complete processing so quickly that the therapist is left wondering if anything happened. As with adults, a set in which an upsetting image is processed will usually take longer than a set used for positive installation.

At present we still assume that eye movements are preferable, but that other forms of alternating stimulation are acceptable. Given this preference, it is worth trying to induce eye movements whenever possible. For example, when providing alternating auditory or tactile stimulation, the client can still be instructed to move her eyes in sync with the other stimulus.

Many younger children, and children who are neurologically challenged, will not be able to accomplish eye movements within the standard format. Other considerations, including increasing interest and sense of control, may also lead to the use of an alternate means of inducing eye movement. It is rare that a child will not be able to work with one or more of the following methods.

Special Object

Use a magic wand or other attractive object with the standard motion. The wand has lovely symbolism, and puts less wear and tear on the therapist's arm. A puppet, small stuffed animal, or plastic sword that has already been part of the session might also serve well. Alternately, the child may be allowed to choose a special object. Anything that helps to maintain the child's focus is worthwhile.

Hand Tapping/Hand Slapping

This is probably the most widely used method with younger children, and many therapists start here without even attempting the standard method. The therapist holds his palms out, and the child, using only one hand, taps the therapist's palms alternately. Many children enjoy this, especially those that get into slapping. Make sure the child is actually moving his eyes. The therapist may have to keep his own hands moving a bit, and say, "You have to watch where you hit, because I'm going to try to trick you by moving my hands, and you don't want to miss." There are some nice prop variations with this one. The child can be asked to tap for the animal he is holding in his lap, or to tap with the animal. If there are toys in the therapy setting, and the child has used a gun or knife to protect himself in play, he can tap with that weapon, whether to install the weapon or to process a trauma.

Finger Popping

Hold a fist up on either end of the child's visual range, and pop up a finger on alternating hands. Children who cannot track across their visual range can often successfully move their eyes back and forth to watch each new finger pop in succession.

Finger Snapping

For those who can't snap their fingers, try using those little metal frogs that click when you press on them. This can be done in the same position as finger popping. The multimodal (visual and auditory) stimulus helps to draw attention and keep the child focused.

Alternate Motions

Some children who have difficulty with the standard side-to-side motion may be able to follow an alternate motion, such as circular, elliptical, diagonal, bumpy line, or a sideways figure 8. This may be helpful for AD/HD or learning disabled children, and may also be tried with children for whom the other methods are ineffective. Some therapists believe that specific motions have specific effects—for example, I may use a circle or sideways figure 8 motion when I want a calming effect—but there is no general consensus regarding such effects, and they have not been formally tested.

Spots on the Wall

Select spots or objects on the wall at each end of the child's visual range, and instruct her to look at them alternately. This is a useful technique in many situations. Children who are oppositional or have a strong need for control of the process may prefer to select the spots themselves, perhaps by drawing marks on the blackboard or by placing colored push-pins on the wall. If the child is distracted by seeing the therapist during eye movements, using the wall may be helpful. Even with children who have been successfully using other methods, switching to this one is a good way to train the child to use EMDR on her own, in specified situations such as waking up from a bad dream, or facing a situation associated with performance anxiety.

Ball Games

There are several ways to use a ball to induce eye movements, while occupying the child with an engaging activity concurrent with conversation (Marshall and Vargas-Lobato 1997). The conversation may be about a traumatic memory or recent upsetting event, or simply about a distressing topic. The child may be asked (or allowed) to throw the ball from one hand to the other, or to throw it up and down, while remaining seated. Alternately, the therapist and child may throw the ball back and forth, perhaps concurrent with the turn-taking in the conversation. When the therapist notices an opportune moment for eye movements, she stops the ball and has the child slap alternating knees, perhaps while counting aloud, "1, 2, 3, 4, 5, 6." If this is too much for the child, the therapist may slap her own knees instead. This method fits eye movements into an active, engaging, free-flowing interaction, and can be particularly helpful with children who might otherwise have difficulty staying focused.

Pushing

For children who need to be in control, they can be instructed to push the therapist's arm or wand, thus guiding the movements. Children may also be instructed to imagine pushing (the arm or wand) with their eyes.

Coloring

For children who have trouble crossing the visual midline, they can color from one side of the page to the other, while following their own hand movement and markings visually.

Hand Touch

The child rests both hands on his knees, palms up or down as preferred, and closes his eyes. The therapist touches the child's hands alternately with her finger, instructing the child to move his eyes accordingly. This is borrowed from the adult repertoire, and is used only in special circumstances due to boundary and vulnerability issues. This method might be considered when the child complains of visual distraction, or of dry and itchy eyes.

Other Alternating Stimuli

As with adults, other alternating stimuli may be used if eye movement is not available. Alternating sound may be accomplished with the finger-snapping method, or by the therapist's tapping her own alternating feet, or slapping alternating knees. Similarly, the hand-slapping method can be used without insisting on eye movement. The child can also be asked to alternately slap his own knees or tap his own feet. When not contraindicated, alternating touch can also be used, most often by touching the child's alternate hands. In general, though, eye movements are preferred.

High-Tech Options

There are now a number of commercially available devices designed to induce eye movements or other alternating stimulation. Those focused on eye movements include a wand with the end lit up, and a box with a beam of light that moves from side to side. A number of clinicians working with children and adolescents have anecdotally reported a preference for non–eye-movement gadgets, which they say some kids find more acceptable and less distracting. For example, alternating auditory stimulation is transmitted via headphones; alternating tactile stimulation is induced by having the child hold small objects that alternately vibrate. Further information on commercially available EMDR-related products can be obtained from the general sources on EMDR information listed in Appendix A.

My personal preference is low-tech and some form of the traditional eye movements, and I have rarely had problems with this approach. However, it is quite possible that some of these gadgets do contribute to a smooth treatment session without losing anything in effect. Until more definitive data are available on this point, individual clinicians are, so to speak, left to their own devices.

7

The Eight Phases
of Treatment for Children
and Adolescents

This chapter, following the format set out by Shapiro (1995), introduces age-appropriate variations on the eight phases of treatment. However, the protocols actually used with children and adolescents may not always follow this pattern. For example, a "safe place" or "safety device" installation is often used prior to desensitization. Such variations and suggestions are included in the description of the techniques and protocols. Further detail, pertaining to specific protocols and populations, is provided in other chapters.

For many adolescents and some older children, the standard adult protocol may be used. However, with young, impatient clients, some steps can be modified in the interest of maintaining engagement with the process. Fortunately, children may compartmentalize their experiences somewhat less than adults, so that the full protocol might not be needed for full effectiveness. With the adult protocol, imagery, cognition, emotion, and sensation are all explicitly identified as simultaneous focal points for processing, in order to gain a holistic, or comprehensive, access to the memory. With children, concentrating on the image alone, or the image and the emotion, often seems to be sufficient to access the entire memory. In general, the younger the child, the more abbreviated the protocol. With experience, the clinician develops a good sense of how much of the protocol to use. Regardless, systematic follow-up can mitigate the risk of incomplete treatment.

PHASE 1: CLIENT HISTORY AND TREATMENT PLANNING

This phase includes the initial intake and assessment. With children and adolescents, it is important to assess the problem context, including family, school, and other potentially significant contextual factors. Then the therapist can work with parents and others to promote an environment conducive to the child's healing. Some EMDR-related approaches to working with the family are included in Chapters 2, 9, and 10. In addition to the clinician's standard assessment, the following items should be specifically addressed:

Problem and Trauma History

Currently the most popular way to use EMDR is as a treatment for distressing memories that have not been effectively processed and have thus led to disturbing symptoms. To identify appropriate targets for processing, the trauma/loss history and problem history can be compared. It is often possible to trace the onset of the presenting problem to a specific event in the child's life. Earlier events may also have contributed to the child's vulnerability, with the index event serving as the final blow. This is why a thorough history of both the problem and the trauma and loss events is necessary to formulating the case in terms conducive to EMDR treatment.

Current Situation

The current parameters of the problem should be carefully defined, including the circumstances under which the problem occurs (and the environmental contingencies), and the circumstances under which it does not. It is particularly worthwhile to learn about how the child defines the problem. Then all concerned can identify treatment goals, and the parents and the child can agree on a plan with the therapist. The specific details of the problem will also be used during the treatment itself.

Useful Information

During treatment, the following information will come in handy, and should be obtained from the parent or the child as appropriate (much information will come from the parent, who may be more comfortable with the interview format in the first session or two): details of the trauma/loss event; the child's strengths, preferences (favorite food, music, activity, subject in school, best friend, role model/ego ideal, etc.); the child's history of successes (accomplishments, positive relationships); and the child's goals.

PHASE 2: PREPARATION

This phase includes an explanation of both EMDR and the possible effects of treatment. Also, the parents and child provide their informed consent for the therapist to use EMDR. Potential obstacles such as fears or secondary gains are explored and worked through. This phase also involves ensuring that the client is able to cope effectively with a high level of stress, so it may be necessary to teach relaxation or other self-soothing skills.

While the EMDR procedure should generally be portrayed in an appealing manner, the potential for the child to experience unpleasant feelings or for EMDR to be ineffective must also be conveyed, or the child may ultimately feel betrayed by the therapist. "The therapist can say, A lot of times kids feel better after, but it's different for everyone. Sometimes other feelings come, and it's hard to tell how it will be for you. It might feel scary at first, but I hope we can get through that part, to a better feeling. And you can stop whenever you want to." Many of the metaphors described in the next section can assist in this preparation.

In some circumstances, EMDR may be intentionally portrayed as very difficult or unpleasant. Adolescents may be motivated by the element of challenge inherent in facing a traumatic memory head on. Also, a resistant and/or oppositional older child or adolescent who may not want to be in treatment at all might be offered EMDR as a potentially painful but quicker therapy option.

> *Therapist:* There are two basic choices we have, and they both usually work. We could meet every week for maybe half a year and keep talking about different parts [of the trauma, the anger, etc.] until finally you feel better and don't have to come here anymore. Or we could do it the fast way in a month or two, but you wouldn't like it.
>
> *Client:* What is it?
>
> *Therapist:* Well, I'll tell you, but you're not gonna like it. It's this thing where you concentrate really hard on the bad things we were talking about. The feelings can get pretty strong sometimes. The good thing is that this way at least you get through the stuff faster.
>
> *Client:* I'd rather get through it faster.
>
> *Therapist:* Well, let me tell you why I don't think you'll like it. First of all, the feelings can be pretty bad, maybe even as bad as it was when the stuff happened. But if you keep going, at least you will probably get through it and feel better. The other thing that a lot of kids

think is weird is that while you're thinking about the bad stuff, you have to move your eyes back and forth.

Client: What do you mean?

Therapist: Well, I'll show you. See, I would move my hand back and forth like this, and you would watch my hand with your eyes. Yeah, that's it. For some reason, that makes it all work better.

Client: That's pretty weird.

Therapist: So your dad told me that you have to keep coming until we all agree that things are okay. But you can decide whether we do it the slow way or the fast way. And whatever way you decide to try, you can always change your mind later.

Client: I'd rather do it the fast way.

Thus, a choice is offered and the EMDR option can represent the means to complete treatment more quickly. Later, the therapist is in a position to say, "That's okay, if you don't want to do this now, we can just talk today." And it is okay. The point is, giving clients choices is therapeutic in itself, and contributes to the therapeutic relationship. In this example, it also builds motivation for EMDR while providing clear information regarding potential associated distress.

This "informed consent" is designed to ensure client control and avoid potentially damaging surprises. However, some practitioners focus more on the positive, to induce cooperation and heighten expectation, and some simply begin the activity with minimal introduction. There is no consensus on the degree of specificity that may be useful to a child in the preparation stage, and clinical and ethical judgment is required.

Screening for Risk Factors

Potential risk factors include current medical or respiratory problems, use of medication, prepsychotic conditions, dissociative disorders, the possibility of disclosure of abuse or neglect, pending litigation, and the client's volatility. These items must be explored and, if necessary, addressed, so that appropriate precautions can be taken prior to using EMDR.

Litigation Issues

Clinicians are sometimes asked to treat children who have been traumatized from an event for which litigation may either be pending or under consideration for some later date, such as when the child is more able to face the prospect of testifying. In such cases, a number of issues must be addressed, including the possible effects of EMDR on memory and on willingness and ability to testify, and the court's perception of the magnitude of damages.

One concern is whether the use of EMDR might damage the client's subsequent credibility regarding the accuracy of the memory. Preliminary data suggest that EMDR can actually enhance recall for details of significant past events, at least during the session (Lipke 1994). For example, one unpublished study (Carol McBryde, personal communication) found that children with verified allegations of abuse were able to provide numerous independently verified additional details regarding the abuse events when EMDR was used following the standard investigational interview. Case law to date (cited in Shapiro 1995) indicates that the courts have so far viewed EMDR as noncontaminating, as opposed to hypnosis, which is viewed by the courts as potentially distorting memory details. However, case law evolves, and subsequent decisions may reinforce or diverge from this precedent regarding memories that have been touched in some way by EMDR. Furthermore, regardless of EMDR's involvement, memory details may not always be entirely accurate (ISTSS [International Society For Traumatic Stress Studies] 1998). Thus, even though EMDR may assist in recall of details, and even though the courts have not yet disallowed testimony following EMDR treatment, neither the validity of the memory details nor the future stance of the courts can be assumed.

The child's testimony may be affected by EMDR in other ways as well. On the one hand, successful treatment can help a child feel more comfortable discussing the event in a courtroom. Many parents will not even consider subjecting their child to the litigation process until they see that she is comfortable talking about the event, following successful treatment. On the other hand, a court case may be jeopardized following the use of EMDR, for two reasons. First, following successful treatment, the memory may become less vivid for some children, potentially leading to more limited recall of detail, as well as less emotionally dramatic testimony. Second, if the child is apparently no longer suffering psychological damage from the event, a monetary award may be reduced if it is based on extent of pain and suffering.

The interface of EMDR and litigation is a complex and still evolving area. At this writing, the recommended procedure includes (1) discussion of these issues with the child and parents/guardians; (2) referral for consultation with an attorney; (3) having the child give a deposition to the appropriate authorities prior to treatment, so that the testimony cannot be said to have been contaminated by therapy; and (4) obtaining written consent for treatment in light of the above issues. In practice, most parents appreciate being informed but have no wish to sacrifice their child's emotional welfare for possible future financial gain.

Volatility

Another frequently encountered risk is the child who is prone to acting out. Parents and children can be told, "Sometimes it gets worse before it gets better," because upsetting emotions may be activated but not completely resolved prior to the end of a

session. Even with an apparently successful session, when the
SUDS score is reduced to 0 or 1, additional distressing material
might arise later. Although this seems to occur less with EMDR
than with other therapy approaches, because of the speed of
resolution, it must still be addressed so that families can prepare
for the eventuality. Predicting this type of difficulty can mitigate
the potential for children and their parents to terminate prematurely, since the therapist has already defined it as part of the
treatment process. (Additional ways of addressing this risk are
described in the Closure section of this chapter, and in Chapter 3.) The clinician should carefully evaluate the potential for
acting out, and consider postponing EMDR until sufficient protective steps have been taken.

Motivation

Many children do not want to be in therapy, and the therapist
can sympathize with them. The parents' concerns must be acknowledged but motivation is enhanced when the therapist can
elicit treatment goals directly from the child. "While you're stuck
coming here, maybe there's something you can get out of it for
yourself. Some kids want to get rid of their nightmares or stop
wetting the bed, some kids want to do better in school, some
kids want to have more friends, some kids want to get in less
trouble so they can have more fun. Do you want anything like
that?" It is rarely advisable to offer the child a choice about being
in therapy, but it can be very useful to find out what she hopes
to gain. With inarticulate, untrusting, or oppositional children,
the therapist is unlikely to hear about goals until rapport and
trust have been established—if even then.

While goals are important for motivation in therapy, other
factors loom large, including family support for treatment and
change, rapport, and minimization of social stigma. Motivation
can build as the child's expectations for benefit increase, through

beliefs regarding the effectiveness of the methods, and as the therapist develops a track record of helping the child to feel better. Also, motivation can be fostered in the moment, by making the activity nonthreatening, fun, and engaging.

Metaphors

Metaphors, with their imagistic and experiential base, can be effectively used to explain the process, mechanism, and potential outcomes of EMDR. Some popular metaphors follow.

REM during Dreaming

"Did you know that when you dream, your eyes move back and forth real fast? Well, scientists think that that's what makes things feel better from dreaming. You know how you might feel bad about something, but when you wake up you feel better? Well, what we're going to do here is have your eyes move fast just like when you dream. That can help you get through the bad feelings so they're not so strong anymore."

VCR

"When we do this, it might be something like watching a movie on the VCR. Do you have a VCR at home? You know how sometimes there's a bad part of the movie, but if you keep watching, that part's over and something else is happening? Well, if we get to a bad part, we don't want to stay there feeling bad, right? So we'll have to remember, don't press 'pause,' keep on going if you can, to get through that part and see what's next."

This metaphor is conducive to further use during the session; for example, the target may be called a "frame" or "snapshot." If processing an entire event sequence is required, it can be described as "running the whole movie." For a long sequence, the use of "fast forward" can be suggested.

Chest of Drawers (Dunton 1993)

"Do you have a chest of drawers at home? Can you remember what's inside? What's in the bottom drawer? How about the top one? We're going to do something with your chest of drawers. Remember, these are your drawers, and you can open and close them whenever you want. Now, what's in your homework (or other problem) drawer?"

This is particularly conducive to client empowerment, and leads nicely from the metaphor into the processing. Children often enjoy reciting the contents of their drawers, which can get them into a cooperative mind set.

Laser Gun

"Sometimes this works like a laser gun that can zap the bad stuff and make it change or disappear. Your job is to help me find all the bad stuff so we can zap it. A lot of times kids feel better after this, but sometimes the bad stuff fights back. If that happens, we can decide what to do about it." This metaphor can be adapted to a video game the child may know.

Dislocated Finger

"Did you ever have a dislocated finger, or see on TV when that happens to a basketball player? It hurts some the way it is, but what really hurts is when you fix it. You have to pull it way out so that it can fall back in where it belongs. And then, suddenly, it doesn't hurt at all! Sometimes this works that way with feelings, that it might feel really bad for a bit, but then it feels a lot better. Sometimes it takes longer to start feeling better, it's hard to tell ahead of time."

Toothache

"Did you ever have a tooth that hurt so bad that it had to be pulled? What was the worst part: the hurting all along, or when you went to the dentist? But I bet afterward it felt a lot better. What we'll be doing with your bad memory is something like that. Now it bothers you a lot every day. When we work on it, it might be even worse for a little while. That would be like going to the dentist. Later, though, if we get through it, it will probably feel a lot better, maybe not even bother you anymore."

Metaphors are often useful, but not always necessary. EMDR can simply be presented as a challenge, or not explained at all. The therapist may introduce it as a game, for example by saying, "Let's play this game now, here's how you do it." In general, metaphors work best when the content is familiar to the child, yet holds some fascination.

Stuffed Animals

There are many constructive ways to use a stuffed animal. The animal can function as a stand-in for the child, the new "identified patient" with the symptom or distressing feelings. This indirect, projective method often helps children to engage more easily around their problems. It's usually worthwhile to find a name of some kind for the animal. Once into animal mode, much therapy can be accomplished without further reference to consensual reality. For example, after eye movements the therapist may ask for the animal's SUDS level. Here are some ways of using an animal to promote the child's involvement and cooperation:

Demonstrate EMDR with the Animal

The therapist does the stuffed animal's voice as well as his own. The animal can be used to help the child become familiar with the activity and to encourage him to participate.

"Sibling" Rivalry

If the issue is one of controlling the session (i.e., the child may prefer a different game) rather than safety per se, the therapist can offer to give the animal another turn! The child may demand a turn, in which case the animal is told to wait. If the child does not cooperate, the therapist can simply turn back to the animal, saying, "I guess you get another turn now. She didn't want hers after all." This works especially well with manipulative children who have neglect or sibling rivalry issues and crave attention, and it is preferable to confrontation and insistence on participation.

The Child Holds the Animal

The child is asked to hold the animal (to provide comfort and safety) while the therapist treats the animal. Instructions are given to the animal, and the child may find himself following along with his own thoughts and eyes. This can be adapted to many eye movement techniques. The child may also be asked to hold the animal and participate in EMDR, to help the animal. For some reason, many children find this request plausible.

Moving the Animal

Ask the child to jump the animal back and forth from one spot to another (inducing eye movement in the child), "to help the animal feel better," while instructing the animal to concentrate on an appropriate target. Then the therapist can ask, "Does [the animal] feel a little better, a little worse, or about the same?"

Fun

Children are more likely to cooperate with the therapist, and be willing to return, if there is some fun in the session. Some examples of fun elements include use of foot tracing for SUDS, alternating EMDR with play, use of stuffed animals, taking big breaths between sets, and using hand slapping for eye movements. Children also may enjoy positive installations, as well as observing the SUDS reductions and feeling better. The EMDR process, while serious in intent, may be presented in a playful form. Some examples follow.

Start and Stop

The therapist begins with a practice session of Stop Means Stop (see Chapter 5). Children who find this particularly amusing might also like to announce when to start and stop the eye movements. Children often enjoy telling a grown-up what to do, consider this a fun game, and benefit from feeling in control of the therapy process. As long as the eye movements are of sufficient duration to maintain progress, this can be an excellent way to proceed with EMDR.

Picture Game

Some therapists introduce EMDR as "the Picture Game." The child is asked to think of a picture, and then the eye movements are introduced. Other techniques can still be used in this context. Children may select their own pictures, with positive or neutral affective loading, as an introduction to the game, or as a break from more difficult work.

Bully, Bargain, and Bribe

For basically intact children with known traumatic experiences that are the focus of treatment, the therapist may be convinced that prompt EMDR treatment is called for. With other children, EMDR might also be deemed desirable. The therapist might obtain cooperation by simply instructing the child to cooperate, and insisting. She might also strike a deal, for example, "If we do something I choose for ten minutes, then we'll do something you choose for the next ten after that. But my time only counts if you're really trying." Some children may be willing to promise for the next session, and have time to emotionally prepare. On more than one occasion I have gambled control of session time in a card game, with the winner choosing the activity.

Incentives can work wonders. Some clinicians offer the child some stickers for playing "the picture game," perhaps at a rate of one sticker for five minutes of EMDR. I occasionally use a small toy or a quartz crystal as an incentive, and draw an outline of the coveted object on a piece of paper. As the child perseveres with EMDR, I fill in more and more of the outline, with the understanding that the child earns the object when the picture is complete. Of course, the picture isn't completed until the processing is. Parents may also contribute to the incentive approach, perhaps by promising a treat after the session if the therapist says that the child worked hard.

This type of approach requires that the clinician be able to balance firm limits and demands with appropriate sensitivity, flexibility, and responsiveness to the child. The trick is to maintain responsiveness in a way that validates the child without letting her sabotage the activity. For example, if EMDR is targeted to an unpleasant memory and the child rolls from the chair to the floor, the therapist can say, "Are you going to do it down there?"

in a playful manner that implies a choice of location or method, even while the activity remains EMDR. Children can accept control and direction if they feel safe, understood, and cared for.

With resistant children, especially those who are reluctant to do EMDR because they understand that it involves facing upsetting memories, this strategy must be used delicately and with fine clinical judgment. Imposing a feared activity may constitute a reenactment of the very trauma that is the focus of treatment. While pushing EMDR may lead to quick resolution when done wisely, misjudgment in this regard can seriously impair therapeutic progress. Safety tactics such as using only positive targets for a session, using a low SUDS target, and the stop means stop option should be considered. In most circumstances, it is worth taking an extra session or two to avoid the risk of retraumatization.

PHASE 3: ASSESSMENT

This phase involves a detailed assessment of the targeted memory, including, in order; the selected image, the negative cognition, the positive cognition and VoC, the emotion and SUDS, and the physical sensation. This phase provides a baseline measurement of the client's response to the memory, while focusing the client on the memory to be reprocessed. With children and adolescents, there is quite a bit of variability in terms of how this phase is conducted, as noted in the previous chapter.

Target Selection

Imagery is the target medium of choice, for both upsetting memories and positive installations. Imagery can effectively represent an experience for a child, in a way that facilitates the necessary concentration and involvement. It is simple, easy to focus on, and usually sufficient. Occasionally an auditory target, such as being yelled at, or kinesthetic target, such as an expressive posture or a physical symptom, may be appropriate. A verbal or cognitive target would normally be useful only on rare occasions, perhaps with an intellectually oriented or older child, or when a maladaptive cognition has been spontaneously articulated. Of course, what the client produces during EMDR is often the preferred target in the next set, in whatever form.

Nightmares and bad dreams are choice symptoms in assessment inquiries and in target selection. Nightmares commonly plague troubled children (and their parents!), and most children will want to cooperate to eliminate them. The child's concerns may be symbolized and condensed in this symptom, and the effects of even recent trauma may be mitigated through EMDR treatment of a bad dream. Of course, EMDR with nightmares may access the traumatic memory. If additional EMDR sessions are required, the therapist who helps the child eliminate nightmares has established a good track record with EMDR, and can expect continued cooperation with more difficult material.

Children may not have the tolerance for the slow pace of the adult EMDR protocol. It is generally sufficient to elicit the worst image from an upsetting memory, ascertain the SUDS score, and begin eye movements. (The adult protocol should be considered for children who are older, more sophisticated, and have developed cognitively beyond a primarily concrete orientation.) The sequence of targets selected is similar to that for adults, in that all related upsetting memories should be completely processed, followed by positive installation. As with adults, more recent traumatic experiences may require processing of the entire sequence, or "movie," rather than just the representative worst moments.

For children who have been abused or scared repeatedly by the same person, that person's face may constitute an excellent target. First, discrete representative memories should be processed, and a few such events may be sufficient. Then the use of the face may help to condense and process the group of experiences more quickly. This principle may be applied to any target that can represent a multitude of similar traumatic memories, such as the location in which repeated abuse occurred.

Target selection may occur in a number of ways. It is important to have a good trauma history from the parent, and it is often possible to "sell" trauma work by tying the trauma to some symptom that the child would like to eliminate. In that case, the therapist can introduce a trauma-related target directly, or offer a choice of targets. In establishing a track record with a child, it is best to begin with positive installation, a low-SUDS target, or a high-motivation target such as nightmares, to maximize the likelihood of cooperation and success.

Target selection may also arise from the flow of art or play therapy, or from conversation. Many therapists may intervene with EMDR whenever an appropriate target arises, by saying, "think of that, and follow with your eyes [or whatever eye movement method works for that child]." In this case, the SUDS may not be used until after the first set, if at all, depending on whether the therapist wishes to complete the processing with EMDR, or to use a set or two to intensify an emotion, gain access to information, or get over a "hump" for other therapeutic purposes.

Visualization of targets may be enhanced by having the child draw a picture of the image to be processed. In the intake session the child may be asked to draw a bad dream or memory as an emotional and material preparation for the next session's work. In play therapy, sand tray work, and art therapy, the target may already be graphically displayed. The child can face this display, rather than the therapist's face or a wall, to enhance concentration during the eye movements. However, simply creating the picture or display, or verbally describing the target, is often sufficient for the child to be able to focus.

The child's failure to articulate or graphically represent the target does not imply inability to focus adequately for processing. Some children who are motivated to do EMDR are unable or unwilling to communicate about the target. The therapist might say, "Do you want to tell me about that bad part of the dream, or just think it?" and accept either response.

If the EMDR is not progressing properly, it may be useful to use a more adult protocol and search for the child's associations during processing, possibly including additional imagery, cognitions, emotions, or sensations. This approach occasionally yields important new targets that can evade focus when only visual image and SUDS are tracked. This may be most useful with children traumatized prior to age 3 or 4, who may have stored the memory kinesthetically. It may also be appropriate with older children, for whom the pure visual focus may not elicit the fullness of the targeted memory.

If cognitions appear to be an appropriate focus, the therapist can say, "What do you tell yourself about that?" For the positive alternative, ask, "If you had a magic wand, what would you tell yourself instead?" or "What do you wish you could be telling yourself?"

Some problems can be creatively externalized and concretized by the therapist, and targeted as such. For example, a bedwetter was trying to overcome the power of the "pee-pee monster," and she used an image of this confrontation as a target. This type of approach has also been reported in the treatment of obsessive-compulsive disorder, by externalizing a bully called "Mr. Clean" who dictated excessive hand-washing (Grosso 1996). The child is asked to co-generate the image, and to visualize it with self-generated detail, thus imbuing it with the necessary personal validity and meaning.

SUDS and VoC

The primary purpose in using SUDS and VoC is to monitor the progress of the processing. These devices also provide the client with a relatively graphic and concrete means of verifying that progress has occurred. Also, the process of assessing one's experience on a SUDS or VoC continuum can constitute training in self-awareness and monitoring, often a goal in therapy.

There is wide variation in the use of SUDS and VoC with children. Most practitioners use SUDS in some form, and do not use VoC, but there are notable exceptions in both areas. Therapists who use EMDR with a cognitive focus (e.g., for preliminary work with abused children), or informally in the flow of play therapy, may not use SUDS at all.

PHASE 4: DESENSITIZATION

In this phase the eye movements are combined with concentration on the targeted memory, as the client works through the various aspects of the memory, including negative affect, imagery, cognition, and sensation. This is continued until every aspect of the memory is completely neutralized, measuring 0 to 1 on the SUDS. The principles are basically the same with children, but again, some steps may be skipped. For example, many children fail to report that anything "came up" or that they "noticed" anything during the previous set of eye movements. Rather than quizzing children incessantly and fruitlessly for a specific response in this situation, it is acceptable to simply continue focusing on the target until the SUDS disappears. (However, those adolescents and older children who report that "nothing" happened during the eye movements can be trained to be more articulate, as described in Chapter 2.) As with adults, the main principle here is to keep going as long as there is movement, and to try to resolve impasses.

Certain additional steps have also proved useful in this phase. Deep breathing is often emphasized between sets, to teach a calming skill, and to enhance the child's sense of self-efficacy and fun in relation to the procedure itself. Following the completion of the initial desensitization procedure, there are several approaches to pursuing additional targets, to ensure that processing is complete and to maximize generalization of effects.

Impasses

Impasses commonly arise when the child is unprepared for the level of distress entailed or not sufficiently motivated. Impasses also occur for no apparent reason. The child may refuse to continue, or there may be no movement despite repeated efforts at processing. Most impasses can be understood in terms of the child's need for a greater sense of motivation, safety, security, and control. The various protocols are designed to address these issues before they become problematic. However, no protocol is problem-proof.

The therapist must take a problem-solving approach, and will generally be able to identify and resolve the problem so that treatment can proceed. First, the therapist should confirm that the child understands the reason for this procedure and is motivated to go through with it. Previously unaddressed fears or secondary gain issues may emerge. Second, the therapist should ensure that the protocol is not unduly slow-paced and burdensome for the child; rather, it should be as entertaining and engaging as possible. Finally, the therapist should make efforts to help the child gain the sense of inner strength needed to continue with the procedure.

Interventions useful in resolving impasses can be found throughout this book. Issues related to understanding and motivation for treatment are addressed in the Preparation section of this chapter, and in Chapter 10. Issues related to the child's sense of safety are addressed in the final section of this chapter. The Installation section of this chapter includes additional interventions to help the child feel secure and strong enough to proceed, as well as cognitive interweave suggestions.

Between Sets

Breathing can serve many useful functions in this treatment. Following an EMDR set, the therapist can give the following instructions: "Now take a big breath in. And when you breathe out, breathe out all the junk." With children especially, the therapist can exaggerate breathing movements, in sync with the child, and then repeat the procedure. The breathing provides an element of playfulness that helps children sustain interest and continue with the activity. Also, in subsequent sessions, the breathing technique can be used to get rid of headaches, master anxiety or fear, and as part of relaxation or visualization training.

There is no standard of practice regarding tracking the thoughts, sensations, feelings, or images that the child may produce during EMDR. Generally it is sufficient, and easiest, to stay with the initial target until no distress remains, then do the installation. There is frequently no alternative, as many children do not articulate any other reactions during processing. When self-awareness is a treatment goal, or when more information and guidance is needed from the child, EMDR productions ("What came up? What did you notice?") are a natural point of inquiry. Tracking these productions may be particularly important when the treatment has stalled on apparently superficial targets, which may be processed without affecting the problem. If available, the guidance from these productions is preferable to therapist hunch and inspiration.

Occasionally children are unable to speak, but are still willing to continue with the activity. These children can point and indicate yes or no. The therapist, then, can ask yes or no questions, and move his own hands from wide apart to close together and have the child stop him at the position that represents the SUDS score. When also trying to help a child learn to articulate emotions, the therapist might have the child point to one of a set of stylized faces with expressions such as scared, sad, mad, happy, mixed up, lonely. Children may not know why they are not able to talk, and may feel overwhelmed with unaccustomed and confusing feelings. It is important to acknowledge that confusing feelings may be difficult to manage, and to give permission to proceed in whatever manner the child may require, including nonverbally.

Following an EMDR set, the child may suddenly want to sleep, play, draw, or see her mother. This is recognizable as a moment of sudden clarity and sureness of purpose, somewhat akin to waking up from a trance. It may signify that a piece of work has been done, and the child may know exactly what she needs to do to actively process what she has just been through. It is probably best to trust the child and follow her lead at this time. Later, if necessary, the therapist can ascertain the SUDS score and continue EMDR with the previous target, add a positive installation, or do whatever is most appropriate. However, if the child has completed the piece of work, and shifted into another modality, that is probably enough EMDR for the day. As with adults, children may need time to process their EMDR experience, and further exposure to EMDR may not be accepted.

After a SUDS Score of Zero Has Been Attained

After the SUDS has reached 0, there may still be more to do, to confirm that the memory has been fully processed, and to locate additional, related targets to enhance treatment effect. The installation, body scan, and reevaluation phases may also provide information about possible additional targets. Here are two additional ways to identify further EMDR targets.

Cleaning Up (Greenwald 1994e)

It can be difficult to confirm with confidence that a child has completed the processing of a memory, even if the full adult protocol has been used.

When a child announces that her SUDS is 0, she is probably sincere, but the usual means of gauging completion—SUDS score, body scan, and possibly VoC—may be insufficient. Some children may compartmentalize aspects of their disturbing memory and be unaware that portions remain unprocessed. Furthermore, even after using EMDR successfully on much of the memory, the child may still prefer to forget about other parts of it, and fail to mention that those parts are still disturbing.

It is worthwhile to routinely seek other potentially distressing aspects of the memory—*after* the SUDS score of 0 has been attained. Every so often, this pays off. It is fairly quick to systematically ask a series of questions that address the various elements of the memory that are likely to be distressing. For example, following EMDR work with the memory of an auto accident, the therapist might say:

> I am going to ask you about different parts of the memory, to see if any parts of it still bother you. What about when you got into the car that day, think about that. Does that feel bad? What about watching your mother drive? What about when the other car hit yours? What about all that noise? The broken glass . . . going to the hospital . . . having your baseball jacket get thrown out at the hospital . . . sleeping over at the hospital . . . when you were alone there . . . the needles . . . what anyone said to you after . . . wondering if it was your fault . . . What about when you get into a car now?

Using EMDR with children can be very fast-paced and confusing, and there is a risk of sloppiness. This extra clean-up effort at the end can help to ensure that the job is really done.

Theme Development (Tinker 1994)

Once the work is done with a particular target, it can be very helpful to treat related targets. This reinforces the treatment effect and reduces the likelihood that additional memories or triggers remain to drive the symptoms. The new targets may be relatively minor events or situations that have not been identified previously. However, they may constitute additional trauma history, or current triggers that should be addressed as a way to enhance the effect of treating the initial target. The child can be asked, "What else makes you [mad, sad, etc.]?" depending on the theme that was the focus of the earlier work. Often, a series of such targets can be processed very quickly.

PHASE 5: INSTALLATION

For installations, as for treatment targets, imagery is the medium of choice, unless a verbal or other form is clearly appropriate. Imagery and cognitions can also be combined. Installations can be used prior to reprocessing, which helps the child access additional resources with which to face the disturbing images (Greenwald 1993a,b), particularly the Safe Place or Safety Device. Installations can also be used to jump-start a session that is stalled, for example when the SUDS score fails to decline. Sometimes installations are used in isolation, that is, without using the rest of the EMDR protocol.

Because installations are used with children at so many points, and because the installation often duplicates the function of the cognitive interweave (even if no cognition is stated), interweaves are included here without distinction. The use of corrective information in interweaves is similar with children and adults.

Safe Place

This widely used installation is often introduced first as a self-soothing technique. The child is instructed to select a "safe place" (or "special place"), based either on experience or from the child's imagination. Typical safe places include being with a favorite caregiver, being in bed, or being at an imagined beach, garden, or mountaintop. The child is asked to notice the details of this location, and notice how relaxed, comfortable, and safe it feels. This is installed by having the child concentrate while eye movements are done. The child can also say "I'm safe" during installation.

It is important to use a safe place that is not contaminated by conflicting memories, which can spoil the effect. The safe place should be a haven. If the child is unable to generate an effective safe place, an alternate installation such as the safety device should be considered.

The Safe Place can be used in several ways. It can be a part of the relaxation training that may precede EMDR. In this way, the eye movements are introduced in a positive context, and not immediately associated with trauma work. The Safe Place can also be installed just prior to desensitization. The child can even be told, "If it gets too hard, you can go to this place." This installation can also be used as part of closure, to help a child calm down prior to leaving the session.

Safety Device (Greenwald 1993b)

This is a fantasy installation, originally developed to deal with a fantasy context: the nightmare.

> *Therapist:* If you were ever in this dream again, what would you need to feel safe? (If the child doesn't know how to respond, the therapist explains again, or gives several examples, such as a special gun, magic wand, and laser sword.) So what would be the best thing for you?
> *Child:* A gun.
> *Therapist:* Okay, take a good look at that gun, what it looks like, what color it is, how heavy it is, how it feels to hold it, how it feels to use it.

Then the therapist installs this image, which can be used prior to processing the nightmare, and certainly should be used after reducing the SUDS score to 0.

The Safety Device can also be installed even if the disturbing target image is memory as opposed to a dream image (Greenwald 1993a). Then the child is told, "I know this really happened, but for a minute let's just make believe that it was a bad dream. If you had to go back into that dream, what would you need?" The rest of the intervention is the same.

This is perhaps the most potent and versatile of the interweave types of installation, because the child is allowed to identify and generate the resource most needed to overcome the target memory. In other types of installations, the therapist provides potentially limiting constraints. There is a place for each. Many therapists routinely install the safety device prior to the desensitization phase, whereas others don't do so until there is an impasse of some kind. This installation may be particularly useful if the child becomes too scared or upset to continue, or if the processing has gotten stuck (SUDS score is not decreasing). A Safety Device may also be used in the treatment of anxiety conditions, where current situations are targeted.

If the child is asked the dream question and gives an answer that is not in an immediately installable format, for example, she may say, "I would need to be stronger," then the therapist must assist the child in converting her answer to a concrete image. In this case, for example, the therapist may say, "What's the strongest animal?" Then the child is asked to concentrate on an image of the strong animal, which is installed. An additional variation is the Role Model installation (see below).

Solution Image

Just as a picture can represent the child's problem, he can also be asked to "draw it all better," and this picture can be used for the installation. The therapist can also ask, "If this problem magically disappeared, what would be different for you?" This difference, if it is positive, can be installed. Another type of solution installation can be obtained by asking, "What would you like to think about instead of [the upsetting image]?"

Fantasy Solution

If the SUDS is stuck at a high level, there is no harm in suggesting a target modification such as fading, shrinking, or exploding it (Shapiro 1995). This can add an element of playfulness while restoring the child's sense of power, allowing for continued progress.

Past Successes and Good Feelings

The child is asked to produce a positive memory that can serve as a counter to the negative lesson of the upsetting memory. For example, after processing a memory involving feelings of fear, lack of protection, and isolation, an appropriate installation might be the image of being tucked in at night by a parent. Past experiences of success can also be installed to counter memories of failure in a related area. For example, a child who has been teased may benefit from the installation of a memory of a more positive social experience. The intake interview, with both parent and child, is a good source of information regarding the child's strengths, interests, and achievements. The therapist may have to suggest possible installations, but the child should be asked to make, or at least accept, the selection.

Future Successes and Good Feelings

If the child can imagine success in a targeted area, this can be installed. It is important to get a clear target, and prompting may be necessary to ensure its adequacy. The therapist can help the child achieve a vivid focus by saying, "Notice how good it feels. Notice where in your body you feel it," or "Notice who's there. Notice what they're saying." The installation may also include, if appropriate, imaginal rehearsal of the actions required to achieve the success.

Generalize Safety

This procedure is used when a child has generalized a fear reaction to many situations or locations (Diane Spindler-Ranta, personal communication). Install the cognition "I'm safe here" first with the formerly distressing traumatic target image, and then with all the other locations in which the child has shown a fear reaction. The therapist says, "Now think of being at your desk at school, and say to yourself, 'I'm safe here.' Now think of being in your bed . . ." This should be done following resolution of the traumatic material.

A variation is to start by pairing the cognition with the safe place, and then repeating the cognition in a series of imagined locations. This can also be done with serial images of people or situations instead of locations. This is also one way to find out if there is unfinished business.

Role Model/Ego Ideal

This is a wonderful adaptation of an intervention used in many other therapy approaches. For children who cannot describe a personal history of success, good feelings, or appropriate actions available for installation, we borrow someone else's. The therapist finds out, either ahead of time or in session, whom the child may particularly admire or respect. This may be an older sibling, peer, teacher, famous athlete, cartoon character, or TV personality. Start by identifying in the role model the specific feeling, quality, or behavioral repertoire that is intended for enhancement in the child. Then install an image of the role model in the act of demonstrating the desired quality.

A more elaborate version of this technique involves having the child imagine becoming the target image (Martinez 1991). The therapist guides this visualization as follows: "So look at him, you can walk up from behind, real quiet, you can get so close that you can hear him breathing. Now, real slow, get so close that you can step right inside. And feel what it is like to be him, to be big and strong and brave." That image is installed.

This installation can also be initiated by converting a particular desired quality into an animal. For example, if the child is asked for a safety device, and says, "I would need to be stronger," the therapist asks, "When you think of a strong animal, what animal comes to mind?" The rest of the intervention is the same.

Another variation is to use an identified role model/ego ideal as the source of a safety device. For example, the therapist might say, "Superman left you a weapon. Can you picture it?" (Cocco 1995). Then the item is intensified as above—"What color is it? What does it feel like to hold it?"—and installed.

Helper

Some children spontaneously choose a helper or comforting companion when asked to visualize a safe place or safety device. However, the therapist can also suggest that the child identify a helper. If the child is unable to do so, the therapist can offer some examples. Favorite helpers include the child's parent, a guardian angel (P. Marvel Logan, personal communication), the role model/ego ideal, or the current self (perhaps older and wiser than the self in the disturbing memory). This helper should be clearly visualized and installed. As with the safety device, the helper can be utilized throughout the desensitization process.

Skills and Knowledge

For children with social or academic deficits, installing specific competencies, or even academic content, can enhance the learning process. The target must be clear and specific. This type of installation can range from assertiveness training to impulse control to math facts. Therapists can be creative in setting up this installation. For example, a child may demonstrate desired behavior in a role play, which can then be installed, along with the imagined consequences such as pride and positive responses from others.

Correction/Polarity

This is a variation of the standard verbal installation, borrowed from the adult repertoire (Rappaport 1992). If a maladaptive cognition has been identified, a corrective cognition should be installed. It's best to elicit this from the child, perhaps by asking, playfully, "Was it your fault?" or "Are you stupid?" Tried prematurely, this intervention can intensify the child's frustration. However, challenging the child in this manner with her own self-attack, from the outside, often serves to help her to break the hold of the negative cognition. This seems to work by eliciting anger, and by bringing the child's adaptive, rational knowledge to bear on the formerly protected, traumatized zone. The response can be elicited several times, with the child increasing the strength of the declaration, before beginning the installation. It may also be installed upon first response, and even continued during the eye movements, having the child continue to respond out loud.

Inner Goodness (Greenwald 1994c)

Some children cannot get past a firm belief in their own basic badness. This is usually based on a history of actual misdeeds, or as a reflection of having received punishment: "My dad hit me, so I know I'm bad or he wouldn't have." The child may be asked, "Is it possible to [do a bad thing; get punished by Dad] and still be a good [boy/girl]?" The child ponders this question during eye movements. This may be sufficient.

Unfortunately, the child may still answer in the negative. Then the therapist can ask, "Deep down inside, do you have a good heart?" or "Deep down inside, is there a part of you that's good?" and have the child answer this (it will normally be "Yes") and then do eye movements. This helps the child access a sense of being a truly good person, often a critical step in treatment. The therapist can also help the parent give more positive messages to the child.

Cognitive Restructuring

More adaptive and positive cognitions can be installed to replace extreme and inaccurate negative ones (Diane Spindler-Ranta, personal communication). For example, if the school day was "terrible," due to one upsetting incident, but the rest of the day was okay, cognitive restructuring can be discussed, and then the therapist installs "The day was pretty good." If the child has enjoyed a game but, after losing, views the whole experience as aversive, the therapist installs, "I had fun playing." Or during a game in which the child is having difficulty managing frustration when losing, "I am having fun playing" or "It's okay" can be installed. This approach can help the child, over time, to abandon overly negative thinking and gain a more balanced and adaptive outlook. This can be used effectively in conjunction with the strength-building approach described in Chapter 1; the child feels stronger when he can tolerate adversity and take things in stride.

Container

A visualized container can be used to store skills or other resources for later use. The child can also rehearse accessing the container in a potentially challenging situation, as part of the installation of a future success. One special use of the container is in preparation for work on a memory that may bring the client's anger to bear on a parent. Many clients are reluctant to proceed in this situation, fearing that they might thereby destroy their love for their parent. Then the container can be used to hold the "good parts" or positive aspects of the parent, to keep them safe during the trauma or grief work. Once the anger and other feared emotions have been processed, the contents of the container can be retrieved.

Installations may be used in succession, for example by combining an installation on schoolwork with a role model installation of someone who is good at taking tests. Correction/polarity (see above) works well as an add-on, either tacked onto the same set or used subsequently.

For children who refuse to consider upsetting memories, or for whom it is most important to focus on building skills and self-esteem, EMDR work may be restricted to positive installations. When EMDR work with a traumatic memory seems stuck, often using a positive installation will get the process moving again.

PHASE 6: BODY SCAN

As with adults, the child is asked to notice any residual physical discomfort, which is then the focus during eye movements. Usually, either this will open up further material for processing, or the sensation will dissipate. This phase can be modified, for example, by saying, "Put a camera inside. Now look all through your body, see if you can find any place where there's a different feeling than usual."

PHASE 7: CLOSURE

In this phase, the therapist helps the child regain composure prior to leaving the session, and helps the child and family prepare for the next session and the intervening period. Although this should be done regardless of whether EMDR was used, there are specific approaches to closure of an EMDR session.

Consolidation

Following the EMDR portion of a therapy session, it can be helpful to consolidate the child's gains through fantasy play, role play, or other means. For example, a child who has worked through fear during EMDR may demonstrate bravery in a confrontation among puppets. The therapist may ask a child who has worked through helplessness to demonstrate physical strength, perhaps by lifting a heavy object or doing push-ups. (Then "I'm getting stronger" can be installed.) A child working on assertiveness can practice in a role play with the therapist. Some consolidation may be accomplished by praising the child's accomplishments in the session when returning the child to the parents in the waiting room.

Container (Dunton 1993)

When a session is nearing the end, and the child is working with still unresolved material, he can be asked, "Where do you want to put those feelings (or this memory) away, until next time?" The image, perhaps of packing them in a box, a safe, or the therapist's file cabinet, can be installed. This may help the child to contain himself following a disturbing session, and make the child's therapy experience less challenging for family members.

Closure

The child should be assisted as needed in regaining composure and feeling good again. Some children use the ritual of putting away the play materials to gain closure in a session. The therapist can also guide the child in a relaxation exercise or do some other calming activity. Positive installations can also be helpful in this effort.

Between Sessions

The child and parents should be prepared for possible disturbance between sessions, and if necessary, management strategies should be discussed. The child and parents should be instructed to observe problems or changes related to the treatment focus, to report at the following session. If progress has been made in the session, homework might be considered involving in-vivo consolidation of gains. The therapist should say that the homework is difficult, so that encountered difficulty will be expected, and success will be perceived as exceeding expectations.

PHASE 8: REEVALUATION

After EMDR has been performed, a reevaluation is conducted to track the effects of treatment, and to determine the next focus or course of action. With children, the reevaluation phase may begin immediately following EMDR, if there is more time left in the session. Children may dramatically portray their current status through their play or other behavior. However, it is also important to track children's response to treatment during the time between sessions. Although some children are able to report articulately on their own experience, it is good practice to maintain regular contact with a parent, either by meeting for a few minutes at the beginning of each session, or talking ahead of time by telephone. The next steps of treatment can be planned on the basis of information from the child and parent, as well as the therapist's own observations.

PART III

SPECIAL APPLICATIONS

8

Infants and Toddlers

In general, the younger the child, the more abbreviated the EMDR procedure will be, and the larger the role the parents will play in the treatment. This is most true with the youngest clients. Parents must remain present during the treatment of infants and toddlers, in order to keep these young clients feeling comfortable and secure, and to facilitate communication. In fact, the parents may conduct much of the child treatment themselves, guided by the therapist.

Infants or toddlers typically present for mental health treatment following a trauma such as auto accident, medical procedure, or maltreatment. There are several issues to address in this treatment approach, including parental reaction to the event, parent education regarding appropriate care, and the child's traumatization. Fortunately, these issues can frequently all be addressed at once, and sometimes even in a single session. In fact, with the tired parents of a screaming infant, a four-session diagnostic routine is inappropriate.

Jesse, a 19-month-old boy, was seen through his mother's employee assistance program. His mother reported on the phone that he had been screaming a lot at night for a couple of weeks, along with increased crying and clinging behaviors. This type of case warrants immediate treatment and relief, because both the toddler and the parents are in distress. I suggested that the mother bring in the entire family—herself, her husband (Jesse's stepfather), and Jesse.

One early goal is to determine the source of the disturbance. When we met, this was easy enough to figure out, as it immediately followed a rare visit to Jesse's biological father, who was known to have poor self-control when he got angry. Jesse's mother speculated that the father had probably yelled at, and possibly slapped, Jesse. Alternately, Jesse may have witnessed a loud or violent confrontation among adults. Considerations regarding Jesse's ongoing safety were simplified by the fact that his father had already left the state and was not expected to visit in the foreseeable future. Jesse's home life appeared to be stable and did not normally expose him to this type of event.

PARENTS' REACTIONS

When a child is hurt in some way, whether physically or emotionally, the parents' reaction can be strong and complex. The parents may hurt in sympathy with the child. They may also be sad or angry that the child was hurt. They may also feel personally responsible for what happened, whether or not the event was actually due to parental negligence. The parents may develop elements of a posttraumatic reaction, such as intrusive imagery, overwhelming affect, denial, numbing, and other symptoms. The parents' reactions can interfere with their appropriate care of the child.

Occasionally, a highly reactive parent may require individual treatment. This would be most likely when the child's trauma has re-stimulated the parent's own traumatic memories, or when the parent had some direct responsibility for the child's trauma. The parents' response is known to play a critical role in the child's development of a posttraumatic stress reaction. If the parents are helped to respond appropriately, the child has an improved chance of recovery.

However, child treatment should not be delayed. Probably the most effective treatment for the parents' secondary posttraumatic reaction is for them to see that the child is okay. The therapist can further help the parents to recover their own sense of effectiveness by giving them an active role in the treatment. This can be accomplished through direct participation in child treatment activities. When the parents can feel less guilty as well as more knowledgeable and effective, the child will receive better care.

Mother: I knew I shouldn't have let him go to his father's house. The man has a temper, he yells, he's hit me before, that's why I left him in the first place. God knows what he did to this poor boy. It's my fault, I shouldn't have let him go.

Therapist: Has he ever done anything to Jesse before?

Mother: No, but he hasn't been around him much. I just thought it would be okay to give them a visit before he left the state.

Therapist: And then Jesse came back all upset.

Mother: Yes. I should have known better.

Therapist: Parents wish they could predict the future, but you can't always know ahead of time when something will go wrong. But now you know! What will you do next time he's in town and wants to see his son?

Mother: I guess I'll just say no unless someone else is there who I can trust to take Jesse away if things get bad.

Therapist: That sounds okay. Is there anyone else who takes care of Jesse that you might have any cause to worry about?

Mother: Oh, no, just us, my mother sometimes, and one babysitter who we know very well.

Therapist: So you made a mistake and you learned from it. Sounds like it's not going to happen again.

Mother: Yes, but he keeps crying and screaming all night.

Therapist: That's what you're here for. You're doing just what a good parent should do—get help when there's a problem you're not sure how to handle.

PARENT EDUCATION

Many parents don't know what is best for their child following exposure to trauma. The therapist can help them find specific ways to help the child recover. With infants and toddlers, this may involve frequent soothing physical contact and proximity. Maintenance of daily routines can also be comforting, as well as verbal praise and reassurance. The therapist will have to evaluate each situation to provide appropriate advice. For example, if the child is hospitalized, the therapist may suggest bringing the favorite teddy bear along, as well as having a parent or other relative be present as often as possible.

Mother: So what should we do when he screams and cries at night? Should we keep on letting him sleep with us? Before this, he was sleeping in his own crib for the last few months. And the doctor had told us then, just let him cry and he'll go to sleep. But now, he just goes on and on. I can't stand it, so I bring him to bed with us.

Therapist: You're doing just the right thing. Right now, because he's been scared, he needs you more than usual. When he gets over it and he's back to normal, he'll be able to sleep on his own again. For now, though, just keep on trusting your judgment and do what you need to do.

PARENT INVOLVEMENT IN TREATMENT

The opportunity to participate in the treatment can help parents regain a sense of themselves as effective caregivers. In fact, their participation is critical to treatment success. EMDR can help, too. Parents can come to believe that their own contribution was paramount in the treatment's success, which is fine because the child needs confident, effective parents.

The EMDR procedure is boiled down to its essence with this population. The therapist or parents say a few key words that remind the child of the trauma, while alternately tapping (typically) on the child's feet. The child sits on the parent's lap. After the trauma words are used, more positive words are used, also with alternating stimulation. For example, after saying, "big bang" for a car accident, "all better" might follow. This series is repeated until the child appears to be happier and more relaxed, and shows no negative reaction to the trauma words. A follow-up session is very important to ascertain the effects of treatment, since such young children cannot verbally report on their inner experience. The follow-up session also provides an opportunity to offer further guidance and support to the parents.

> *Therapist:* What words can you think of that might remind him of what happened to him?
> *Mother:* Daddy. Whenever we mention Daddy he cries again.
> *Therapist:* Good. Anything else?
> *Mother:* Well, maybe yelling. When we raise our voices at home he doesn't like it lately.
> *Therapist:* Okay. And what do you tell him to let him know that you're happy with him, or that things are okay?
> *Mother:* Well, we say "good boy" or if he's had a cut or a bump I kiss it and say "all better."
> *Therapist:* Okay, I want you to just keep on holding him on your lap like he is now. (To Jesse): Is it okay if I touch your feet, like this? (Child nods. Therapist taps

feet lightly, alternating, and continues for the following dialogue. To mother): Now remind him of the bad
thing. Go ahead.

Mother: Jesse, remember when you went to Daddy's house?
Did Daddy yell? Did he yell loud?

Therapist: Good. Now tell him that it's okay, he's safe with
you now.

Mother: Good boy, good boy Jesse. All better! You're safe
now, safe with Mommy.

Therapist: No more Daddy?

Mother: No more Daddy. All better now. (Therapist stops
tapping.)

Therapist: Good. We'll give him a little break, and then go
through the whole thing another time or two. Did you
see how he got all tense at first but seems happier now?

The family returned about ten days later to report that the
nightmares and clinging had basically ceased. Jesse was already
sleeping in his own crib again. In that follow-up session, we did
the EMDR procedure again just for good measure, but no further distress was evident. We discussed a couple of more general parenting questions and the treatment was over.

In other cases, the child may not respond so completely to
the first treatment attempt, and at follow-up the entire protocol
would be repeated. This would start with a review of the parents' response to the precipitating event, their approach to the
child, and any problems they are continuing to encounter. If the
parents seem to be sufficiently comfortable with the situation as
to be able to care for the child effectively, then the therapist
can repeat the EMDR procedure, perhaps searching for additional key words to ensure that all aspects of the trauma are
being accessed.

If the parents have not been able to provide appropriate
therapeutic care, then that should be the primary focus. The
therapist may help the parents view the situation in a more

adaptive manner, or may help to solve a specific problem. For example, if the father becomes so upset when the child cries that the father yells at the child, the therapist may teach the father to remove himself prior to yelling. In some cases, the parents may be so reactive that they exacerbate the child's posttraumatic reaction rather than soothe it. Sometimes EMDR with such parents can be helpful, targeting either the precipitating event, events that trigger their reactivity (e.g., the child's screams), or earlier memories that may pertain. Even when the parent is the primary focus, it can still be useful to repeat the EMDR procedure with the child. This may help the child to recover more quickly, which can also help the parent.

SLIGHTLY OLDER CHILDREN

EMDR can be used with very young children in other ways also, for example, in the context of a play therapy session. But there are special problems. These children may not have the capacity to maintain sufficient concentration to cooperate with the procedure. They may not have the perspective to place the EMDR experience in the context of a broader healing process. If the processing momentarily intensifies unpleasant feelings, they may not be willing to proceed. Premature stoppage of EMDR can constitute retraumatization, even if a portion of the healing has already occurred. This may threaten the relationship, and lead to increased disturbance outside the session. But relationships can be repaired and disturbance can be treated in other ways, and it may be worthwhile for the healing that does occur prior to the stoppage. This is a judgment call.

Very young children with pervasive trust issues should probably not be exposed to EMDR very early in the course of treatment, except for one-shot treatments following an isolated trauma experience such as an accident or scary movie. It is more prudent to establish a relationship with the child, through parent collaboration and play, prior to direct EMDR trauma work. This treatment is analogous to a mother washing a cut; when painful, it is only tolerated on the strength of the relationship.

Eye movements may be too difficult for very young children. Hand tapping without eye movement is acceptable and fun. If even hand tapping is a challenge, the child can use both hands, one over each of the therapist's, and can be trained by the therapist saying, "Hit this hand. Good. Now hit this one." (Tinker 1994). With even younger children, the therapist may use alternating sound or touch. For example, while the child is in her mother's arms, the therapist may tap alternating feet.

Targets for processing should also be simplified. For example, the child can be asked to repeat emotionally laden words related to the trauma or anxiety, such as "car," "bang," or "doctor" (Tinker 1994). Alternately, the therapist can state the words (Lovett 1995). Thorough information must first be obtained from the parent, in order for the therapist to understand the nature and details of the targeted memory.

9

Young Children

The successful use of EMDR with young children (ages 4 to 7) requires that special attention be given to effective parental involvement and to the child's willingness to proceed when the work may become uninteresting or painful. The EMDR procedure itself is simplified in some ways, while other features of the protocol are modified to fit the younger child's needs. This approach typically begins with family work and leads into using EMDR.

ASSESSMENT

Assessment of the child's problem is straightforward if the parent is insightful and a good observer of the child. For example, a parent may accurately report that the child's symptoms began following an identified trauma or loss. Regardless, the therapist should obtain a developmental history, including any major loss or trauma, as well as any history of significant shifts in the child's attitude, mood, or behavior. This helps the therapist understand why the child is having the presenting problem and account for the problem in terms that the parent can relate to. Trauma-fo-

cused standardized measures (see Appendix B) can also be helpful, both for obtaining information and for presenting it cred-
ibly to parents. The assessment should also include the parent's
description of parent–child interactions as well as behavioral
observation. Then the therapist will be prepared to make appropriate interventions with the child, and to encourage the parents to more effectively support the child's improvement.

DISCUSSING THE PROBLEM

The parents should be seen without the child if possible, to reinforce the adult–child boundary ("There are some things it's
best not to say in front of children") and to preclude, as far as
possible, the parents' embarrassing the child in front of the
therapist. This also gives the therapist an opportunity to reframe
the problem, if necessary, so that when the therapist and parents present a treatment plan to the child, they can share a philosophical approach. The concepts are presented to the child, in
a simplified form.

Two perspectives seem to be most helpful in explaining
children's problems, whether to the parent or to the child. Parents are typically concerned that there may be something inher-
ently wrong with their child that will not resolve. The therapist's
formulation can help transform the parents' view of the child
from bad to mad, sad, or immature. One effective way to portray children's problems is to describe the problems as a normal reaction to specific trauma and/or loss experiences. It can
also be useful to describe the child's problems as reflecting
immaturity; the child just "needs to learn." These trauma, loss,
and developmental issues are resolvable, and lead to specific
therapeutic responses on the parts of the parents as well as the
therapist.

> *Therapist:* It sounds like your daughter can get pretty hard
> to handle sometimes.

Mother: Oh yeah, she gets me going. It's like she's just asking to get smacked, until finally sometimes I do it, just to shut her up.

Therapist: You know how she had to see you and your husband fighting those times, and then he left? When kids go through that kind of thing, they get really scared inside. Like the world's not safe anymore, anything can happen. And then, even much later, they're still worried that something else bad might happen anytime. Did you know that could happen, those bad feelings staying stuck inside?

Mother: No, I hadn't thought of that, but it makes sense.

Therapist: So when she gets nervous, wonders if things are still safe, she asks you, by acting bad. Then if you can show you're in charge, in control, she feels safe again.

MAGICAL THINKING

The more fully the parents can understand the child's experience and needs, the more likely they will be able to participate as effective members of the therapeutic team. More sophisticated parents may benefit from learning about the role of magical thinking in the child's development and in the child's experience of the presenting problem. This is what I say to parents:

> When a baby is born, she doesn't even know she's a baby or that someone else is someone else. Then when she realizes, "Oh, I'm me, and I stop at my skin, and beyond that it's 'not me,' " well, even then, she figures, "But I control everything in the world." Of course, the world is only what she can see, and she *does* control it. Just think it and it happens. "I'm hungry, Mom feeds me; I'm cold, Mom puts a blanket on me." The thing is, at first she doesn't even know that she's communicating by crying; she doesn't really wonder, "How does Mom know what I want?" Just think it and that makes it happen.

This is called magical thinking. Later on, of course, kids learn even more, and realize that things don't happen from thinking, but from doing. And that they can't always control things. That's what the Terrible Twos is about, the tantrums, when they realize they can't always get their way. But some of that magical thinking stays, maybe a little less every year, but even grown-ups still have it a bit.

One thing about kids, though, is that they have very strong, all-or-nothing feelings. When they love you you're the best person ever; when they hate you, they want to kill you. Not that they even understand what that means, it's just that the feelings happen that way, very strong. The problem is that when something really bad happens, like someone actually dies or goes away, or there's a bad accident, or someone does something bad or scary, the child thinks she did it. It's that magical thinking, she says to herself, "I got mad at him and then he did that. It's my fault. I made it happen." So then she feels guilty, that she's the cause of everything bad, and she feels dangerous, like if she has any more bad feelings, she'll make more bad things happen.

The best thing you can do at home is help her learn what kids learn when they're 2. That you're the adult, that you're in charge. That she's just not that powerful. Then she won't have to be so guilty, or so dangerous, afraid of her own bad feelings. If she learns this enough times, then maybe she'll start to believe that she didn't cause those other things, either.

PARENT TRAINING

Once the parents accept and understand the therapist's trauma/loss-oriented formulation, the therapist can begin to engage them in implementing corrective activities. (A parent-training approach is discussed in detail in Chapter 2; an additional, age-appropriate intervention is described below.) This helps to reinforce, for the parents as well as the child, the notion that the parents are in charge, and that this translates into increased safety and security for the child. This intervention is not needed in every case, so clinical judgment must be exercised.

Sometimes the child has taken on a parental role, perhaps as the confidant, caregiver, or boss. The therapist highlights this role confusion to the point of absurdity, which may jar family members into a new perspective on their interactions. First the confusion itself is presented, and then elements of resolution are addressed sequentially. Once the parent is demonstrated to be bigger, older, and stronger, she is qualified to be in charge. Once she can prove that she is really in charge, she can use this parental role to help her child feel more safe and secure.

> *Therapist:* You might think I'm stupid, but I'm getting confused here. Which one of you is the real mother?
>
> *Child:* She is!
>
> *Therapist:* I'm not so sure. When Mom tells you her troubles, then you're the mom. (Then to the mother): Do you have any adult friends you can tell your troubles to, so that Sara doesn't have to be your mother?
>
> *Mother:* Yes, I talk to my neighbor sometimes, and to my sister.
>
> *Therapist:* That's good. You want to keep grown-up talk with the grown-ups, so that your daughter can be a kid. But I'm still confused about who the mom is. Remember a little while ago, when you (to mother) told her to put the markers away, and she kept on using them? She was the boss then. I always know who the real mom is by seeing who's in charge. So I'm still confused. (To the child): Are you in charge sometimes, when maybe your mom is supposed to be?
>
> *Child:* Sometimes I don't listen good.
>
> *Therapist:* Oh, so you might be confused sometimes, too. No wonder I'm confused now.
>
> *Mother:* Well, I tell her, but she doesn't always listen.

Therapist: Right, that's why we're all so confused. But it's really important to know who the mom is, to know who's in charge. Let's see, a mom should be bigger, older, stronger. (To child): Mom, stand up.

Child: I'm Sara!

Therapist: Oh, I'm sorry! Got confused. Okay, Mom—no, I mean Sara—stand up. And (to mother) Mom, you stand up too. Okay, good. Now which one of you is bigger?

Child: She is!

Therapist: Hmm. Let's see, you go up to here (puts hand by the top of child's head), and you go up to here. Yup, she is bigger. Now who's older?

Child: She is!

Therapist: Are you sure? How old are you?

Child: I'm 6.

Therapist: And how old are you?

Mother: I'm 27.

Therapist: Bigger and older. Well, maybe you are the real mom. But let's see who's stronger. (To child): Go over and lift her up off the ground.

Child: I can't.

Therapist: Well, you never know, if you were the mom you could. Go give it a try.

Child: (tries) I can't.

Therapist: Okay, good try. Now (to mother) you lift her off the ground. (Mother does so.) Oh, bigger, older, and stronger, too! Well, she might really be the real mom. But let's find out who the boss is! (To child): What I want you to do is tell her to jump up and down, see if you can make her do it. (To mother, in a whisper): Don't do it.

Child: Jump up and down.

Mother: No (smiles and does not move).

Therapist: (to mother) Good job. Now, how does she get

her way sometimes? I know! (To child): Tell her again, maybe she'll change her mind. (To mother, whispering): Don't do it.

Child: Jump up and down.

Mother: No (smiles and does not move).

Therapist: You're both doing a good job. (To child): Keep telling her again and again, I bet you can get her to change her mind. (To mother, whispering): Don't do it.

This role play provides an excellent opportunity to emphasize the appropriate parental authority role. Children tend to enjoy this activity even if they are unable to articulate that they feel more secure when their parents take charge. The parent can become somewhat inoculated to the child's coercive strategies, by going through each one systematically, with the child's playful participation.

Therapist: Hmm, I guess that's not working. What can we do? I know! Make that face that you make, you know (makes face), no, you do it better, go ahead, make that face and tell her again.

Child: (makes face) Mom, jump up and down.

Therapist: Boy, she's tough, isn't she? Can you think of anything that might get her to do what you say?

Child: Maybe if I cry?

Therapist: Good idea, try that (by now, mother understands her role and does not need prompting to stand her ground).

Child: I can't.

Therapist: That's okay, just do your best, make believe.

Child: (moans) Mom, jump up and down.

Therapist: That was pretty good, but she's still not doing it. How about yelling? Will that work?

Child: I don't think so.

Therapist: Well, let's try one last thing. This time, yell at her to do it, and stomp your feet too. (Child stomps and yells.) Well, I guess this is the real mom after all. She's older, bigger, stronger, and it turns out that she's in charge, too. You can't boss her around. That's good news.

Once the parent is established as the more powerful person in the parent–child relationship, this should be immediately tied to the protective function. This can be done through discussion or role play, and can be modified to reflect any identified fears the child may have. The therapist can say, "Well, your mom seems pretty tough to me. Do you think she's tough enough to handle monsters [robbers, etc.]?" Then the therapist may direct a role play in which the parent is able to successfully protect the child from the feared object.

Therapist (raising arms and baring teeth): Here comes the monster! I like to eat little children. I think I see one! (walks slowly toward the child). (Whispers): You think your mom can save you?
Mother: Go away or I'll shoot!
Therapist: Ha, ha! Here I come!
Mother: Bang! Bang!
Therapist: (falls down) I'm dead.

If the therapist is uncomfortable in playing the monster role, a puppet or other prop can be used. Props can also be used for weapons or other means of protection. This role play may be repeated a number of times, with variations, for example, "Oh no, now there are two monsters coming!"

Although the child is the most direct beneficiary of this game, the parent is also learning how important the strong parental role appears to be to the child. This can help to overcome parental ambivalence about taking charge. This provides a positive context for implementing effective and consistent discipline with the child. Therefore, the goal of this intervention is to prepare the parent for the parent training, and to convey to the child that discipline translates to increased security and safety. A successful disciplinary approach enhances the child's sense of security, which is the essence of this phase of treatment.

INTRODUCING AND DOING EMDR

Once there is some indication that the child's environment is becoming more conducive to healing, an individual focus is likely to be productive in treating trauma or loss. Many elements of the standard protocol are omitted, for several reasons. Young children don't want to hear explanations about why EMDR might be effective; they just need some kind of warning that they might feel bad for a little while, and to know that they can stop if they want to. The session will probably go more smoothly to the extent that the therapist is able to maintain good pacing (not too slow) and a sense of fun. It can also help considerably to harness the child's own motivation in whatever way possible. These elements of effective treatment tend to get jumbled together in various ways. Here is one example of how to use these principles in practice:

> *Therapist:* You were saying that you wanted to stop wetting your bed so you could go sleep over at your friend's house.
> *Child:* Yes. Mommy says that if I don't wet my bed for one whole week, I can go to my friend Jennie's house and stay overnight.
> *Therapist:* There's something we can do that might help you to stop wetting your bed. But before I tell you about it, I have to tell you the rule. The rule is, if it gets too hard, you can stop. Do you know how a cop stops traffic with her hand?
> *Child:* (holds hand out, palm forward).

Therapist: That's right, just like that. Now I'm going to make some noise, and see if you can make me stop, by doing that with your hand. Ready? Blah blah blah blah blah. (Child holds out hand.) You did it! This time, I'm going to wave my arm back and forth, and see if you can make me stop (waves arm). You did it again. So you know what to do if you want to stop?

Child: (nods).

Therapist: Okay. Now for the next thing, let's see if you can do it, or if it's too hard. Which hand is your best hand to use for things?

Child: This one.

Therapist: (holds out his own hands, palms up) Okay, use just that hand, now hit this hand (motions with his right hand; child touches it). Good, and now hit this one (motions with left hand; child touches it). Good. Now go back and forth. Good. Was that easy or hard?

Child: Easy.

Therapist: Okay, good. Now I'm gonna make it harder. This time, I want you to think of where you feel the most safe. What's the safest place you know?

Child: At home.

Therapist: Where at home? What part of the house?

Child: In my room.

Therapist: Do you feel safest in your room at a certain time? When you're alone or with someone?

Child: When my mom is telling me goodnight.

Therapist: Okay, this time, think about being in your room, with your mom telling you goodnight. Now keep thinking of that, and hit my hands again like before. (She does.) Good. Was that easy or hard?

Child: Easy.

Therapist: And what did it feel like?

Child: Good.

Therapist: Did it make you feel safe?

Child: Yeah.

Therapist: This time, I'm going to make it even harder. Think about your mom telling you goodnight, and say to yourself, "I'm safe." And now hit my hands. . . . Good. Were you able to concentrate on all that at the same time?

Child: I think so.

Therapist: Okay. Every time I give you something hard, it seems like you can do it. But here comes the hardest part, because there might be bad feelings for a while. But first, I want to check: Do you remember how to make it stop?

Child: (holds out hand in the stop sign).

Therapist: Good. Now, you know your mom told me about the bad things your babysitter did to you. I want you to think about the worst thing that happened. Do you have a picture in your mind?

Child: (nods).

Therapist: Do you want to tell me what the picture is, or just think it?

Child: Think it.

Therapist: Okay. Now I want you to show me how bad the feeling is that goes with the picture. This would be a lot of bad feeling (holds hands widely spread), this would be a medium amount (holds hands partially spread out), and this would be just a little bad feeling (holds hands close together). Now when you remember the worst thing your babysitter did to you, show me with your hands how bad the feeling is.

Child: (hold hands as wide as possible).

Therapist: Oh, that must be a very bad feeling. Now keep thinking of that, and hit my hands like before. . . . Okay, now take a deep breath, and breathe out (therapist exaggerates a deep breath in and out to demonstrate). Good. Now, next time, when you breathe out, if you have any bad feelings or other junk, just breathe it out then. Let's try that again, breathe in (both breathe in) and now breathe out the junk (both blow air). Good. Now, think about that picture again, ready? And hit my hands. . . . Okay. Now a deep breath in, now breathe out the junk. Good. Now, show me with your hands how bad that picture feels now.

Child: (holds hands about halfway apart).

Therapist: Okay, now think of that picture again, ready? And hit my hands. . . . Good. Deep breath, breathe out the junk. . . . Think of that picture again, ready? And hit my hands. . . . Good. Deep breath, breathe out the junk. . . . How much bad feeling is there now?

Child: (holds hands very close together).

Therapist: Okay, now think of that picture again, ready? And hit my hands. . . . Good. Deep breath, breathe out the junk. . . . How much bad feeling is there now?

Child: (claps hands together) All gone!

Therapist: Wow! What happened to the bad feeling?

Child: (shrugs) I breathed it out?

Therapist: So what happened to the babysitter? Can he do any more bad things to you?

Child: No, he's not allowed to come over anymore. If he does, my mom will call the police and they'll take him to jail.

Therapist: Think of that (holds out hands for child to tap). What happened then?

Child: He tried to come over, and my mom called the police, and they came, and knocked him down and put him on handcuffs, and they took him to jail.

Therapist: So are you safe now?

Child: (nods).

Therapist: Think about that (holds out hands for child to tap). What happened this time?

Child: Nothing.

Therapist: Say to yourself, "I'm safe now" and think of being in your room with your mom telling you goodnight (holds out hands for child to tap). What happened this time?

Child: Good.

Therapist: A good feeling? Feel safe? (Child nods.) This time, think of that picture you were thinking of before, with your babysitter, and say "I'm safe" (holds out hands for child to tap). What happened this time?

Child: I'm safe. He can't get me anymore. (Gets up.) Can we play Candyland?

Therapist: We can play for a few minutes. Then I have to tell your mom how good you did. I didn't know if it was going to be too hard for you.

Child: I'm blue, you be red. Can I go first?

The vignette began by identifying a motivating factor; she is interested in cooperating so that she can stop wetting her bed and go to her friend's house. Then she learns, through experience, that she can make the therapist stop. This exercise adds an element of fun, and many children ask to do this again and again. However, it also helps to prevent the child from being retraumatized by virtue of recalling the traumatic memory—this time, she's in charge. Then the EMDR procedure was introduced, one step at a time, in a way that made the child feel proud of herself; she could prove to the therapist that nothing was too hard for her!

The eye movements (in this case, the hand taps) were first tried with a positive image, which brings up good feelings right away. This serves several functions. The "safe place" helps the child to access her own sense of security, a good foundation from which to face a traumatic memory. This also begins a good-bad-good sequence, with the bad being the traumatic memory, and the final good being the elimination of target-related distress, the reintroduction of the positive perspective, getting to play a game, and the therapist praising the child to her parent. This type of experience is likely to teach the child that therapy is a place where bad feelings can be addressed in a safe, contained way that ends with feeling good.

The therapist in this vignette cannot yet know to what extent the traumatic memory may be resolved. He stopped because the child was clearly done for the day, and because, having apparently achieved resolution at least on the initial target, it was a good stopping point. However, the therapist will then observe the child's play, ask the parent whether any changes were noted in the child in the days following this session, and ask the child herself, at the next meeting, how bad the targeted image feels now. The therapist will also explore the child's reaction to a number of related memories and images (e.g., the face of the babysitter).

This vignette did not necessarily show the complete resolution of a traumatic memory. It demonstrated an approach to using EMDR with young children, by showing part of a single session.

10

Families

Many therapeutic approaches to working with children empha-size the importance of the family. EMDR-related family interven-tions are primarily used to support the child's progress in therapy, to encourage the child specifically to engage in EMDR, and to provide credible corrective information. When parents can assist in their child's healing, the parents feel better too, which in turn is good for the child. In this chapter I offer guide-lines and techniques for encouraging parents to help their chil-dren through an EMDR session. I also include a few more elabo-rate planned interventions.

Although these interventions are intended to have systemic impact as well as supporting the child's treatment, they are not appropriate for every family. For example, if the family is orga-nized around the child's symptom as a means of diverting pa-rental conflict, it may be counterproductive to attempt to heal the child prematurely (Szapocznik et al. 1989). Similarly, if the parents blame the child or believe in the child's badness, their statements to the contrary will not be credible. Therefore, these interventions should only be attempted when such obstacles are not present, or have been substantially resolved. The therapist's determination that individual child treatment is appropriate must take into account whether the family is indeed in a position to support it.

PARENTS AND EMDR

There is no consensus on whether to tell parents specifically about EMDR, even giving them reading material about it, or just talk about therapy in general, with EMDR as one of many techniques. It may depend on how sophisticated the parents are, and how much they want to know. There is consensus, however, on the need to be in communication with the parents about the progress of the child, about any unusual behavior, symptoms, or special events occurring between sessions, and about how the parents are handling the child. Teachers, social workers, or foster parents may also serve some parental functions for the purpose of this discussion. As with other child therapy, parental support of treatment is critical.

Bringing the Child for Therapy

The parent handing the child over to the therapist gives a clear message that the child is to cooperate, and that the therapist is "approved" by the parents and is on their "team." The therapist can enhance this effect by further demonstrating a treatment alliance with the parents. For example, the treatment goals can be discussed with the parent and child together. Later, the therapist can invoke the parents' authority and support of therapy by saying, "Your mother told me that . . ."

Providing Information

The parents are a primary source of information about the child. Essential information includes a detailed trauma history; observed behaviors indicative of such emotions as fear, anxiety, anger, and sadness; and information about the child's heroes, likes, dislikes, interests, strengths, and weaknesses. This information is needed for initial assessment, to track the child's progress, and to select targets and installations for the child. The child should be asked for help in selection, but often this effort confirms the value of collecting information elsewhere!

Demonstrating EMDR

Like the king's food taster, the parent can try EMDR first, in front of the child, to confirm its safety. The child may also be motivated to cooperate due to the appeal of imitating the parent. "I was talking with your mom, and she was telling me that you've been having some bad dreams since [the trauma]. Is that true?" Child nods. "Well, there's something we can do that might help to make your bad dreams go away. Would you like to try it?" Child nods. "I'm going to show you how it works with your mom, and then let you try it. Okay? Watch now." The therapist winks and says to the mother, "Think of the bad part of your dream, and follow my fingers with your eyes." The therapist moves his hand several times. Then he asks the child, "Do you think you could do that?"

Staying with the Child

Some very young or fearful children are more comfortable with their parent present, or at least very accessible nearby. A fearful child may only be able to do EMDR while sitting in the parent's lap. In that case the parent may even perform the hand tapping while the child watches. The child's sense of security is more important than the therapist's sense of how things are supposed to happen. If the therapist can show support for the parent staying with the child in such a case, the family will feel cared for, and generally respond by trusting more in the therapist.

Communicating

The parents should communicate with the therapist on a regular basis, giving feedback on progress and any pertinent events or concerns. It's optimal to have at least a brief check-in with the parent—in person or by phone—just prior to each meeting with the child. This will help the therapist to know how the child has responded to the previous session, and to become aware of fresh material that might be useful to address. As the parent–therapist relationship progresses, the therapist may also have increased access to information, and increased opportunity for consultation, family therapy, or referral.

Parent Therapy

Parents are often willing to undergo therapy themselves if the focus is limited to parenting issues, such as difficulty in setting limits and reactivity to specific child behaviors. In the latter case, EMDR can help to desensitize the parents, enabling more appropriate parenting responses. Even one or two sessions can be worthwhile. If family of origin or marital issues emerge, they can be addressed in more depth according to relevance and client interest. Most often, though, work with parents tends to focus on helping them to understand their child's problems from a more productive angle, and helping them to become more consistent in handling their child (see Chapters 2 and 9).

OTHER FAMILY INTERVENTIONS

Sometimes further intervention is required to mobilize and emphasize parental support for the child's healing. The following interventions involve helping the parents actively provide corrective information to the child. This information may be needed to help the child begin to engage in the treatment, or to move forward most productively. As noted above, parents may also benefit from participating in these interventions, leading to more favorable family dynamics.

Invoking the Rules (Lovett 1995)

Rules can have enormous stature in the mind of a child. Therefore, rules can be very useful as a child is learning either to be assertive or to increase self-control. For example, a child who has had difficulty in standing up to aggressive peers may find it relatively easy to proclaim, "The rule is: no hitting." The child is, in essence, borrowing the adult's authority for enhanced self-confidence.

The therapist, parent, and child can collaborate to formulate a rule or two that would be most appropriate and useful to the child's progress. The parent can then be asked to emphatically state the rules in session and at home. The rules can be installed, first with the memory of the parent's statement, then with the image of the child's similar statement. Finally, challenging situations can be rehearsed (and imaginally installed) in which invocation of the rules may be useful.

Getting Better Might Be Risky (Greenwald 1994c)

This intervention directly addresses possible secondary gain issues for the child, and should be considered as a routine component of preparation for EMDR. Following a careful assessment of the child and the family, individual child treatment may be deemed appropriate. After introducing EMDR as a potentially helpful activity, the therapist can express concern regarding possible risks of successful treatment. The child may then acknowledge concern that getting better might lead to losing parental attention and/or family closeness. Once the child admits to this—sometimes only following specific questioning—it can be discussed. Typical outcomes include contradiction by the parents, who assert that relationships will actually improve; discussion of specific ways of tracking possible changes in relationships; and a family commitment to exploring this issue following individual treatment.

> *Therapist:* Before we get too far, I just want to check and make sure that going ahead will be okay. (To child): If you get better, what would be the worst thing about that?
>
> *Child:* Nothing.
>
> *Therapist:* Some kids worry that if their mom and dad don't have to worry about them anymore, they might not be as close, might not spend as much time together. Is that a worry for you?
>
> *Child:* I guess so.
>
> *Therapist:* (to parent) Is that a worry for you too?
>
> *Parent:* Of course not. If I didn't have to deal with all this, we could spend time doing fun things instead.
>
> *Therapist:* Like what kinds of things?
>
> *Parent:* Oh, watching movies, going to the park, playing games.
>
> *Therapist:* You mean that if he didn't have this problem, he'd get just as much time with you, but doing more fun things?
>
> *Parent:* That's right.
>
> *Therapist:* (to child) Would that be okay with you?
>
> *Child:* That would be better.
>
> *Therapist:* Well, it sounds good to me too, but I'm still just a little worried. Can we make a deal? After the problem is gone, can we get back together and make sure that things are going well in the family? Then if something went wrong, we can fix it.
>
> *Child:* Okay.
>
> *Parent:* Okay.

Therapist: (to child) So what would be the best thing about getting better?

This intervention helps the child to feel permission, support, and safety in attempting to relinquish symptoms. It also may serve to promote the use of EMDR, with the therapist's paradoxical worry about success leading to increased motivation. The awareness of family dynamics generated by this discussion may also help the family reorganize in support of the child's changes.

"What a Good Boy/Girl" (Greenwald 1994c)

This intervention addresses the child's underlying sense of badness, and is used when the child's inner resources have been insufficient for healing with EMDR. For example, a child's memory of an angry, punishing, or upset parent may constitute irrefutable evidence of badness, limiting progress accordingly. The therapist should introduce corrective information from the most authoritative source available: the parents. In a family session the therapist questions the parents, who must repeatedly insist that the child is "a good boy/girl" even if sometimes making mistakes or requiring punishment. (Some parents may need to be prepared for their role.) Specific upsetting past events may be brought up, perhaps asking the parents if the child was at fault (they say no). After such a session, children tend to integrate this information easily during EMDR, often leading to dramatic changes.

This intervention also tends to have multiple effects. Not only does the child acquire a needed healing resource, but the parents may become more able to distinguish their positive feelings about the child from their negative feelings about the child's behavior. The parents' inclusion here may help them discover their child's goodness, and to feel empowered to continue to support their child's healing through praise and positive interaction.

The Story of the Child (Lovett 1995)

One of the problems when a child has been traumatized is that
the parent can be a secondary trauma victim, with feelings of
guilt, helplessness, and other symptoms. This can cause ongoing distress to the parent, possibly interfering with his capacity
to support his child's healing. This intervention allows the parent a major role in the treatment, while also providing the child
both useful information and encouragement for doing EMDR,
so both parties can be healed simultaneously. This story approach
can be used even with very young children, and up to about age
8.

Following initial assessment, as homework the parent is
asked to prepare a short, written, fairy-tale type of story in which
the main character has an experience similar to that of the traumatized child. The story must have the following features:

- The protagonist should be the same age and sex as the
  child, and have a similar family makeup. However, the
  name should be different, thus giving the child the option of hearing it in either the third or the first person.
- The language should be age-appropriate so the child can
  easily follow along.
- The most important features of the child's traumatic
  memory should be included.
- The story should start by portraying a positive life situation, and, following the trauma portion, should resolve
  to a recovery of the positive.

The therapist should review the prepared story, and modify
it as necessary, prior to using it with the child. The parent's
ability to follow instructions in this matter may also be diagnostic of their ability to be supportive of the child's therapy. A
parent who provides a blatantly inappropriate story will probably
need extra help.

When the story is ready, and the child and parent have been prepared for the EMDR session, it proceeds as follows. The parent reads the story aloud to the child, a line or two at a time as per the therapist's signals. After each part has been read, the therapist has the child perform eye movements. It is permissible to continue with eye movements for more than one set if this is not too uncomfortable for the child. This reading and stopping for eye movements continues until the story is done. Then the whole process is repeated until there are no more distressing parts of the story, and the child feels sure of the happy ending.

The structure of the story resembles a trauma protocol for using EMDR with young children. It starts with a positive image (or safe place), then goes through the traumatic memory, and finishes with another positive image (or installation). This intervention offers a particularly elegant way of integrating the individual and family treatment components.

11

Bed-Wetting

Whether bed-wetting is the primary presenting complaint or one of many problems, it remains an excellent target for treatment. Children and parents are motivated to end this ordeal, and success is tangible. Sometimes bed-wetting simply ceases following trauma resolution, especially when a child who was not wetting had begun following trauma. Often, though, additional interventions are required to overcome this habit. I prefer a shotgun approach, utilizing a number of interventions simultaneously. Advantages include greater chance of success, possible quicker resolution, and increased sense of self-efficacy for the parents and the child, who may each feel that their active contribution made a difference.

As with all physical or physiological symptoms, a medical consultation may be required to rule out a physical cause such as allergy or constipation. There are also drugs that can help some children to become continent, and there are some children who are developmentally slow in acquiring night continence. However, the following cluster of interventions will be more than sufficient to help most children stop wetting their bed. Although this does not represent exhaustive coverage of effective interventions for this symptom, many facets of this issue are addressed, including trauma, sleep hygiene, behavioral contingencies, and physical and emotional development.

ASSESSMENT

Assessment of bed-wetting should cover the many possible contributing factors. Did the child stop wetting the bed at some point, and then later start? What other event coincided with restarting? Does the bed-wetting occur every night, or only under certain circumstances? What are the consequences of this symptom, including penalties as well as possible secondary gain? How does the parents' disciplinary style interact with the child's trauma/loss history, and how does it affect the contingencies surrounding the symptom? What are the child's habits pertaining to sleep, and might these habits contribute to the problem? Finally, what are the child's goals, and how will overcoming this symptom move the child closer to those goals?

TRAUMA

Bed-wetting is one of the classic symptoms of child trauma, and in many cases trauma resolution eliminates this symptom. Furthermore, if bed-wetting does represent a posttraumatic response, failure to address the traumatic memory will undermine other otherwise effective interventions. Therefore, trauma resolution should be at the top of the agenda. This can be accomplished by using EMDR with all significant trauma and loss memories. This approach is described in detail in other chapters, according to the age of the child. Nightmares and night fears should probably be targeted, via trauma work and then directly if necessary, prior to focusing directly on the bed-wetting. These sleep-related disturbances can serve as retraumatizing experiences, so this would be considered part of the trauma treatment.

POSITIVE PARENTING

One important aspect of trauma work entails assisting the parents in establishing and communicating a safe environment for the child. Otherwise, the child may be subject to ongoing punitive shaming, or other stressful experiences that serve to retraumatize in a minor but potentially debilitating manner. This portion of the treatment is also important in that the parents may be asked to implement a behavior modification program, which requires habits (skills, behaviors, and attitudes) that are taught with positive parenting. This approach is described in detail in Chapter 2.

SLEEP HYGIENE

The therapist should find out whether the bed-wetting is nightly or more irregular, and whether it occurs in relation to other events in the child's life. For example, some children may tend to wet their beds most often after having watched a scary movie, on early-to-bed nights, or following stress or excitement. Any discernible patterns of this kind should be addressed and rectified to reduce the frequency of the bed-wetting. Good sleep hygiene should also be followed, including maintaining a regular schedule of meals, exercise, and sleep; avoiding late-night eating; limiting intake of liquids after dinner; emptying the bladder just before going to bed; and avoiding exposure to stress or excitement in the hour or so before bedtime.

Some parents have a habit of waking the child up later at night to use the toilet. If this is convenient and effective, it should be continued during the treatment, even if it may be discontinued later. Success contributes to treatment progress, so the more success the child experiences, even with this type of extraordinary support, the better. Also, success can help the child shift from a habit of incontinence to a habit of continence.

However, if the parents are not waking the child, it is probably not a practice worth initiating.

POSITIVE DEVELOPMENTAL APPROACH

Having a dry bed is something that older kids can do; bed-wetting is for babies. Children can easily accept the idea that when they get bigger and stronger, they will be more like an older kid and able to stay dry at night. Treatment is presented as a way of helping the child build up strength. The therapist portrays increased strength as representing increased maturity, and children generally accept this concept. This theme can be developed in many ways. For example, the child can be encouraged to exercise more, and to demonstrate increasing strength by doing push-ups or by arm-wrestling with the therapist. Imagery of doing exercise, eating good meals, and other healthful activities can be installed along with a cognition, such as "I'm getting stronger."

In some cases, the child may be having problems in other areas that can be related to this theme. For example, progress on issues such as poor impulse control or failure to complete household responsibilities can be characterized as other ways in which the child can show that he is becoming more mature. During eye movements, appropriate behavior in the targeted area can be imaginally rehearsed along with positive outcomes, as well as a related cognition, such as "I'm getting stronger."

A positive role model can also be used to support the positive developmental approach. The role model is presumably someone the child can identify with, who does not wet the bed. This can be installed by imagining the role model doing some strength-building activity, and then waking up in a dry bed; then the same activities can be installed with the child imitating the role model.

MUSCLE DEVELOPMENT

Consistent with the positive orientation of symptom resolution through normal development—perhaps enhanced in the therapy process—children can practice exercises that help to develop their continence muscles. This may be presented to the child both as an exercise and as a challenge, in which the child is asked to continually surpass the previous personal best. This intervention varies by gender, and the intervention for boys is a lot more fun. Boys can practice by sinking Cheerios in the toilet. They are instructed to put a Cheerio in, sink it with their urine stream, then stop urinating long enough to put in the next Cheerio. The quicker they can stop, the less wasted "ammunition," and the more Cheerios they can sink. Girls can practice "stopping your pee" by urinating and then stopping. Start, stop. The therapist says, "See how many times you can stop at one sitting. Try to beat your record." Girls who report difficulty in stopping themselves can be instructed to imagine urinating in a public bathroom, and then having a man open the door to their stall. Most girls can make themselves react to this shock by stopping.

Bladder capacity can be expanded by having the child drink a large glass of water in the morning, and then refraining from urinating for about five minutes after feeling the need to do so. This can be practiced at least on a daily basis.

EXTERNALIZE THE PROBLEM

This intervention involves helping the child personify the problem as being an entity separate from herself. This entity should have a name, physicality, and character. Once the child has described and/or drawn this entity, it can be processed with EMDR. The child may, for example, have a battle with "the peepee monster," make friends with it, trap it in a cage, or send it away.

INCENTIVE PROGRAM

The use of incentives can be very helpful. A positive focus can be maintained by having rewards only, not punishments. The program should include a quick experience of success so that the child can feel encouraged, while also including a substantial incentive sufficient for strong motivation. Therefore, there may be more than one level of incentive, to meet both of these requirements. For example, each dry night might earn a star on a chart, with five dry nights earning the child a trip to the ice cream store.

The effect of incentives can be maximized when just the right balance of tension and comfort can be found. For example, it is okay to require the child to face reasonable consequences for wetting the bed, such as washing the sheets. However, this should be presented as a fair responsibility, not as a punishment, which would just add stress and interfere with treatment. Parents should be trained to use the incentive approach effectively by being encouraging but not overly involved or reactive. The ideal incentive program may evolve from trial and error. For example, some children respond to the challenge of earning the reward for five consecutive dry nights. But others may feel too much pressure and thus stress, so the conditions should be modified so that, for example, the reward can be earned when five dry nights are accumulated, consecutively or not. Later, when the child is more successful, the achievement levels can gradually be raised.

12

Special Treatment Settings and Populations

This chapter addresses treatment issues and approaches pertaining to special treatment settings and populations. Many techniques mentioned in this section have already been described in detail.

SETTINGS

Outpatient Treatment

With high-functioning children, whose problems are relatively circumscribed, it may be appropriate to begin EMDR as early as the second session. The following routine works well in such cases.

In the intake session, the therapist interviews the parents about family structure and dynamics, the child's strengths and interests, trauma history, current problem and symptoms, and how this is managed by the child and the family. In a separate interview with the child, the therapist explains the reason for treatment and what the treatment entails. The therapist begins to develop the child's motivation and selects potential targets and installations. This is a good time to have the child draw the problem or some symbol of it, and to identify some positive images and feelings. Therapy goals may be discussed, and the child can be tested for which eye movement method is most effective, using a neutral or positive target. The intake session is used for assessment, but also to get both parent and child on track for their participation in treatment.

Subsequent sessions are structured as follows:

> Parent check-in (5 minutes): parent consultation, to monitor the child's progress in treatment-related areas, learn of any recent significant events in the child's life, and encourage the parent's support of the child's healing.
> Child check-in (10 minutes): child-initiated activity, typically drawing or playing. Verbal check-in when possible.
> EMDR (20 minutes): guided by treatment goals and new information.
> Play (15 minutes): child-initiated activity, to facilitate consolidation of the gains.

This routine seems to make good use of several modalities. There is wide variation in individual cases, with some younger children only doing a few minutes of EMDR, and some older children doing little or no play.

Other therapists report using a flexible structure, in which EMDR is introduced at opportune moments that arise during the course of the session. For example, a child may draw a picture expressing hurt, or enact a puppet drama with an angry scene, and the therapist may intervene to induce eye movements while the child remains in the emotional moment.

Adjunct Treatment

Clinicians trained in EMDR are frequently asked to provide adjunct treatment in a variety of situations. This can work well, but it is important to clarify relationships and expectations ahead of time, and to create conditions conducive to client safety and treatment success.

Providing adjunct treatment in an outpatient therapy context makes the most sense when there is already another established therapy relationship, and when help is being requested to address a specific and discrete identified trauma or other obstacle to therapy progress. The EMDR therapist must evaluate the case, since the referring therapist may not fully understand the issues related to EMDR treatment. This evaluation may be done with the child and family, or in some cases by discussing the case with the primary therapist. If the EMDR therapist chooses to proceed, it should be explicitly as a consultant, with the primary therapist maintaining responsibility for the case and resuming treatment after the consultation. It is often helpful for the primary therapist to be present during the EMDR, so that the child can feel more comfortable and the therapist will know what occurred.

It is normally inadvisable to provide adjunct treatment in cases where the EMDR therapist is likely to become the primary therapist. For example, if the referring therapist is just beginning a case where the bulk of the work is identified as resolution of a discrete trauma or loss, the case should probably be passed on to the EMDR therapist. If a referring therapist has a well-established relationship with a multiply traumatized child in long-term treatment, the best solution may be for that therapist to learn EMDR. Those without EMDR training may not be sure how to use an EMDR-trained consultant, and it is up to the consultant to ensure that she is being used effectively and appropriately.

Providing adjunct treatment in an inpatient or other residential context is becoming more common as EMDR becomes better known, while the in-house clinicians may not yet be trained to use it. Again, the EMDR therapist should make sure that she is fully aware of treatment issues, and does not blindly accept instructions to "do EMDR on the trauma." With good collaboration, and with other treatment needs being met, adjunct treatment can be both helpful and efficient in this context.

Milieu Treatment

In a milieu treatment setting, EMDR may be applied as soon as practicable following a negative behavior that has been targeted for treatment. After intervening, establishing safety, removing the child from the situation, and helping the child regain composure, the recent experience of extreme reactivity constitutes a high-interest target for processing. Installations such as role model/ego ideal would also be useful in helping children to achieve their goals. However, this in-the-moment intervention works best when the EMDR therapist has a prior relationship with the child, and when they meet for therapy at scheduled times as well.

Although the clinician may not have the authority to initiate changes in the structure and daily workings of the milieu setting, these factors can play a major role in supporting or inhibiting the child's healing. Most obviously, if the child is subject to harsh or brutal treatment, either by staff or peers, he is not likely to feel safe enough to face traumatic memories. In many settings, for example, an outmoded style of physical restraint is used, so that what should be an intervention to establish safety is actually an aggressive act in itself. Other more subtle elements of a program can also make a real difference. For example, in many settings well-meaning staff acquire the prison-guard mentality because their responsibilities push them to focus on bad behavior.

Programs that support healing have many things in common with supportive family environments. Good programs are of small size and focus on the individuals; larger programs should be subdivided into smaller units. Good programs are driven by a vision or theory, such as trauma orientation, that guides policy and practice and makes for a coherent, systematic approach. Good programs also focus on the positive, for example, by providing the residents with engaging and productive activities, and by basing privileges and promotions on achievement. Finally, staff support and training are critical to ensure consistent and effective practice.

Schools

The school setting is conducive to treatment because it is a normative environment, and thus therapy goals may be framed in comfortable terms, for example, helping the child do better in school. There are a few steps that will help a therapist be successful in a school environment.

The therapist should establish "insider" status, so that the school accepts the therapist as an integral staff member and a resource to be tapped. This status helps not only in gaining access to the child, but also in operating as part of a team including the child's parents and teachers. To gain insider status the therapist must understand and respect the school's mission, which is to educate children. Teachers and administrators tend to believe that class attendance is important, and disruptions to educational activities should be minimized. In fact, many in schools seem to believe the therapist should not compete with teachers for the child's time or compromise or expand the school's mission in any way. Although they may also understand that mental health issues can interfere with the child's ability to benefit from school, territoriality and defensiveness may prevail. It is not the therapist's job to win the battle over the child; in fact, that approach is usually more damaging than helpful. Rather, the therapist should emphasize his recognition of the school's authority, and his support of the school's goals and mission. The need for mental health services should be framed in that way; for example, the boy needs to get over the death of his uncle so he can concentrate on school again and stop being disruptive.

The teachers should be consulted as to when it would be most convenient for the therapist to see the child, perhaps during a class the child is doing well in, or during one in which he is refusing to participate. The logistics of getting the child to and from therapy should be as nondisruptive as possible. Every effort should be made to facilitate closure at the end of each session, so that the child is not disruptive in class after the therapy sessions.

The therapist often has an opportunity to provide consultation to the teacher, which may make the classroom more supportive to the child. The therapist must show respect for the teacher's knowledge about the child as well as for her classroom management skills. When the teacher is feeling respected, she may be open to suggestions or even ask for them. However, if the therapist approaches the teacher to give advice, the teacher may become defensive.

EMDR can be helpful in many aspects of the treatment, including trauma work, training in coping skills, and enhancement of studying skills and practices. EMDR can also be particularly helpful in addressing routine school-related frustrations, and in effecting end-of-session closure.

Medical Hospitalization

EMDR is generally not the first order of business when treating a hospitalized child. The parents must be helped to cope with their own response to hospitalization (and related circumstances), so that they can effectively support the child. Pain control takes priority over psychotherapy, and is a good way to establish a track record with the child. In an acute setting such as an emergency room, panicked patients can sometimes be calmed by the soothing voice of a caring person, combined with alternating tapping on an accessible body part such as feet or shoulders.

EMDR can be used in several ways in the hospital setting, such as installing visualizations of the internal healing process and then teaching the child to repeat this with self-practice. EMDR may be helpful in processing changes in self-image or life plans that may be associated with the medical condition. EMDR may play a role in preparing the child for scary procedures, and in securing compliance with treatment. If the child is hospitalized following a traumatic event, EMDR can be used to process that event. It is important to remember that hospitalization can itself constitute a trauma, or can extend the duration of the experiencing of a traumatic event.

Often the period of hospitalization is too brief, and too physically uncomfortable, to permit psychotherapy treatment. Parents should be helped to support the child's emotional recovery at home, and to recognize posttraumatic symptoms that may require professional treatment. Written information can be provided including signs of posttraumatic symptoms and suggestions for responding (see Appendix A).

Disaster, Accident, or Other Critical Incident (Greenwald 1993d)

Following a critical incident, and once urgent needs are met, all affected parties should have an early opportunity to debrief. Parents may feel overwhelmed, guilty, and stressed out, and they may need help with their own responses in order to effectively care for their children. They also may need assistance with securing basic needs. Finally, they may need education about their children's posttraumatic responses, and how best to support their child's healing.

In a family or community crisis, it seems appropriate to treat troubled children with EMDR, even if these children are not the primary problem, and even if they could be expected to recover on their own over time. If a family is under stress, a child who is fearful, acting out, or waking up at night constitutes an additional stress. Any intervention that reduces the stress level is worthwhile, and may ultimately help the family become stronger.

This population is a particularly gratifying one for the EMDR practitioner, as results tend to be quick and dramatic, and the preventive value immense. The target may be nightmares, new fears, or memories of the traumatic event. With recent events it may be necessary to process the entire sequence rather than focusing on just the highlights. The therapist should be prepared to work with prior traumatic material that emerges during processing. Given our understanding that posttraumatic symptoms often reflect the cumulative effect of multiple adverse experiences (Greenwald 1997b), prior trauma and loss should be sought and treated if time permits.

PROBLEMS AND POPULATIONS

AD/HD and Learning Disorders

Dunton (1993) stresses the importance of being sensitive to physiological limitations as well as the child's sensitivity to frustration, failure, and threats to self-esteem. Her approach is a gentle, step-by-step self-efficacy model that accommodates special needs. The approaches described in the chapters on disruptive behavior disorders includes many methods appropriate for this population, in addition to those described below.

Dunton suggests an emphasis on positive installations designed to build self-esteem, social skills, and learning skills. For example, after working through a performance anxiety, she will install a memory of a good or successful feeling. If the child cannot locate one, she helps to create this capacity, by installing ego ideals or role models. This method is also useful in installing appropriate social skills. She also installs specific academic skills, such as spelling words or math facts, preferably in a visual or sensory form, for example by having the child write them first.

These children may have special difficulty tracking, so multiple-stimulus or variable-direction methods are often required. Particularly effective are hand slapping, finger snapping, or moving the hand in an elliptical or figure-8 motion. "Spots on the Wall" is also good because it facilitates the child's gaining additional control. For children who cannot track, clicking on alternate sides of the head may be sufficient for processing.

If the child is having an unpleasant physical reaction, or doesn't like the experience, it may be best to stop EMDR, even if, with an adult, the therapist would process the reaction and go on. Continuing might make the child feel unsafe, damaging the therapeutic alliance and limiting future cooperation.

These children often have an extensive history of minor traumatic experiences. Focusing on the most recent problem or incident conveys respect, since that is what often feels most relevant to the child. One approach is to start with the current concern (e.g., "I hate the teacher"), process that, and then ask, "Have you felt this way before?" working back through traumatic experiences one at a time.

An alternative, cognitive-behavioral approach retains the focus on the recent event. Following processing of the associated negative aspects, a behavioral choice point is identified, and the child is asked to furnish a positive alternative action. This positive choice is rehearsed and installed, along with the more positive outcome. This approach can be used systematically to address easier to progressively more difficult types of situations. Finally, EMDR may be taught as a self-calming tool, using spots on the wall to reduce anxiety and emotional reactivity in stressful situations.

Abused Children

EMDR is useful with this population, but may be complicated, as many abused children have incurred extensive damage beyond the obvious PTSD manifestations. The family may be a focus of treatment, and in individual treatment a substantial corrective-relationship component may be required. Treatment of children with extensive abuse histories should err on the side of caution in introducing EMDR, as premature use may constitute retraumatization and damage the therapeutic alliance. While many of the safety-oriented interventions can be used, there may be no substitute for the passage of time. As with other techniques used with this population, client pacing and sense of control is critical to safety and trust.

Facts regarding current safety may serve as a safety device for abused children. For example, the child may visualize the perpetrator in jail (if he is), while saying, "I'm safe now" during eye movements. Trauma targets may include discrete events, and some children only need to work through a few of the worst. Then, the face of the abuser, or the location of the abuse, may be an excellent target, and help to condense the remaining processing. The events can be scanned in a batch, with the child going through each one as slowly or quickly as desired. Often, when the first, worst, and most recent events have been reprocessed, and then the face, location, or other key targets have been neutralized, the final run-through of remaining memories can be completed in minutes.

Many abused children, particularly those exposed to cult and/or sexual abuse, have been pressured, lied to, and tricked in a variety of ways. Add to this the child's own adaptive responses, including assumption of guilt, dissociation, distortion, and denial, and there is a real possibility that the child's memory, cognitive processes, and sense of reality will be seriously compromised. For such children, a major treatment focus may be the recovery of their history and validation of their experience, with the therapist as a witness and co-investigator. Children with damaged memory may experience flashbacks or have memory fragments that they find confusing, disturbing, and scary. Sutton (1994) suggests that it may be desirable to work on a cognitive level for memory reconstruction, before doing intensive emotional work, in order to maintain a sense of safety and control.

When the child explores the memory during EMDR, details of the memory may become filled in, so that the story can become more organized and coherent. The full EMDR protocol might be contraindicated in this process; if the child is not prepared to tolerate strong painful emotions, it should just be used as necessary to gain information.

Although EMDR does seem to facilitate access to memory details (see Preface), there is no reason to assume that such memory details, or any memory details, are entirely accurate (ISTSS 1998). Whereas the client's psychological truth is valid and important to address within the treatment context, independent corroboration of memory details is normally required for other purposes, such as litigation.

EMDR may also be used in the usual manner, with the traumatic memories as the target. However, this will probably not preclude the need to develop a solid therapy relationship, in the context of which the reconstructive work may proceed.

EMDR may be appealing to some abuse victims who are initially reluctant to describe the incidents to the therapist. They can be given the option of processing the material without telling the story aloud.

Dissociative Disorders

Children can be screened for dissociative disorders by inquiring about symptoms such as memory loss, surprise at finding things bought or accomplished, and unexplained headaches, particularly in conjunction with a known extensive trauma history such as chronic abuse. As with adults, children with dissociative disorders should be treated carefully, by clinicians with specialized training, in a manner that fosters as much consent and participation as possible by the various component subpersonalities that may be present. Children who dissociate may be very sensitive to criticism, or to other therapist features that may constitute warning signs for the child, triggering a dissociative episode.

As with adults, lesser dissociative disorders may be treated more directly. The therapist should be prepared for unusual reactions during processing, such as intense headache or a sudden need to sleep. Even if using EMDR with memories becomes too problematic, it can still be used to treat ongoing symptoms, and the child can learn to self-soothe using eye movements in distressful situations. The anecdotal reports with this population have been positive regarding EMDR results.

Reactive Attachment Disorder

Reactive attachment disorder (RAD) is a complex condition requiring a highly specialized treatment approach. Although some clinicians now view EMDR as a central component of treatment for RAD children and adolescents (Greg Keck, personal communication), it should be applied only within the context of a comprehensive treatment approach. RAD children may experience trauma in a unique manner, as the attachment orientation, with expectation of safety and care, has already been impaired. During EMDR for trauma work, the dominant focus may be the child's rage, as opposed to the range of responses one might otherwise expect.

EMDR has been reported to be particularly helpful during a "holding" intervention, which involves nurturing physical restraint by the adoptive parents, with therapist support, during the child's uncontrolled rage episode. The addition of EMDR seems to help provide a bridge between rage and acceptance of a new attachment relationship (Marshall and Vargas-Lobato 1997, Joanne May, personal communication). EMDR may also be used during individual work with a cognitive focus, to help the child move from "I am bad/evil" to "I deserve to be loved." This is often followed by another cognitive shift regarding parent figures; for example, the birth parents will be recognized as irresponsible, and the adoptive parents may be viewed more openly as possible sources of love and security.

EMDR is also used at certain points in the process of developing the attachment to the new parents (Joanne May, personal communication). For example, the therapist may induce eye movements (or tap alternate feet) while the new parent is holding the child, and "reinvent the narrative" by saying, "If I were there when you were born, I would have smoothed your hair, I would have counted your toes, I would have . . ." As the new relationship progresses, and the child becomes hopeful, fear of losing the parent will arise. The therapist can help the child concretize the fear (e.g., Mom will die when she goes on vacation), and then process with EMDR.

Obsessive-Compulsive Disorder

There is some speculation that those suffering from obsessive-compulsive disorder (OCD) may have unique neurological features that are incompatible with EMDR (Rothbaum 1992). On the other hand, there have been anecdotal reports of success with EMDR. For example, Grosso (1996) describes a case in which he helped a 6-year-old girl externalize and personify her OCD as a character named "Mr. Clean" who would tell her what to do. They also identified the triggers that accompanied this, such as anxiety and a sensation in her stomach. The various bullying behaviors of Mr. Clean, with the girl's associated responses, became the targets for EMDR. Coping behaviors were also installed, such as telling Mr. Clean to go away. In that case, EMDR was used in conjunction with supportive behavioral interventions in the home.

Tourette's Disorder

Abruzzese (1995) suggests using EMDR in combination with guided imagery to help children to move an embarrassing tic to a less noticeable location, for example, from the neck to the big toe. Have the child "find the place where the tic comes from, the control center" and guide the child through having the tic sent to the alternate location. Since tics become more active in response to stress, sources of stress can also be addressed. EMDR may be used for trauma work, self-control, relaxation, and self-efficacy. Special attention should be paid to the specific situations in which the child's tics tend to become more active. These situations should be processed with EMDR, either by having the child imagine a "movie," or by having the therapist recite a script of the typical sequence of events, during eye movements. Other problem-solving and coping approaches also pertain.

Somatic Disorders

Somatic disorders can entail a range of issues that may be at least partially addressed with EMDR, including pain management, trauma and grief reactions, treatment compliance, stress reduction, and adjustment to new limitations. The general approach across conditions might include family support, trauma/grief work, adjustment work, and problem solving around current and anticipated challenges. However, immediate concerns take precedence; for example, a child experiencing pain should first be taught pain management techniques, and only later helped to reduce the stress that may be exacerbating the pain. Otherwise the client may be too distracted by pain to concentrate on the therapy, or she may be too disgusted with the therapist, who insists that her pain is caused by memories.

Pain

Standard pain management approaches include distraction, self-hypnosis, relaxation, and general stress reduction. EMDR can contribute to stress reduction in many ways, as described below. Generally strategies for immediate relief are taught first. It is essential that the therapist act is if the pain is real and respond accordingly. Once the therapist has gained the client's confidence in this way, there may be more leeway to try additional interventions.

Sometimes pain seems to serve as a physical container for psychological pain. If an identified traumatic source for the pain is available (e.g., a car accident), the memory can be processed with EMDR. This may or may not eliminate or reduce the pain. When a pertinent pain-related memory is not available, it can be worthwhile to use EMDR with the standard multimodal focus (image, cognition, emotion, sensation) on the pain itself. This can yield a startling array of responses, which can be processed as usual.

This approach may be used with pain as well as other somatic conditions such as headache, tension, and stomachache, as long as proper medical care has been given. Sometimes focusing on areas of somatic distress may access traumatic memories. Therefore, care should be taken to establish a relationship capable of supporting such disclosure and subsequent processing. The possibility of a dissociative disorder should also be considered.

Trauma and Grief

It is generally worthwhile to address trauma and grief issues as early as practicable in the treatment. EMDR with these targets can contribute to reduced reactivity and lower stress, which may mitigate a variety of stress-responsive ailments such as asthma, chronic pain, and some headaches. Furthermore, unless the trauma and grief related to the medical condition has been resolved, it will be very difficult to make progress in other related areas such as stress management, treatment compliance, and rehabilitative efforts.

There are a number of potential trauma sources associated with somatic disorders, such as the memory of the accident or assault causing the current injury, and related upsetting events, perhaps associated with subsequent medical treatment or the response of significant others. For those suffering from a serious or terminal illness, the discovery of this condition may have been traumatizing. Grief reactions are likely to accompany awareness of terminal illness as well as any seriously limiting condition such as partial paralysis or disfigurement.

Adjustment

Some somatic disorders entail adjustment to reduced capacity or some other impairment, which can be perceived as substantially limiting expectations regarding quality of life. For example, a preadolescent who has acquired facial scars may believe that he will never have a girlfriend or get married. To address this issue it is critical that related trauma and loss have been resolved as much as possible, because otherwise those issues will interfere. Other facets of treatment may be done before or after addressing adjustment issues, depending on the situation. For example, the boy with the scarred face may develop increased hope for the future once he learns how to cope with his classmates who now look at him differently. However, he may not even be willing to discuss coping skills until he believes that he may have a social future worthy of his investment. The sequencing of interventions requires clinical judgment.

Helping the child adjust to impairment entails several steps, beginning with trauma work regarding the source of the impairment. Then the feared future can be addressed by targeting it with EMDR—as if it were a memory—and using the standard procedures. As the potency of the feared future diminishes, more positive alternatives will generally emerge. Sometimes additional resources can be brought to bear, for example, by introducing a newly blind child to blind adults who may serve as positive role models. Finally, the positive future can be developed and strengthened by imaginally rehearsing (with eye movements as well as cognition, emotion, and sensation) not only the "happy ending," but the various realistic steps that may be required to get there. These steps may include some of the treatment compliance and problem-solving behaviors addressed in other facets of this treatment approach.

Stress Reduction

Stress reduction is of particular importance for stress-responsive disorders such as asthma, which will serve as the example here. In conjunction with appropriate medical care, a number of interventions may be used to reduce the frequency of asthmatic attacks by reducing the child's tendency to experience a high level of distress. Family therapy should be considered if family dynamics create undue stress. Since traumatization often leads to magnification of normal responses to stress, trauma work with EMDR may lead to generally reduced reactivity. Memories of serious asthma attacks should be considered as possible targets along with other trauma and loss. The child's circumstances should be thoroughly evaluated for any undue sources of stress, which should be addressed if possible.

Problem Solving

Problem solving contributes to stress reduction as well as positive adjustment. Problems to be addressed may include those related to the medical condition, as well as any other problem that may contribute to undue stress or interfere with functioning. Current typical challenging situations can be targeted, first by processing with EMDR, and then be imaginally rehearsing more adaptive coping strategies, also with eye movements. Anticipated challenges can be addressed in a similar manner. Typical problem areas include treatment compliance, interactions with family members and peers, learning/school difficulties, and coping with formerly normal situations that are now altered in some way.

One problem that may be targeted in some situations is the somatic disorder itself, especially if the child is engaged in some activities designed for healing. The basis for this intervention is the visualization for healing (Simonton and Creighton 1982) in which the child imagines internal biological forces engaging in healing activities. For example, a child with leukemia might practice visualizing white blood cells eating up the malignant cells. This may be done with anatomically accurate imagery, or with symbolic imagery such as, for example, soldiers in white uniforms representing the white blood cells. As with other types of visualizations, the child should generate as much of the content and detail as possible. Once the imagery is developed and then practiced with eye movements, the child can be taught to self-practice, perhaps by using spots on the wall or by moving the eyes under closed lids. There is anecdotal support for this EMDR-enhanced visualization approach with an adult (Greenwald 1998a).

Once this visualization has been taught and practiced, it may be incorporated into other elements of the treatment. For example, treatment compliance may be encouraged by having the child imaginally view a "movie" during eye movements, in which treatment compliance activities (taking medicine, doing exercises) are followed by the visualized healing. This combination of treatment compliance followed by visualized healing can also be incorporated into a broader movie, perhaps leading to more positive adjustment and realization of various goals over time.

Appendix A: EMDR and Child Trauma Resources

The EMDR International Association (EMDRIA) is an independent non-profit organization dedicated to the promotion, development, and responsible use of EMDR. EMDRIA's numerous activities include providing referrals, supporting research, accrediting training programs, publishing a newsletter, and organizing an international conference every year. EMDRIA is an excellent resource and clearinghouse for information. Interested clinicians might also consider becoming members. The address is P.O. Box 140824, Austin, TX 78714-0824; e-mail, emdria@aol.com; and telephone, (512) 302-9943.

The Internet is now an excellent way to learn about EMDR-related books, gadgets, training opportunities, and research findings, as well as child trauma information, assessment, and treatment resources. Here are the best sites:

> The EMDRIA home page, www.emdria.org, includes a wealth of information related to the organization and the various types of information and other services it provides.
> The EMDR Institute, the first and still the dominant source of EMDR training, also has an excellent home

page at www.emdr.com, including information on EMDR, training, and a frequently updated bibliography of EMDR-related studies.

David Baldwin's Trauma Pages, www.trauma-info.com, provide comprehensive information and links regarding all aspects of trauma, including treatment methods.

Ricky Greenwald's Child Trauma Home Page, www.childtrauma.com, offers a range of information, clinical aids, and links on both child trauma and EMDR, for parents, clinicians, and scholars. The page includes brochures, parent education handouts, newspaper and scholarly articles, and child trauma measures.

Many other important trauma and EMDR-related Internet resources can easily be found via links listed at the above sites.

Appendix B:
The Trauma Orientation
and Child Therapy

This appendix explains the empirical and theoretical bases of the trauma orientation to conducting therapy with children and adolescents. The focus is on how current knowledge about child trauma prevalence, effects, assessment, and treatment may be relevant to a broad range of child problems. This is not to say that every child has been severely traumatized, nor that every child problem represents posttraumatic stress disorder (PTSD). However, I will argue that most children have been exposed to some upsetting experiences that are relevant to the presenting problem and resemble trauma sufficiently for principles of trauma treatment to apply.

DEFINITION OF TRAUMA

Child trauma generally refers to an experience of overwhelming horror, fear, or pain, along with helplessness (Krystal 1978). Typical examples include auto accident, physical or sexual assault, house fire, and witnessing violence. Such extreme events often lead to PTSD, although many outcomes are possible.

Children may also be exposed to a variety of other upsetting events that do not meet the *DSM* criteria for trauma. Such events may include the death of a family member, family breakup, serious illness, geographical displacement, and a range of other challenges. Traditionally, the child's symptomatic response to this class of event, when recognized as such, has been called an adjustment disorder. The research on adjustment disorders of childhood suggests that this is a misnomer in many instances. For example, children's symptoms following family breakup are suggestive of a posttraumatic reaction (Heatherington et al. 1989), although this may be complicated by ongoing family dynamics. As with PTSD, so-called adjustment disorder symptoms also frequently fail to resolve within the specified 6-month period, and may be sustained indefinitely (Newcorn and Strain 1992). Another similarity is that, even when acute symptoms diminish, the internal damage is often maintained.

For children, at least, there may be relatively little difference between an unexpected traumatic experience and an unavoidable major loss experience that has been anticipated. Although a loss experience does not typically lead to an increased state of arousal (Pynoos 1990), the overwhelming fear and helplessness may be present in either case. Furthermore, many children develop similar reactions to chronically occurring but relatively minor upsetting events, such as repeated verbal abuse or school-related frustration. Thus, virtual posttraumatic responses may arise from many types of events. The clinician's concern is not with how bad the trauma was according to some objective criteria, but rather with how the trauma is affecting the child now.

As a clinician I prefer to define trauma in the broadest sense, to include any upsetting experience that has been incompletely integrated. This definition would not be acceptable in a research context, and much of the following discussion refers specifically to the more extreme types of traumatic events. I am also not trying to suggest that one child's adjustment reaction is likely to represent the same degree of distress as another child's PTSD. However, this inclusive definition of child trauma is arguably the most clinically relevant, since recognizing trauma's contribution to a child's problem may enrich the treatment plan, regardless of specific diagnosis.

VULNERABILITY TO TRAUMA

Severity of Exposure

Since Terr's (1979) landmark study of a group of kidnapped children, there has been considerable interest in children's responses to traumatic incidents such as accidents, abuse, exposure to violence, and natural disasters. It is widely recognized that virtually all children exposed to extremely traumatic events retain posttraumatic reactions for over a year (if untreated), and perhaps indefinitely (Greening and Dollinger 1992, Holaday et al. 1992, Nader et al. 1990, Newman 1976, Terr 1979, van der Kolk 1987). Vulnerability is increased with severity of exposure (Lonigan et al. 1991, Nader et al. 1990, Pynoos et al. 1987). Posttraumatic sequelae phenomena such as hospitalization or separation from parents may extend the exposure to trauma, constituting continued traumatization (McFarlane 1987). Other associated loss or displacement experiences may function similarly (Cohen 1988). Lesser exposure may also entail posttraumatic response, but typically involving lower frequency and severity of symptoms.

The severity of exposure to a traumatic event is mediated by perception, personal meaning of the event (Milgram et al. 1988), and emotional reactivity (Schwarz and Kowalski 1991). Such mediation may reflect developmental level (see below), as well as prior traumatization or psychopathology, which have also been found to increase risk (Burke et al. 1982, Earls et al. 1988).

Developmental Level

Children may be particularly vulnerable in general, as they are more helpless and easier to frighten than adults, who have more fully developed physiques, knowledge, social status, emotional resources, and perspectives of the situation. However, developmental level per se has not been found to differentiate children in their vulnerability to traumatization (Newman 1976, Terr 1979). For example, the cognitive distortion and regression associated with traumatization is found across developmental levels (Schwarz and Kowalski 1991, Terr 1979). However, the child's level of development may influence the nature of the traumatic experience. Coping efforts are affected by current developmental-phase–specific issues, capacities, and influences. For example, the ability to regulate affect and to obtain extrafamilial emotional support normally increases with age. Level of development may also have some effect on the way an experience is understood (Newman 1976). For example, very young children may not accurately perceive their lives as being threatened in a dangerous situation (Green et al. 1991).

Personality Styles

Personality styles that are more prone to avoidance, denial, and external locus of control, as opposed to actively facing and integrating experience, may also increase vulnerability (Gibbs 1989, Hyman et al. 1988). This predisposition may lower the threshold at which an upsetting event constitutes a trauma rather than being effectively processed. Along with severity of exposure, peritraumatic dissociation (during and after the event) is now considered one of the best predictors of subsequent posttraumatic stress problems (Michaels et al. 1998, Shalev et al. 1996).

Although temperament undoubtedly makes some contribution to this tendency, early development involves a pattern of parent–child interactions through which the child learns the extent to which painful emotions are tolerable, or must be feared and avoided (Mahler et al. 1975, Winnicott 1965). Thus, an avoidant processing style may already represent a low-grade chronic posttraumatic reaction. Similarly, for reasons discussed below, prior discrete traumatic experiences also predispose to vulnerability to posttraumatic reactions.

Environmental Factors

The child's social environment following a critical incident can also be influential in supporting or limiting expression of feelings and integration of the traumatic memory (Cohen 1988, Galante and Foa 1986, Jones 1991). The nature of family interaction may be particularly important. When one or both parents "fall apart" or give the message that they cannot tolerate exposure to the traumatic memory (perhaps expressed as overprotection, avoidance, or denial), this may confirm and reinforce the child's own defensive posttraumatic reaction. Furthermore, the child may move into an emotional caregiver role (parenting the parents), leading to loss of feeling cared for, reduced opportunity for processing, and increased disturbance (Bloch et al. 1956, Green et al. 1991, McFarlane 1987).

PREVALENCE OF TRAUMA

Some of the data on the prevalence of traumatic events in childhood are indirect and suggestive, yet persuasive and alarming (e.g., Pynoos 1990). Recent research has found astonishingly high incidence rates for prior experience of at least one criterion A (extremely traumatic) stressor among young adults, most of which presumably occurred during childhood or adolescence. For example, Riise and colleagues (1994) found an 85 present incidence among a young military population (only a minority of which were military trauma), and Vrana and Lauterbach

(1994) found an 84 percent incidence among college students, presumably a relatively well-protected population. Among disadvantaged urban populations, exposure to criterion A events appears to be a regular occurrence (Campbell and Schwarz 1996, Jenkins 1995). Trauma during childhood and adolescence is now so common as to be normative.

When major loss experiences as well as chronic minor trauma are also taken into account, it becomes increasingly clear that child trauma, broadly defined, is ubiquitous. In clinical practice it is unusual to encounter a child who has not been touched by at least one significant adverse life event. Although the majority of children and adolescents do not develop the full PTSD syndrome, a high percentage may carry symptoms of posttraumatic stress (Cuffe et al. 1998, Greenwald and Rubin 1999), sometimes sufficient for the development of other mental disorders.

EFFECTS OF TRAUMA

Trauma involves an intense experience of helplessness and fear, frequently including physical or emotional pain. If this becomes intolerable to the child, an extraordinary effort may be made to escape these feelings. The scope of this effort is represented in the variety of symptoms a traumatized child may develop (described below). These symptoms provide partial relief from the intolerable feelings, but have the paradoxical effect of deferring true relief, since they prevent the child from fully facing and processing the traumatic memory. Failure of integration leaves the traumatic memory in a fresh, raw state–a constant threat.

In effect, the traumatic experience constitutes such a shock to the system that it is, in some way, rejected from the normal processing routine. Instead of facing and gradually working through the upsetting aspects of the memory, it is experienced as too overwhelming, and pushed aside. Avoidance, a hallmark of PTSD, can include many strategies such as repression, distraction, self-medication, emotional numbing, emotional withdrawal, and behavioral avoidance of reminders.

Meanwhile, the traumatic experience persists in an active unprocessed state, constantly threatening to intrude, as if still happening. The memory is preserved, perpetually waiting for a chance to go through the normal processing system and enter long-term memory storage. When something thematically similar arises, the traumatic memory may become stimulated and then reemerge in part or whole, as if to say, "I'm still here, can I finally come through the system?" This may be experienced directly as an intrusion of imagery from the traumatic memory, or as an intrusion of belief and/or affect, in the form of an overreaction to the current stimulus. Because the person may be unaware of overreacting, the danger value of the current stimulus, or "trigger," is experienced as being magnified. This unwanted intrusion of memory aspects is another hallmark of PTSD.

Not only does the unprocessed trauma contribute to overreaction and an experience of increased environmental threat, the memory itself is aversive. Indeed, some children find many aspects of their life threatening merely because they never know when the memory will intrude. The traumatized child may develop a sense of the world as more dangerous, along with a sense of her own mind as being dangerous by, in essence, attacking her with the traumatic memory, often without warning. The child may become hyperalert to possible threat, developing symptoms such as anxiety, worry, tension, a hostile attribution bias (misinterpreting neutral communication as threatening), and exaggerated startle response. This hyperarousal, or "survival mode" state (Chemtob et al. 1988) is another hallmark of PTSD. The hyperarousal also contributes to reactivity, as the child is already in a state of tension.

Avoidance in many forms becomes a priority, driven by the urgency of survival instinct. Intrusions may continue to drive overreactivity and infect the child not only with general fear, but also with specific thoughts and feelings arising from the unprocessed traumatic memory. For example, the child may come to feel more generally helpless and ineffective, and so become apathetic. Thus, the child's response to the trauma becomes a primary organizing principle for personality, mood, and behavior.

This combination of avoidance, intrusion, and hyperarousal creates an extremely unfortunate dynamic for the traumatized child. Whenever the traumatic memory is stimulated, it sets off a process resulting in the reinforcement of the avoidance response. The avoidance response precludes facing and working through the memory, which is required for recovery (see below). To the extent that the spectrum of avoidance symptoms are effective in providing a measure of relief, they are self-reinforcing and may be maintained indefinitely.

The effects of trauma in individuals may be concealed or expressed in a number of ways. Posttraumatic symptoms in children are often manifested quite differently than in the classic adult PTSD picture; for example, children's reactions may include somatic symptoms, regressive behavior, or acting out (Fletcher 1993). Trauma effects, broadly defined, arguably form the basis of most nonorganically based psychopathology (Brom 1991, Conaway and Hansen 1989, Famularo et al. 1992, Flisher et al. 1997, Green 1983, Kendall-Tackett et al. 1993, Malinosky-Rummell and Hansen 1993, Terr 1991, van der Kolk 1987). Traumatized children may better fit behavioral criteria for diagnostic categories other than PTSD, such as AD/HD, generalized anxiety disorder, depression, or oppositional defiant disorder. Child trauma effects may frequently be mislabeled with a diagnosis that accurately describes behavioral attributes but does not address the root of the disturbance. Note that trauma may also lead to lasting symptoms in lieu of any formal diagnosis (Cuffe et al. 1998, Fletcher 1996, Sullivan et al. 1991, Terr 1991).

The special problem of chronic trauma frequently entails even more pervasive changes in personality organization, including the classic PTSD denial, numbing, and hyperarousal as well as dissociation, self-hypnosis, and rage. This pervasive reaction has been implicated as the basis of such adult pathology as borderline personality disorder, dissociative identity disorder (van der Kolk 1987), and complex PTSD (Herman 1992).

The Burden of Traumatization

Here is a conceptualization of the process underlying the apparent cumulative effect of traumatization (Figley 1985, Peterson et al. 1991). Trauma increases reactivity to thematically similar stimuli, to the extent that the current reaction encompasses prior unprocessed painful emotions as well as those evoked by the new event. The nonintegrative response style, used to avoid the painful emotions, increases in value at each successive trauma, as the amount of pain in the reaction accumulates with each additional traumatic experience. Thus, as the *trauma burden* increases, so also does thematically related reactivity and predisposition to a nonintegrative response style.

This concept of the trauma burden may explain the "sleeper effect" shown by those without apparent long-term effects from trauma, when challenged in a thematically related area (Kantor 1980, Wallerstein et al. 1988). Recent research has also shown increased vulnerability to posttraumatic reactions, following a traumatic experience, among those with prior trauma history (Riise et al. 1994, Scott and Gardin 1994). At some point of critical mass, the burden of reactivity may simply overwhelm the containment mechanisms (or competing schemas) and become more generalized and apparent, manifesting in symptoms of depression, anxiety, or PTSD.

It has become increasingly clear that children mature in a healthy way from experiences, even upsetting ones that they can integrate; but they become psychologically crippled from traumatization (Pynoos and Nader 1988, Terr 1991). That symptoms may eventually diminish in prominence is not in itself indicative of recovery; instead it may reflect the child's effectiveness in defensive containment (or keeping a secret). The underlying damage may remain, impairing the child's future coping capacity, and perhaps altering the nature of career goals, future relationships, mood, or sense of self. The scope of the damage may be pervasive, or quite circumscribed, so that similar reactivity would only arise in thematically similar situations. Many traumatized children's symptoms do not subside.

ASSESSMENT OF TRAUMA

There are many appropriate approaches to trauma assessment, which vary according to the situational context. Rather than outlining a particular assessment protocol, I will review the issues to be considered more generally in conducting an assessment of posttraumatic stress.

The Time Factor

Children assessed with intensive clinical methods soon after a traumatic event tend to show disturbance more consistently, whereas both nonclinical assessment methods and greater time lapse since the event are associated with a decline in detected disturbance rates (Sugar 1989). For many children, acute symptoms are more intense and noticeable than long-term symptoms. Also, immediately following a traumatic event, it is easier for the child and others to identify new symptoms as related to the event. Later, the child's personality may to some extent be organized around the posttraumatic symptoms, making the symptoms stand out less. Nonetheless, the child's posttraumatic response can certainly contribute to symptoms long after the acute response has faded. Clinical observations in adult populations also suggest that apparent recovery from childhood trauma may not constitute true recovery, with the adult remaining vulnerable in thematically related areas (Greenwald 1997b, Kantor 1980).

One of the best ways to ascertain the possible contribution of specific past events to current symptoms is to obtain a history including both upsetting events and symptom development. Other factors should also be considered, including history of head trauma and other medical problems as well as situational factors such as changes in neighborhood, school, family, lifestyle. It's astonishing how frequently the presenting symptoms are found to have developed, or escalated, immediately following a major trauma or loss, without anyone in the family having previously made the connection.

Sources of Information

Children are generally the best informants regarding their internal states, but tend to be poor observers of their own behavior. Parents, on the other hand, often underestimate their child's internal distress, but they are fairly good observers of the child's behavior (Belter et al. 1991, Burke et al. 1982, Earls et al. 1988, Handford et al. 1986, Loeber et al. 1990, Yule and Williams 1990). Therefore, it is necessary to obtain multiple sources of information.

Parent and child reports are generally correlated, but not always. Some traumatized children may maintain exemplary behavior to keep their parents from worrying, or to keep from being singled out, and intentionally avoid displaying their ongoing distress (Bradburn 1991). With such children, self-disclosure of posttraumatic symptoms may be the best indicator. On the other hand, some children may deny, or simply lack awareness of, their posttraumatic status, and fail to acknowledge any posttraumatic symptomatology. With such children, the parent's report may be most useful.

An additional source of information may also be telling. For example, evidence is stronger when the teacher and parent describe the same cluster of problem behaviors across settings. It is also informative if a traumatized child misbehaves at home, where the discipline is inconsistent, but behaves well in a highly structured classroom setting. The situation could also be reversed, for example, when a child does poorly in the classroom of an overly harsh or lax teacher, but does well at home.

The Family Environment

The family environment may contribute to the development and persistence of posttraumatic symptoms, and can contribute to recovery. Assessment of the family context is therefore critical. Although parent and child interviews can be helpful in this regard, nothing can replace direct observation of family interaction.

As noted above, when parents are reactive to trauma-related material, the child may experience further traumatization, or at least get an unfortunate message regarding the trauma. For example, if the child reports a rape and the parents respond with avoidance and denial, the child may feel rejected and discounted. If, following an auto accident, the parents manage their own guilt by indulging the child and retreating on discipline, the child may feel that he is seen as damaged or less capable. Parents who discourage the child from talking about the event, ostensibly to keep the child from feeling bad, may be impeding resolution by giving the child the message that the event is too scary to bring up. Following a major trauma or loss, many parents are so overwhelmed with their own reactions that they find it difficult to attend to their child's emotional needs. When this co-occurs with the traumatized child's increasingly difficult behavior, a cycle of negative interactions can easily develop and become entrenched.

Ongoing family dynamics may also be contributing to the persistence of the child's posttraumatic symptoms. For example, a girl who had been raped by her babysitter was being regularly retraumatized, in a minor but significant way, when her older brother bullied her. A father who no longer beat his children retraumatized them with his yelling; they would cringe and bring an arm up in front of their face in self-defense. Probably the most common of the destructive family dynamics involve parental loss of control (yelling, angry physical discipline, unreasonable punishment) along with inconsistent discipline. Ongoing interactions like these give the traumatized child the message that things still aren't safe, meaning that the trauma could happen again at any time. This makes recovery much more difficult.

Supportive elements of the family context should also be evaluated. Most families provide elements of routine, security, support, and safety. It is generally not too difficult to discern concrete evidence of parental caring and concern as well. These strengths, elements conducive to healing, can be developed and built upon in the treatment plan.

Current Safety Issues

Assessment of current safety issues is critical to developing an appropriate treatment plan. Attempting to treat a child's post-traumatic reaction while the child is exposed to continued risk for trauma makes as much sense as repainting a damaged ceiling without first fixing the leak in the roof that caused the damage. The goal of trauma treatment is achieved when the child can say, "That's over, and now I'm safe." Therefore, major safety issues must be identified and resolved as far as possible, before attempting trauma resolution work. More subtle safety issues such as parental consistency with discipline may be addressed either first or simultaneously, according to clinical judgment.

Objective Measures

Until fairly recently, reliable identification of traumatized children has been cumbersome, involving extended clinical interviewing (McNally 1991), because assessment of trauma via instruments designed to detect anxiety, depression, or general psychopathology can be very sloppy. However, there are now a number of trauma-focused objective measures available that can be very useful in efficiently screening for posttraumatic symptoms as well as tracking progress in treatment. Objective measurement cannot replace clinical assessment, but it can make a real contribution. Since resources in this area continue to develop, I will only mention a few here, and refer interested readers to the sources listed in Appendix A.

There is no single best child trauma measure. Rather, the purpose of the assessment and the conditions under which it is conducted guide selection of the most appropriate instrument for the situation. There are several issues to consider:

Trauma History

There are a number of available trauma history instruments, ranging from checklists to extended structured interviews. Some are keyed to assess qualification under criterion A, whereas others assess a broader range of adverse life events. The briefer questionnaires, while convenient to administer, are not generally scorable, and are best used as a guide for follow-up questions during a clinical interview. The structured interviews are much more detailed, but they are relatively tedious and would generally be most appropriate for research settings. Children's and parents' reports of the child's trauma history may not be entirely consistent, either in the specific events reported, or regarding the child's response to the events.

Identified Traumatic Event

Sometimes a trauma assessment is conducted specifically to determine the child's response to an identified event, such as a hurricane, a school shooting, or recently disclosed abuse. The

Impact of Events Scale is the only well-established instrument that assesses posttraumatic response to an identified event, and there is subset of eight items (IES-8) that have been thoroughly validated for use with children and adolescents (Dyregrov and Yule 1995). Although the IES-8 can be useful in screening for posttraumatic stress and for tracking recovery, it does have limitations. The first is the same as its strength: it only assesses response to the identified event, and may fail to pick up posttraumatic symptoms associated with other, perhaps unidentified, trauma history. The other major limitation is that the IES-8 only taps two classic posttraumatic symptoms—avoidance and intrusion—and does not address the full spectrum of posttraumatic responses that may occur.

PTSD vs. Posttraumatic Symptoms

Some instruments may be keyed to *DSM* criteria for PTSD. Although this approach is useful both for research purposes and to help determine PTSD diagnosis, the *DSM*'s PTSD criteria does not address the full range of children's actual posttraumatic responses (Fletcher 1993). For clinical purposes a more comprehensive full-spectrum symptom assessment is preferable. At this writing, the Trauma Symptom Checklist for Children (Briere 1996) is preferred by many clinicians and researchers, as it features good psychometrics and includes a broad-symptom coverage as well as relevant subscales. The Los Angeles Symptom Checklist–Adolescent (Foy et al. 1997) also has good psychometric properties, and has been used extensively with urban teens. Both of those instruments also have PTSD subscales. The Child Report of Posttraumatic Symptoms and the Parent Report of Posttraumatic Symptoms (Greenwald and Rubin 1999) feature brevity, full-spectrum symptom coverage, sensitivity to change in posttraumatic status, and the perspectives of both parent and child. However, as a newer instrument it is not as well established as the others mentioned.

In sum, selection of objective measures, as well as the general assessment approach, will be determined by the purpose of the assessment, the age of the child, and availability of suitable resources. For example, a kindergartner is not likely to be able to complete any of the available trauma-focused self-report measures, but her parent will be able to complete a parent report form as well as providing relevant history and behavioral observations. Many clinicians prefer to combine various approaches, for example, by following a screening for trauma history and symptoms with a clinical interview.

I must emphasize the importance of routinely assessing for trauma/loss history and posttraumatic symptoms, whether in an identified posttrauma context or as part of the initial assessment of mental health and behavioral problems (Greenwald 1997b). Many traumatized children are currently not identified as such (Burke et al. 1982, Earls et al. 1988, Handford et al. 1986, Kendall-Tackett et al. 1993, Terr 1983). This unfortunate trend permits an immense amount of preventable impairment and suffering. Effective identification of traumatized children is a critical step in helping the children to recover.

RECOVERY FROM TRAUMA

Factors favoring ease of recovery include an integrative processing style (Gibbs 1989, Hyman et al. 1988), coupled with opportunities to discuss the event and express the associated feelings with supportive family members, peers, and/or counselors (Bloch et al. 1956, Cohen 1988, Galante and Foa 1986, Jones 1991). These findings imply that, for some period of time following an upsetting experience, the support or inhibition of processing may be quite influential in determining whether the memory will become integrated or remain problematic.

The urgency of self-protection that posttraumatic symptoms represent may render the traumatized child impervious to parents and others who try to help the child recover. Such children must often be treated by psychotherapists who are specially trained to facilitate the recovery process. Those children not treated will probably continue to suffer, and will be at higher risk for psychopathology, emotional distress, maladaptive life choices, and additional traumatization (Krystal 1978, Pynoos 1990, Sugar 1989, Terr 1979, 1991). Although treatment of the traumatized child may be a gradual, arduous process, it can be essential to the child's continued healthy development.

The posttrauma treatment approach may entail a number of intervention modalities, taking into account the cultural, community, social, family, and developmental contexts of the child's life before, during, and after the event (Cohen 1988, Pynoos and Nader 1988, Terr 1989). Interventions involving media (Terr 1989), school (Chemtob and Nakashima 1997, Jones 1991), family (Cohen 1988), and group (Chemtob and Nakashima 1997, Galante and Foa 1986, Yule and Williams 1990) continue to develop. Early intervention is most advantageous because the traumatic reactions are still readily apparent and clearly trauma related, treatment may be more appealing, and recovery more rapid (Pynoos and Nader 1988). Later treatment is possible, but over time the trauma effects become more integrated into personality and lifestyle (Horowitz 1986). Periodic treatment at transitional developmental phases may be necessary when the event creates a long-term developmental challenge, for example following the death of a parent (James 1989).

For many children, individual treatment is required, whether as the sole intervention or in conjunction with other approaches. The format typically includes talk, play/art, and/or exposure modalities. Despite the many variations in form and timing, these treatments are nearly identical in underlying structure, including reexperiencing the trauma in a safe, controlled setting; working through emotional reactions; restructuring cognitive appraisals; and enhancing the child's sense of efficacy (James 1989, Peterson et al. 1991, Pynoos and Eth 1986).

Although individual treatment may be essential to trauma recovery for some children, it may not be sufficient. In particular, environmental support may be required to help the child to legitimately feel more safe. This may involve a range of efforts, for example, imprisoning a rapist, expelling a perpetrator of abuse from the home, or advocating for the child's school to crack down on bullying. As noted above, the family environment is also potentially a primary source of support for the child's recovery, if the parents can convey that the child is safe at home. This may entail an exaggerated effort at conveying safety, in consideration of the child's trauma-related hypersensitivity. Safety is reinforced by fairness, predictability, and a sense of control. When parents understand the reasons for the therapist's suggestions regarding their behavior, they are generally quite motivated to improve their own self-control and consistency in discipline.

The Trauma Orientation

Although much of this discussion has referred to extreme trauma, I have suggested that the dynamics of traumatization, as well as the principles of treatment, apply to a wide range of children's experiences and presenting problems. The data support this contention, since many children in treatment suffer from at least some posttraumatic symptoms. One of the advantages to the trauma orientation is that the experiential sources of children's problems are likely to be addressed. Another advantage is that trauma-based case formulations can be nonblaming and nonstigmatizing, eliciting a sympathetic view of the child. Finally, such case formulations tend to be successful in engaging children as well as parents in productive treatment-related activities.

  This book describes the integration of EMDR with a comprehensive trauma-oriented therapy approach. Shapiro's (1995) accelerated information processing theory, intended to guide the selective use of EMDR, is consistent with the broad conceptualization of trauma and related dynamics described above. For the trauma-oriented child therapist, EMDR can enhance treatment effectiveness and efficiency.

References

Abruzzese, M. (1995). *The use of EMDR for children with disruptive behavior disorders.* Workshop presented at the EMDR annual conference, Pacific Grove, CA, June.

American Psychiatric Association (1994). *Diagnostic and Statistical Manual of Mental Disorders (DSM-IV).* Washington, DC: Author.

Belter, R. W., Dunn, S. E., and Jeney, P. (1991). The psychological impact of Hurricane Hugo on children: a needs assessment. *Advances in Behaviour Research and Therapy* 13:155–161.

Bloch, D. A., Silber, E., and Perry, S. E. (1956). Some factors in the emotional reaction of children to disaster. *American Journal of Psychiatry* 113:416–422.

Bradburn, I. S. (1991). After the earth shook: children's stress symptoms 6–8 months after a disaster. *Advances in Behaviour Research and Therapy* 13:173–179.

Briere, J. (1996). *Trauma Symptom Checklist for Children (TSCC) Professional Manual.* Odessa, FL: Psychological Assessment Resources.

Brom, D. (1991). The prevalence of posttraumatic psychopathology in the general and the clinical population. *Israel Journal of Psychiatry and Related Sciences* 28:53–63.

Burke, J. D., Borus, J. F., Burns, B. J., et al. (1982). Changes in children's behavior after a natural disaster. *American Journal of Psychiatry* 139:1010–1014.

Campbell, C., and Schwarz, D. (1996). Prevalence and impact of exposure to interpersonal violence among suburban and urban middle school students. *Pediatrics* 98:396–402.

Chambless, D. L., Baker, M., Baucom, D., et al. (1998). Update on empirically validated therapies, II. *Clinical Psychologist* 51:3–16.

Chemtob, C., and Nakashima, J. (1996). *Eye movement desensitization and reprocessing (EMDR) treatment for children with treatment resistant disaster related distress.* Paper presented at the annual meeting of the International Society for Traumatic Stress Studies, San Francisco, CA, November.

Chemtob, C. M., Roitblat, H. L., Hamada, R. S., at al. (1988). A cognitive action theory of posttraumatic stress disorder. *Journal of Anxiety Disorders* 2:253–275.

Cocco, N. (1995). *EMDR in the treatment of darkness phobia in children.* Paper presented at the EMDR annual conference, Pacific Grove, CA, June.

Cocco, N., and Sharpe, L. (1993). An auditory variant of eye movement desensitization in a case of childhood post-traumatic stress disorder. *Journal of Behavior Therapy and Experimental Psychiatry* 24:373–377.

Cohen, A., and Lahad, M. (1997). Eye movement desensitisation and reprocessing in the treatment of trauma. In *Community Stress Prevention*, vol. 2, ed. M. Lahad and A. Cohen, pp. 160–165. Kiryat Shmona, Israel: CSPC Publications.

Cohen, R. E. (1988). Intervention programs for children. In *Mental Health Response to Mass Emergencies: Theory and Practice*, ed. M. Lystad, pp. 262–283. New York: Brunner/Mazel.

Conaway, L. P., and Hansen, D. J. (1989). Social behavior of physically abused and neglected children: a critical review. *Clinical Psychology Review* 9:627–652.

Cuffe, S. P., Addy, C. L., Garrison, C. Z., at al. (1998). Prevalence of PTSD in a community sample of older adolescents. *Journal of the American Academy of Child and Adolescent Psychiatry* 37:147–154.

Datta, P. C., and Wallace, J. (1996). *Enhancement of victim empathy along with reduction in anxiety and increase of positive cognition of sex offenders after treatment with EMDR.* Paper presented at the annual meeting of the EMDR International Association, Denver, CO, June.

Dunton, R. (1993). *Applying the EMDR model to children and adolescents with school related behavior and learning issues.* Workshop presented at the EMDR annual conference, San Jose, CA, March.

Dutton, P. (1996). *Superkids: Practical Child Management.* Dollar, Scotland: Psynapse.

Dyregrov, A., and Yule, W. (1995). *Screening measures: The development of the UNICEF screening battery.* Paper presented at the annual meeting of the International Society for Traumatic Stress Studies, Boston, MA, November.

Earls, F., Smith, E., Reich, W., and Jung, K. G. (1988). Investigating psychopathological consequences of a disaster in children: a pilot study incorporating a structured diagnostic interview. *Journal of the American Academy of Child and Adolescent Psychiatry* 27:90–95.

Famularo, R., Kinscherff, R., and Fenton, T. (1992). Psychiatric diagnoses of maltreated children: preliminary findings. *Journal of the American Academy of Child and Adolescent Psychiatry* 31:863–867.

Feske, U. (1998). Eye movement desensitization and reprocessing treatment for posttraumatic stress disorder. *Clinical Psychology: Science and Practice* 5:171–181.

Figley, C., ed. (1985). *Trauma and Its Wake: The Study and Treatment of Post-Traumatic Stress Disorder.* New York: Brunner/Mazel.

Fletcher, K. E. (1993). *The spectrum of post-traumatic responses in children.* Poster presented at the annual meeting of the International Society for Traumatic Stress Studies, San Antonio, October.

——— (1996). Childhood posttraumatic stress disorder. In *Child Psychopathology*, ed. E. Mash and R. Barkley, pp. 242–276. New York: Guilford.

Flisher, A. J., Kramer, R. A., Hoven, C. W., et al. (1997). Psychosocial characteristics of physically abused children and adolescents. *Journal of the American Academy of Child and Adolescent Psychiatry* 36:123–131.

Foy, D. W., Wood, J. L., King, D. W., et al. (1997). Los Angeles Symptom Checklist: psychometric evidence with an adolescent sample. *Assessment* 4:377–384.

Galante, R., and Foa, D. (1986). An epidemiological study of psychic trauma and treatment effectiveness for children after a natural disaster. *Journal of the American Academy of Child Psychiatry* 25:357–363.

Gibbs, M. S. (1989). Factors in the victim that mediate between disaster and psychopathology: a review. *Journal of Traumatic Stress* 2:489–514.

Green, A. H. (1983). Child abuse: dimension of psychological trauma in abused children. *Journal of the American Academy of Child Psychiatry* 22:231–237.

Green, B. L., Korol, M., Grace, M. C., et al. (1991). Children and disaster: age, gender, and parental effects on PTSD symptoms. *Journal of the American Academy of Child and Adolescent Psychiatry* 30:945–951.

Greening, L., and Dollinger, S. J. (1992). Illusions (and shattered illusions) of invulnerability: adolescents in natural disaster. *Journal of Traumatic Stress* 5:63–75.

Greenwald, R. (1993a). Magical installations can help clients to slay their dragons. *EMDR Network Newsletter* 3(2):16–17.

——— (1993b). Treating children's nightmares with EMDR. *EMDR Network Newsletter* 3(1):7–9.

——— (1993c). *Using EMDR with children.* Pacific Grove, CA: EMDR Institute.

——— (1993d). *Using EMDR with children: critical incidents.* Workshop presented at the EMDR annual conference, San Jose, CA, March.

——— (1994a). Applying eye movement desensitization and reprocessing (EMDR) to the treatment of traumatized children: five case studies. *Anxiety Disorders Practice Journal* 1:83–97.

——— (1994b). Eye movement desensitization and reprocessing (EMDR): an overview. *Journal of Contemporary Psychotherapy* 24:15–34.

——— (1994c). Family interventions to enhance child EMDR treatment. *EMDR Network Newsletter* 4(2):7–8.

——— (1994d). The therapeutic relationship and *EMDR. EMDR Network Newsletter* 4(1):10–11.

——— (1994e). Using EMDR with children: "cleaning up" afterwards. *EMDR Network Newsletter* 4(3):8.

———— (1995). Eye movement desensitization and reprocessing (EMDR): a new kind of dreamwork? *Dreaming* 5:51–55.

———— (1996). The information gap in the EMDR controversy. *Professional Psychology: Research and Practice* 27:67–72.

———— (1997a). A better approach to training: why you should teach EMDR in your home town. *The EMDR Practitioner* (Available on the Internet: http://www.geocities.com/HotSprings/Spa/1999/).

———— (1997b). Children's mental health care in the 21st century: eliminating the trauma burden. *Child and Adolescent Psychiatry On-Line* (Available on the Internet: http://www.Priory.com/psychild.htm).

———— (1997c). *EMDR for adolescents with disruptive behavior disorders.* Workshop presented at the annual meeting of the EMDR International Association, San Francisco, CA, July.

———— (1998a). EMDR cures kidney stones: a case report. *EMDRIA Newsletter* 3(3):32.

———— (1998b). Eye movement desensitization and reprocessing (EMDR): new hope for children suffering from trauma and loss. *Clinical Child Psychology and Psychiatry* 3:279–287.

———— (1998c). *A trauma-focused individual therapy approach for adolescents with conduct disorder.* Manuscript submitted for publication.

———— (in press). Suggestion is still powerful: response to *EMDR and Mesmerism: A Comparative Historical Analysis. Journal of Anxiety Disorders.*

Greenwald, R., and Rubin, A. (1999). Brief assessment of children's post-traumatic symptoms: development and preliminary validation of parent and child scales. *Research on Social Work Practice* 9:61–75.

Grosso, F. C. (1996). Children and OCD: extending the treatment paradigm. *EMDRIA Newsletter* 1(1):10–11.

Handford, H. A., Mayes, S. D., Mattison, R. E., et al. (1986). Child and parent reaction to the Three Mile Island nuclear accident. *Journal of the American Academy of Child Psychiatry* 25:346–356.

Heatherington, E. M., Stanley-Hagan, M., and Anderson, E. R. (1989). Marital transitions: a child's perspective. *American Psychologist* 44:303–312.

Herman, J. L. (1992). Complex PTSD: a syndrome in survivors of prolonged and repeated trauma. *Journal of Traumatic Stress* 5:377–391.

Holaday, M., Armsworth, M. W., Swank, P. R., and Vincent, K. R. (1992). Rorschach responding in traumatized children and adolescents. *Journal of Traumatic Stress* 5:119–129.

Horowitz, M. J. (1986). *Stress Response Syndromes,* 2nd ed. Northvale, NJ: Jason Aronson.

Hyer, L., and Brandsma, J. M. (1997). EMDR minus eye movements equals good psychotherapy. *Journal of Traumatic Stress* 10:515–522.

Hyman, I. A., Zelikoff, W., and Clarke, J. (1988). Psychological and physical abuse in the schools: a paradigm for understanding post-traumatic stress disorder in children and youth. *Journal of Traumatic Stress* 1:243–267.

ISTSS (International Society for Traumatic Stress Studies) (1998). Childhood trauma remembered: a report on the scientific knowledge base and its applications. Chicago: Author.

James, B. (1989). *Treating Traumatized Children: New Insights and Creative Interventions.* Lexington, MA: Lexington.

Jenkins, E. J. (1995). Violence exposure, psychological distress and risk behaviors in a sample of inner-city youth. In *Trends, Risks, and Interventions in Lethal Violence: Proceedings of the Third Annual Spring Symposium of the Homicide Research Working Group, Atlanta,* ed. C. R. Block and R. L. Block, pp. 287–297. Washington, DC: U.S. Department of Justice, Office of Justice Programs, National Institute of Justice.

Jones, C. A. (1991). Who takes care of the caretakers? *Advances in Behaviour Research and Therapy* 13:181–183.

Kantor, D. (1980). Critical identity image: a concept linking individual, couple, and family development. In *Family Therapy: Combining Psychodynamic and Systems Approaches,* ed. J. K. Pearce and L. J. Friedman, pp. 137–167. New York: Grune & Stratton.

Kendall-Tackett, K. A., Williams, L. M., and Finkelhor, D. (1993). Impact of sexual abuse on children: a review and synthesis of recent empirical studies. *Psychological Bulletin* 113:164–180.

Krystal, H. (1978). Trauma and affects. *Psychoanalytic Study of the Child* 33:81–116. New Haven, CT: Yale University Press.

Lee, C. W., Gavriel, H., and Richards, J. (1996). Eye movement desensitisation: past research, complexities, and future directions. *Australian Psychologist* 31(3):168–173.

Leeds, A. (1997). *In the eye of the beholder: reflections on shame, dissociation and transference in complex posttraumatic stress and attachment disorders.* Workshop presented at the annual meeting of the EMDR International Association, San Francisco, CA, July.

Lipke, H. (1994). Eye movement desensitization and reprocessing (EMDR): a quantitative study of clinician impressions of effects and training requirements. Reprinted in F. Shapiro (1995), *Eye Movement Desensitization and Reprocessing: Basic Principles, Protocols and Procedures*, pp. 376–386. New York: Guilford, 1995.

Loeber, R., Green, S. M., and Lahey, B. B. (1990). Mental health professionals' perception of the utility of children, mothers, and teachers as informants on childhood psychopathology. *Journal of Clinical Child Psychology* 19:136–143.

Lonigan, C. J., Shannon, M. P., Finch, A. J., Jr., et al. (1991). Children's reactions to a natural disaster: symptom severity and degree of exposure. *Advances in Behaviour Research and Therapy* 13:135–154.

Lovett, J. (1995). *EMDR with children: eleven months to eleven years.* Workshop presented at the EMDR annual conference, Pacific Grove, CA, June.

Mahler, M., Bergman, A., and Pine, F. (1975). *The Psychological Birth of the Human Infant.* New York: Basic Books.

Malinosky-Rummell, R., and Hansen, D. J. (1993). Long-term consequences of childhood physical abuse. *Psychological Bulletin* 114:68–79.

Marshall, T. J., and Vargas-Lobato, M. (1997). *Reactive attachment disorders and EMDR.* Workshop presented at the annual meeting of the EMDR International Association, San Francisco, CA, July.

Martinez, R. (1991). Innovative uses. *EMDR Network Newsletter* 1(1): 5–6.

McFarlane, A. C. (1987). Posttraumatic phenomena in a longitudinal study of children following a natural disaster. *Journal of the American Academy of Child and Adolescent Psychiatry* 26:764–769.

McNally, R. J. (1991). Assessment of posttraumatic stress disorder in children. *Psychological Assessment* 3:531–537.

Mendoza-Weitman, L. (1992). Case study. *EMDR Network Newsletter* 2(1):11–12.

Michaels, A. J., Michaels, C. E., Moon, C. H., et al. (1998). Psychosocial factors limit outcomes after trauma. *Journal of Trauma* 44:644–648.

Milgram, N. A., Toubiana, Y. H., Klingman, A., et al. (1988). Situational exposure and personal loss in children's acute and chronic stress reactions to a school bus disaster. *Journal of Traumatic Stress* 1:339–352.

Nader, K., Pynoos, R., Fairbanks, L., and Frederick, C. (1990). Children's PTSD reactions one year after a sniper attack at their school. *American Journal of Psychiatry* 147:1526–1530.

Newcorn, J. H., and Strain, J. (1992). Adjustment disorder in children and adolescents. *Journal of the American Academy of Child and Adolescent Psychiatry* 31:318–327.

Newman, C. J. (1976). Children of disaster: clinical observations at Buffalo Creek. *American Journal of Psychiatry* 133:306–312.

Pellicer, X. (1993). Eye movement desensitization treatment of a child's nightmares: a case report. *Journal of Behavior Therapy and Experimental Psychiatry* 24:73–75.

Peterson, K. C., Prout, M. F., and Schwarz, R. A. (1991). *Post-Traumatic Stress Disorder: A Clinician's Guide.* New York: Plenum.

Puffer, M. K., Greenwald, R., and Elrod, D. E. (1998). A single session EMDR study with twenty traumatized children and adolescents. *Traumatology* 3(2). (Available on the Internet: http://www.fsu.edu/~trauma/v3i2art6.html)

Pynoos, R. S. (1990). Post-traumatic stress disorder in children and adolescents. In *Psychiatric Disorders in Children and Adolescents,* ed. B. D. Garfinkel, G. A. Carlson, and E. B. Weller, pp. 48–63. Philadelphia: W. B. Saunders.

Pynoos, R. S., and Eth, S. (1986). Witness to violence: the child interview. *Journal of the American Academy of Child Psychiatry* 25:306–319.

Pynoos, R. S., Frederick, C., Nader, K., et al. (1987). Life threat and posttraumatic stress in school-age children. *Archives of General Psychiatry* 44:1057–1063.

Pynoos, R. S., and Nader, K. (1988). Psychological first aid and treatment approach to children exposed to community violence: research implications. *Journal of Traumatic Stress* 1:445–473.

Rappaport, J. (1992). Innovative uses. *EMDR Network Newsletter* 2(1):14.

Riise, K. S., Corrigan, S. A., Uddo, M., and Sutker, P. B. (1994). *Multiple traumatic experiences: risk factors for PTSD.* Poster presented at the annual meeting of the International Society for Traumatic Stress Studies, Chicago, IL, November.

Rodriguez, G. (1997). Medical conditions in children and EMDR. *EMDR Association of Australasia's Saccades Newsletter* 2(1):5.

Rothbaum, B. (1992). How does EMDR work? *Behavior Therapist* 15:34, 46.

Rubin, A., and Bischofshausen, S. (1997). *EMDR outcomes in a child guidance center: preliminary findings.* Paper presented at the annual meeting of the EMDR International Association, San Francisco, CA, July.

Scheck, M. M., Schaeffer, J. A., and Gilette, C. S. (1998). Brief psychological intervention with traumatized young women: the efficacy of eye movement desensitization and reprocessing. *Journal of Traumatic Stress* 11:25–44.

Schwarz, E. D., and Kowalski, J. M. (1991). Malignant memories: PTSD in children and adults after a school shooting. *Journal of the American Academy of Child and Adolescent Psychiatry* 30:936–944.

Scott, S. T., and Gardin, M. (1994). *Multiple traumas and the development of post-traumatic stress disorder.* Poster presented at the annual meeting of the International Society for Traumatic Stress Studies, Chicago, IL, November.

Shalev, A. Y., Peri, T., Canetti, L., and Schreiber, S. (1996). Predictors of PTSD in injured trauma patients: a prospective study. *American Journal of Psychiatry* 153:219–225.

Shapiro, F. (1989a). Efficacy of the eye movement desensitization procedure in the treatment of traumatic memories. *Journal of Traumatic Stress* 2:199–223.

——— (1989b). Eye movement desensitization: a new treatment for post-traumatic stress disorder. *Journal of Behavior Therapy and Experimental Psychiatry* 20:211–217.

——— (1991a). Eye movement desensitization and reprocessing: a cautionary note. *Behavior Therapist* 14:188.

——— (1991b). Eye movement desensitization and reprocessing procedure: from EMD to EMD/R—a new treatment model for anxiety and related traumata. *Behavior Therapist* 14:128, 133–135.

—— (1995). *Eye Movement Desensitization and Reprocessing: Basic Principles, Protocols and Procedures.* New York: Guilford.

—— (1996a). Eye movement desensitization and reprocessing (EMDR): evaluation of controlled PTSD research. *Journal of Behavior Therapy and Experimental Psychiatry* 27:209–218.

—— (1996b). Errors of context and review of eye movement desensitization and reprocessing research. *Journal of Behavior Therapy and Experimental Psychiatry* 27:313–317.

Simonton, O. C., and Creighton, J. (1982). *Getting Well Again.* New York: Bantam.

Soberman, G. S., Greenwald, R., and Rule, D. (1998). *Eye movement desensitization and reprocessing (EMDR) for traumatic memories in the treatment of boys with conduct disorder.* Manuscript submitted for publication.

Stickgold, R. (1998). *REM sleep, memory, PTSD and EMDR.* Paper presented at the annual meeting of the EMDR International Association, Baltimore, MD, July.

Sugar, M. (1989). Children in a disaster: an overview. *Child Psychiatry and Human Development* 19:163–179.

Sullivan, M. A., Saylor, C. F., and Foster, K. Y. (1991). Post-hurricane adjustment of preschoolers and their families. *Advances in Behaviour Research and Therapy* 13:163–171.

Sutton, J. (1994). *EMDR with sexually abused children.* Workshop presented at the EMDR annual conference, Sunnyvale, CA, March.

Sweet, A. (1995). A theoretical perspective on the clinical use of EMDR. *Behavior Therapist* 18:5–6.

Szapocznik, J., Rio, A., Murray, E., et al. (1989). Structural family versus psychodynamic child therapy for problematic Hispanic boys. *Journal of Consulting and Clinical Psychology* 57:571–578.

Terr, L. (1979). Children of Chowchilla: a study of psychic trauma. *Psychoanalytic Study of the Child* 34:547–623. New Haven, CT: Yale University Press.

—— (1983). Life attitudes, dreams, and psychic trauma in a group of "normal" children. *Journal of the American Academy of Child Psychiatry* 22:221–230.

—— (1989). Treating psychic trauma in children: a preliminary discussion. *Journal of Traumatic Stress* 2:3–20.

———— (1991). Childhood traumas: an outline and overview. *American Journal of Psychiatry* 148:10–20.

Tinker, R. (1994). *Using EMDR with children and adolescents.* Workshop presented at the EMDR annual conference, Sunnyvale, CA, March.

van der Kolk, B. A. (1987). The psychological consequences of overwhelming life experiences. In *Psychological Trauma*, ed. B. A. van der Kolk, pp. 1–30. Washington, DC: American Psychiatric Press.

van Etten, M., and Taylor, S. (1998). Comparative efficacy of treatments for posttraumatic stress disorder: a meta-analysis. *Clinical Psychology and Psychotherapy* 5:126–145.

Vrana, S., and Lauterbach, D. (1994). Prevalence of traumatic events and post-traumatic psychological symptoms in a nonclinical sample of college students. *Journal of Traumatic Stress* 7:289–302.

Wallerstein, J., Corbin, S. B., and Lewis, J. M. (1988). Children of divorce: a ten-year study. In *Impact of Divorce, Single-Parenting, and Stepparenting on Children,* ed. E. M. Heatherington and J. Arasteh, pp. 198–214. Hillsdale, NJ: Lawrence Erlbaum.

Weinberg, R., and Caspers, S. (1997). *Using EMDR with students who have a learning disability to improve reading skills.* Paper presented at the annual meeting of the EMDR International Association, San Francisco, CA, July.

———— (1998). *Using EMDR with students who have a learning disability to improve reading skills.* Paper presented at the annual meeting of the EMDR International Association, Baltimore, MD, July.

Winnicott, D. W. (1965). *The Maturational Processes and the Facilitating Environment.* New York: International Universities Press.

Yule, W., and Williams, R. M. (1990). Post-traumatic stress reactions in children. *Journal of Traumatic Stress* 3:279–295.

Index

Disruptive behavior disorders
(male), latency-aged, 25–73.
See also Latency-aged
disruptive behavior disorders
(male)
Dissociative disorders, special
problems, 265–266
Dollinger, S. J., 277
Dreams, EMDR treatment phases,
177
Dunton, R., 178, 201, 262
Dutton, P., 51–52
Dyregrov, A., 289

Earls, F., 277, 285, 290
Early warning system, conduct
disorder (adolescent), 96–98
Ego ideal, installation, 196–197
EMDR
accelerated information
processing effect, 25–26
childhood applications, 138–151.
See also Childhood
applications; EMDR
components (childhood)
children and adolescents, xii–xvii
defined, ix
history and current status, x–xi
mechanism of, xi–xii
memory and, xi
traumatic memory, case
vignettes, 6–22
EMDR components (childhood),
155–165
emotion, 158
eye movements, 160–165
imagery, 155–156
physical sensation, 160

positive cognition, 157
Subjective Units of Disturbance
Scale (SUDS), 158–159
validity of cognition, 157–158
EMDR International Association
(EMDRIA), 273–274
EMDR standard protocol, 119–133
accelerated information
processing theory, 119–120
advanced applications, 130–133
components, 121–126
emotion, 124
eye movements, 125–126
imagery, 122
negative cognition, 122–123
physical sensation, 125
positive cognition, 123
Subjective Units of Distress
Scale (SUDS), 124–125
validity of cognition, 124
treatment phases, 126–130
assessment, 128
body scan, 129
closure, 129–130
desensitization, 128–129
history and planning, 127
installation, 129
preparation, 127
reevaluation, 130
EMDR treatment phases, 169–203
assessment, 183–187
body scan, 200
closure, 201–202
desensitization, 187–192
history and planning, 170–171
installation, 192–200
cognitive restructuring, 199
container, 200

About the Author

Ricky Greenwald is a clinical psychologist who has been working with children, adolescents, and their families since 1985. He received his Psy.D. from the Forest Institute of Professional Psychology in Honolulu, completed post–graduate training in couple and family therapy at the Kantor Family Institute in Cambridge, MA, and completed a post–doctoral fellowship in child and adolescent trauma at the Community Services Institute in Springfield, MA. He currently serves as Senior Psychologist for the Mokihana Project, which provided mental health services through the public school system on Kauai, HI.

Dr. Greenwald has published extensively on EMDR, family therapy, developmental psychology, and child trauma assessment and treatment, and maintains a child trauma web site. He has taught at Chaminade University, Tompkins–Cortland Community College, and the American School of Professional Psychology, Hawaii Campus.

A leading authority and innovator on using EMDR with children and adolescents, Dr. Greenwald is the founder of the EMDR International Association's special interest group on children and adolescents, was elected to EMDRIA's board of directors, and is the International Editor for EMDRIA's newsletter.